In search of Butch Cassidy

Butch Cassidy

Larry Pointer

In search of
BUTCH CASSIDY

Constable London

First published in Great Britain 1979
by Constable and Company Limited
10 Orange Street London WC2H 7EG
Copyright © 1977, 1979 by The University of Oklahoma Press
ISBN 0 09 462770 3
Printed in Great Britain by
REDWOOD BURN LIMITED
Trowbridge & Esher

British Library CIP Data

Pointer, Larry
  In search of Butch Cassidy.
  1. Cassidy, Butch   2. Outlaws – United States
  – Biography
  I. Title
  364.1'55'0924   F595.C362

  ISBN 0–09–462770–3

Preface

WHEN PAT AND I were married in Lander, Wyoming, in early 1972, our best man was Allan Robertson, a Lander businessman whose family roots go back to the very origins of the community. Allan's grandmother, the former Dora Lamorreaux, had been one of several girlfriends of the young cowboy "George Cassidy" before he became known as Butch Cassidy, leader of the notorious Wild Bunch, or Hole-in-the-Wall Gang of western desperadoes. Allan and his father Bill often mentioned Dora's claims that Cassidy had returned to visit Lander friends in the 1930s, long after he was supposed to have died in South America in a bloody shootout with a Bolivian cavalry troop.

The Robertsons, we were to find as we visited with area pioneers, were not alone in their claims. Consistent in the local tales of Cassidy's visit to the Lander area was mention of the former outlaw's use of the alias, William Phillips. We were told the man had spent the last years of his life in Spokane, Washington, until his death there in 1937. We also learned that other, less numerous old-timers believed that Phillips was an imposter who had hoped to stumble across rumored caches buried by Cassidy and his outlaw band.

Once introduced to the intriguing Butch Cassidy–William Phillips identity controversy we were hooked. The riddle was too compelling to be dropped. Beginning with an exhaustive literature search at the University of Wyoming Western History Research Center during the 1972 summer session, the investigation was to command the next five years of our lives, and to change the very course of our future.

In 1973 our research put us in contact with a Spokane reporter, James K. Dullenty, who had been assigned by the *Spokane Daily Chronicle* to write an in-depth series exploring the controversy over William Phillips' identity. Dullenty's series of articles gained widespread local attention and the reporter was contacted by several

Spokane area residents who had known Phillips. Also located in the community was the man's adopted son, William R. Phillips.

Of particular importance was Mrs. Blanche Glasgow, who, with her first husband, William Lundstrom, had been close Spokane friends with Phillips. Interested in the feature series, Mrs. Glasgow called the newspaper and contacted the reporter. In her possession was a hand-transcribed copy of a manuscript entitled, "The Bandit Invincible, the Story of Butch Cassidy," written by William Phillips. William Phillips' "Bandit Invincible" was to play a crucial role in our investigation into the life of the outlaw.

As research continued Dullenty was invited to merge with our effort in the hope that a mutual venture could more efficiently piece together the details of Butch Cassidy's life. Mrs. Glasgow and William R. Phillips, the Spokane man's adopted son, then assigned to Dullenty and me the exclusive rights to use of the William Phillips manuscript, along with photographs and other materials. The joint venture was not successful, however, and after several abortive attempts at collaboration the reporter and I terminated the merger, with each retaining full rights to all the shared material, including the "Bandit Invincible" manuscript.

When Blanche Glasgow first showed the Phillips manuscript to reporter Dullenty, much of the pencilled copy was faded to the point of being illegible. As he attempted to read the narrative, the reporter began tracing over the words written in the notebooks. In his zeal, Dullenty unwittingly committed a serious error. When he came to a misspelled word in the original, he corrected the spelling in his tracings. When the names of people and locations were indecipherable, the reporter—unfamiliar with Cassidy's outlaw career—substituted guesses, often obliterating the faint original markings.

Restoring the document to its original form as transcribed by the Lundstrom family has been a tremendous, but rewarding task. With few exceptions the original markings have been deciphered and reconstructed. The William Phillips "Bandit Invincible" passages included herein are as the Lundstroms hand-copied them some forty years ago.

Fitting together the colossal puzzle of retracing the events in Cassidy's life has involved five years and thousands of miles. Pioneers and their descendents were interviewed, and our correspondence spanned the globe. Countless hours were spent pouring over information and documents in archives, courthouses, penitentiaries, museums, libraries, and back rooms of newspaper offices throughout the West. Voluminous notes were compiled; every lead had to be traced, and verified. The grains of truth have been carefully winnowed from the chaff. And, like Ramon Adams, the great bibliographer of the American West, I hope that with this book I have done my small part to help the reader distinguish fact from fiction, legend from history, in Western Americana.

L. P.

Acknowledgments

To THOSE pioneers and their descendents whose shared recollections have contributed to text and footnote, a very humble thank you for helping set the record straight.

To libraries, historical societies, archives, and newspaper offices throughout the West, appreciation for preserving the primary records, documents, and narrative accounts so extensively relied upon. A special thanks is given for the assistance and guidance from such interested and sincere professionals as Eleanor Gehres, Fred Yonce, and the staff of Denver Public Library's Western History Collection; William Linn, vice president of Pinkertons; Dolores Renze, retired Colorado state archivist; Duane Shillinger, Wyoming State Penitentiary assistant warden; John Stewart, executive secretary of the National Outlaw and Lawman History Association; and Robert Svenningsen, chief, Denver Archive Branch and Record Center, National Archives.

Gratitude is expressed to Blanche Lundstrom Glasgow, Ione Manning, and William R. Phillips for supplying pieces of the Butch Cassidy–William T. Phillips puzzle; to Colin Rickards, Pearl Baker, and James Dullenty for sharing related research; and to Jeannine Zimmerman for conscientious professionalism in laborious handwriting analysis.

To Justo Piernes, of the Buenos Aires *Clarin,* for a thorough investigation into Butch Cassidy's Argentine activities, and to Patsy Hamilton, for translating that research, the author is especially indebted.

To Luther Wilson and Doris Morris of the University of Oklahoma Press, for writing guidance and editing of the final manuscript, and to Dorothy Nicholson of the National Geographic Society, for mapping direction, deep appreciation is expressed.

To John Little, to my wife Pat, and to so many others, thank you for the encouragement in seeing this work to its fruition.

Contents

Illustrations

Maps

In search of Butch Cassidy

Introduction

"NOT that it matters, but most of what follows is true."

With this prelude William Goldman launched the 1969 film sensation *Butch Cassidy and the Sundance Kid*. The film depicted the waning career of an over-the-hill Butch Cassidy, former leader of the infamous Hole-in-the-Wall Gang, once the most effective predator upon the financial institutions of the frontier before the turn of the century. Unable to turn back the encroachment of an increasingly impersonal, industrialized, and mercantile society, and relentlessly pursued by law enforcement officers from the Mexican border to Montana's boundary with Canada, Cassidy with the Sundance Kid, last of his once awesome band, escaped to South America, "where picking the banks was easier than picking up the language." Bantering and bickering to the end, the two amiable rogues met their demise at the hands of a troop of Bolivian *rurales,* in what perhaps was the most spectacular shootout ever filmed.

The sterling performances of Paul Newman as the affable Butch Cassidy, Robert Redford as his sharpshooting sidekick, The Sundance Kid, and Katherine Ross as the Kid's ravishing consort, Etta Place, captivated the American and British public. Smashing box office successes have secured for *Butch Cassidy and the Sundance Kid* a place among the all-time moneymakers in cinema history. With the picture's accolades came three Oscars, a spate of television take-offs, and the escalation of Robert Redford to super-star status. With impetuous enthusiasm America affectionately embraced its new folk hero—Butch Cassidy, Robin Hood of the West.

This new star in the sky of Western Americana was heralded with mixed emotions. Movie critics found it "hard put to believe that the real-life Butch and Sundance could have had much in common with the suave affability of Newman and Redford. Their interior life has never been opened to us. Instead, as they lie dying, they remain somehow vague, unfinished emblems of romance, youth and indi-

3

viduality, once again beaten by 'the system.'" Yet, as Abraham Lincoln once so aptly observed, "What people think is, is more important than what actually is so."

Americans historically have made legends of such frontier characters of less than heroic stature as Buffalo Bill, Wild Bill Hickok, the Earp brothers, and Billy the Kid. This adulation of the raucous and wicked is not new. In Tombstone, that crossroads of frontier life, one journalist noted in lament the "class of persons who cannot restrain a sort of admiration for a stupendous criminal. One who has murdered many and shown no mercy—who has hesitated at no deed of darkness and inhumanity—is sure to be admired as a sort of remarkable character who approaches the measure of a genuine hero."

Nor is Butch Cassidy the first horseback outlaw to be decorated with the Robin Hood epithet. The most classic example is Jesse James, whose deadly application of Civil War guerrilla tactics in private life both terrorized and titillated the populace of the border states during the reconstruction era. Even in his day, James and his band of "loafers, braggarts, bullies and easy-money boys" were heralded with admiration by a sympathetic press still stinging over the ignominious defeat of the Confederacy. The *Kansas City Times* hailed the gang as Missouri's version of the Knights of the Round Table and alluded to one particular James robbery as a "deed so high-handed, so diabolically daring.and so utterly in contempt of fear that we are bound to admire it and revere its perpetrators."

Comparison of Jesse James' outlaw career with that of Butch Cassidy reveals interesting parallels and marked contrasts. Both bandits rationalized their lawless deeds as justified retribution for the mercenary sins of the rich, and both were folk heroes of the poor and oppressed. While James was lauded by post-CivilWar southerners chafing under a yoke of external rule, Cassidy was championed by small homesteaders struggling for existence in a raw frontier dominated by cattle barons and railroad magnates. In this context criminologist Walter Lunden has written that western society "maintains the power of force in law, whereas the real power rests in the social obligations of moral relationships between people. When the natives in a developing country are forced to comply with a legal system not based on their living law, conflicts appear and criminality is the natural result." In each situation this lack of consensus in values gave license to the bandit and made his Robin Hood image possible, much as the tyranny of King John in twelfth-century England gave rise to the legendary Robin Hood of Nottingham.

Jesse James' lawless activities of record spanned fifteen years, from 1866 to 1881; those of Cassidy covered a nineteen-year period from 1889 to 1908. Some twenty-six robberies covering eleven states netted an estimated 500,000 dollars for the James gang, while Cassidy and his Hole-in-the Wall associates gleaned a similar amount from banks, railroads, and mine payrolls across at least a dozen western states and the southern tier of South American countries. Yet, while murder and violence marred the raids of the James band from their very first reported robbery, Cassidy reputedly never killed a single person throughout his entire outlaw career, until his reported death in Bolivia.

In his extensive annotated bibliography on western outlaws and gunmen, *Six-Guns and Saddle Leather,* Ramon Adams cites some 330 books and pamphlets pertaining to Jesse James as compared to 78 entries touching on Butch Cassidy. Authors giving significant coverage to Cassidy's outlaw activities totaled a mere half dozen. Critical analysis of this literature reveals a bewildering tangle of limited scope, restricted local coverage, gaps in information, personal bias, and even absolute misinformation.

Such confusion is not uncommon among treatises on western outlaws. Adams, who devoted his entire career to untangling fact and legend in Western Americana, astutely noted, "Nowhere has research been so inadequate or writing so careless as in the accounts of western outlaws and gunmen. Indeed, many chroniclers seem to delight in repeating early sensational and frequently untrue stories without any real attempt to investigate the facts."

"The truth is dramatic enough, without the window dressing applied through tall tales, faulty reminiscences, and just plain fiction."

There is a danger in emulating a hero created from more than truth. Examination in the stark light of reality most often reveals the man to be less than the legend. To make a folk hero more than human is to diminish ourselves. Butch Cassidy the man must be separated from Butch Cassidy the myth. We owe him and ourselves that dignity.

Yes, William Goldman, the truth really does matter.

Chapter I
The Legend of Butch Cassidy

ARTHUR CHAPMAN started it. Chapman is the fellow who penned the immortal "Out Where the West Begins." He should have stayed with poetry.

In the April 1930 issue of the *Elks Magazine,* Chapman immortalized Butch Cassidy as a swashbuckling Robin Hood of the West, jousting with cattle barons, dragons in banker's clothing, and the smoke-belching behemoths of land-grabbing railroad tycoons. For more than a decade this flamboyant champion of small homesteaders sallied forth from that impregnable bastion of outlawry, the Hole-in-the-Wall, leading his infamous Wild Bunch in guerrilla raids upon the mercenary monsters of the West.

With pursuing hordes of sheriffs, Pinkerton operatives, and cavalry troops snapping at his heels, Cassidy miraculously escaped certain annihilation and, with his most trusted confidant Harry Longabaugh, the Sundance Kid, and Sundance's devoted moll Etta Place, romped away to Argentina again to take up his crusade in behalf of the oppressed.

Now, every school child knows that justice reigns eternal, and even Butch Cassidy must have his comeuppance. Sure enough, a Bolivian troop of *rurales,* no less, rushed to the call of moral service and, well, let's let Chapmen tell it. After all, it's his story.

> . . . the captain himself walked into the room where Cassidy and Longabaugh were eating and drinking.
>
> "Surrender, señors," came the demand from the brave captain.
>
> The outlaws leaped to their feet. Longabaugh was drunk, but Cassidy, always a canny drinker, was in complete command of his senses.
>
> The captain had drawn his revolver when he entered the room. Before he could fire, Cassidy had shot from the hip. The captain fell dead and Cassidy and Longabaugh stationed themselves where they could command a view of the patio.

6

A sergeant and a picked body of cavalrymen rushed through the gate, calling upon the outlaws to surrender. Revolvers blazed from door and window and men began to stagger and fall in the courtyard. The first to die was the sergeant who had sought to rescue his captain.

Cassidy and Longabaugh were firing rapidly, and with deadly effect. Those of the detachment who remained on their feet were firing in return. Bullets sank into the thick adobe walls, or whistled through the window and door. Other soldiers began firing from behind the shelter of the courtyard wall.

"Keep me covered, Butch," called Longabaugh. "I'll get our rifles."

Shooting as he went, Longabaugh lurched into the courtyard. If he could only reach the rifles and ammunition which they had so thoughtlessly laid aside, the fight would be something the outlaws would welcome.

Blood was settling in little pools about the courtyard. The sergeant and most of his file of soldiers were stretched out dead. A few wounded were trying to crawl to safety. The mules had broken their halters and galloped out of the yard.

Soldiers were firing through the open gate and from other vantage points outside the wall. Longabaugh got half-way across the court yard and fell, desperately wounded, but not before he had effectively emptied his six-shooter.

When Cassidy saw his partner fall, he rushed into the courtyard. Bullets rained about him as he ran to Longabaugh's side. Some of the shots found their mark, but Cassidy, though wounded, managed to pick up Longabaugh and stagger back to the house with his heavy burden.

Cassidy saw that Longabaugh was mortally wounded. Furthermore, it was going to be impossible to carry on the battle much longer unless the rifles and ammunition could be reached. Cassidy made several attempts to cross the courtyard. At each attempt he was wounded and driven back.

The battle now settled into a siege. Night came on, and men fired at the red flashes from weapons. There were spaces of increasing length between Cassidy's shots. He had only a few cartridges left. Longabaugh's cartridge belt was empty. So was the dead Bolivian captain's.

The soldiers, about 9 or 10 o'clock in the evening, heard two shots fired in the bullet-ridden station. Then no more shots came.

Perhaps it was a ruse to lure them into the patio within range of those deadly revolvers. The soldiers kept on firing all through the night and during the next morning.

About noon an officer and a detachment of soldiers rushed through the patio and into the station. They found Longabaugh and Cassidy dead. Cassidy had fired a bullet into Longabaugh's head and had used his last cartridge to kill himself.

Chapman's tale was picked up by the press, and in an item date-lined New York, April 23, 1930, the *Washington Post,* that "shaper of public opinion" no less, excerpting the *Elks Magazine* article, proclaimed to the world, BUTCH IS DEAD.

The Chapman story was believable. He wrote with authority, appearing to have researched his subject well. Too, his account of Butch Cassidy went unchallenged because people wanted to believe it. With sensational style, contrived dialogue, and lurid detail, he gave a Depression-weary public an escape to the fantasy land of the dime novels of their youth. He painted the west just the way Americans had grown to believe it really was. It was the stuff of which story books are made.

For half a century books passed off as authentic western history have expanded on Arthur Chapman's time-worn saga. In passing the legend on, writers have been content to repeat his sensational account without investigating available records to verify its authenticity.

Most significant of these "histories" is Charles Kelly's *Outlaw Trail,* written in 1938. Kelly, an outspoken Utah printer with a penchant for western history, spent several years in retracing Cassidy's outlaw activities and recording stories told by Utah pioneers who had known the outgoing bandit. Until recently Kelly's book, complete with Chapman's version of Cassidy's South American adventures and violent death, was considered the final word on the life of Butch Cassidy.

Arthur Chapman, however, was not without his detractors. In Wyoming, some five years after his article's release, rumors began circulating that Butch Cassidy had not died in South America, but had returned to the United States and had even revisited old Wyoming friends from his outlaw days. In July 1936 Wyoming's treasurer, Mart T. Christensen, received the following note from the Register of the U.S. Land Office, William G. Johnson:

> During the summer of 1935, Butch Cassidy bought a bill of grub from Harry Baldwin, pioneer merchant at Lander. He then had 2 Lander men deliver him somewhere in the Indian Reservation. At a certain point, Butch dismissed his companions and proceded alone. Soon thereafter departed for his home in Seattle, Wash., where he is known as William Phillips. He now has cancer of the stomach and is not expected to live much longer.[1]

Johnson's findings were generally corroborated by Wyoming historian Tacetta B. Walker, who also wrote Mart Christensen in 1936 concerning Cassidy's reported visit to the Lander vicinity, "two years ago."[2]

In addition to his other civil duties, Christensen also headed the Wyoming Writers Project, a federally funded WPA program. As one goal of the project was to reconstruct the history of the state of Wyoming, Christensen assigned several of his writers to investigate these recurring stories of Butch Cassidy's return.

At the same time Christensen was assembling information on the outlaw, Utah historian Charles Kelly was preparing his *Outlaw Trail*. Kelly was convinced of the authenticity of the legendary battle at San Vicente. The Utah author had interviewed Wyoming pioneers and was aware of the claims Cassidy had returned to visit his old haunts, yet he dismissed the accounts as fiction. When his research placed him in contact with Wyoming historians, a lively exchange of correspondence developed.

Wyoming researchers made serious efforts to get Kelly to reevaluate the stories. Tacetta Walker, in 1936, was among the first to write Kelly of Cassidy's return, stating that Lander pioneers had told her that Cassidy "was back in the country over there two years ago. One old timer who roomed with him claimed he recognized him by a scar on his head. Another one told me that Cassidy did not tell him he was Butch Cassidy until he told him he knew him. Then he told him a story that only he, Butch Cassidy, and one other knew. The third party was dead so that left only Cassidy and himself as knowing the story."

"This same man told me he believed Cassidy was going by the
name of Bill Phillips in Spokane, Washington. . . . And from what
they say, he would probably not admit being Cassidy."[3]

After evaluating research compiled by members of his Wyoming
Writers Project staff, Mart Christensen—convinced the stories were
true—joined Mrs. Walker in appeals to Kelly to reconsider the
accounts of Cassidy's visits to Wyoming in the Thirties.[4]

When, in return, the Utah author made it known to Christensen
that he did not deem the information worth much and that he
preferred to believe Chapman's account of Cassidy's death in San
Vicente, the incredulous Wyoming official sent a heated reply,
elaborating on the findings of his project researchers:

> I will not burden you with the details of Cassidy's visit there in
> the summer of 1934 but it is enough to relate that an old friend of
> Cassidy's by the name of Hank Boedeker, 78, but very alert and
> active for his age, spent the best part of a day with Butch Cassidy
> on that occasion. It is common knowledge in that entire vicinity
> that Butch Cassidy did visit there during 1934 and the purpose of
> his visit. He talked to Harry Baldwin, Wyoming merchant, who
> sold him a bill of grub and to Ed Farlow, a former mayor of
> Lander, who knew him during his early days. Now, if I were
> interested enough in the life of Butch Cassidy to write a book I
> would forthwith visit Hank Boedeker, Ed Farlow, and Harry
> Baldwin in Lander. . . . It will explode all the "bunk" put out by
> the several writers who finish the life of Cassidy in South America
> with such dramatics.
>
> Hank Boedeker, then peace officer in Lander, took Cassidy to
> Rawlins [actually Laramie] the time he went to the penitentiary.
> It would be preposterous to assert to any of the people I have
> named that they are mistaken. George LeRoy Parker, alias Butch
> Cassidy—now known as William Phillips, in the state of
> Washington—was alive six months ago and resides in
> Spokane. . . .
>
> Butch Cassidy related to Hank Boedeker some details of the
> fight you describe, in which he is supposed to have been killed.
>
> The men I have named, who live at Lander, Wyoming, are
> reputable, well-known and responsible citizens and not the type
> who would exploit any sort of story for publicity or for gossiping
> purposes. They knew Butch Cassidy well and they are not mis-
> taken about this whole matter.[5]

Although he viewed the stories of Cassidy's return as a preposterous hoax, Charles Kelly did eventually investigate further, after a September 1937 Wyoming newspaper story announced the death of William Phillips, "the real Butch Cassidy," in Spokane, Washington. A query letter to the Washington Bureau of Vital Statistics brought forth a copy of the death certificate of one William Phillips, a Spokane resident who died of rectal cancer on July 20, 1937, just one month after Christensen's scathing letter.

There was no question this was the man referred to by Wyoming pioneers as "the real Butch Cassidy," Although early reports as to his residence varied from Seattle to Spokane, there had emerged a consistent mention of Spokane, His age, listed as seventy-two on the death certificate, would have been comparable to that of the outlaw, and William G. Johnson's note that Phillips had cancer of the stomach is remarkably similar to the attending physician's statement of cause of death as cancer of the rectum.[6]

Continuing to delve into the mystery, Kelly located the Spokane man's widow, Gertrude Phillips. In October 1938, finally responding to the Utah writer's persistent inquiries, Mrs. William T. Phillips wrote an account of her controversial husband's life:

> . . . it came to my mind last eve. that at least I could do as you suggested and give you a brief outline of Mr. Phillips' life; tho' am afraid there will be little in it of interest to you, because I am unable to give you an account of the part of it in which you, naturally, are most interested, viz, the few years in which he knew and rode the range with Cassidy.
>
> Wm. T. Phillips was born and raised in an eastern state until he reached the age of 14 years; at which time (owing to dime novel influence) he ran away and headed for the Black Hills, where he was greatly disillusioned in regard to many things, as he was bound to be; after a few months of seeing his small hoard dwindle away, and failing to find work because of his youth and inability to convince anyone he could hold down a man's job, he became homesick and started out to make his way back home.
>
> It was in the fall of the year, and he finally succeeded in obtaining work on a ranch during harvest, and (tho I've heard him tell about it), I'm not sure just where that was, but in the corn belt, for he often laughed at the speed he acquired in husking corn. He enjoyed the people with whom he found himself, and

stayed till the following Spring, when, having survived his homesickness, decided to stay a while longer in the west, and again headed for the Black Hills. It was after that, of course, that he fell in with Cassidy; but not having it all in detail, I can not give you much satisfaction as to how it all came about, except that it was at the time of the Johnson County War, and I've heard him express himself as being in sympathy with the "little fellows" instead of the stock association. He thought he knew Cassidy very, very well; and considered he was much more sinned against than sinning. As to just how long he was associated with him I am unable to say, for my memory is none to good as to dates, etc. and I haven't that all in detail, as I have his account of Cassidy, in which he makes no mention of himself.

Later, he did mural decorating in New York City for two or three years; at one time had a machine shop in Des Moines, Iowa, for about seven or eight years. After he and I were married, we lived in Arizona for a year; came to Spokane, and have been here ever since, until his death last year.

That, in brief, is the story of my husband. I wrote you that we each knew Cassidy; so we did; I knew his family, but I can tell you little, I think, that you do not already know; however both Mr. Phillips and myself came originally from the east; *not the middle west.*

So, I'm afraid there is little of interest that I can acquaint you with, concerning the western experiences, tho' I wish I could, for I would very much like to figure out some way whereby I could better myself financially; the depression of '29 is responsible for my present circumstances; we have a son who is not old enough yet to become established in business; and present conditions are not too favorable for young fellows of his age; however, we hope to weather through, and if war does not yet break out, we, as others, have a better chance.

Thanking you for your interest, and wishing you success with your book, I am, sincerely yours,

Mrs. William T. Phillips. [7]

With receipt of this letter, Charles Kelly closed the subject, concluding William Phillips to be a hoax. That same year he published *Outlaw Trail,* re-entrenching Arthur Chapman's dramatic tale as a historically accurate account. Quoting portions of Gertrude Phillips' story of her husband's life, Kelly pronounced benediction on the issue with a terse summary of his own findings in Wyoming:

> Phillips, representing himself as Cassidy, searched the mountains near Fort Washakie with Bill Boyd for $70,000 supposed to have been buried there by Butch. He met Hank Bedeker of Dubois, who knew Cassidy well in the old days, but was not recognized as an imposter. He also fooled several old-timers in the vicinity of Lander and Wilcox, who swore they could not be mistaken. . . . The preceding stories are given for what they are worth, merely to complete the record.[8]

Christensen released to the news media the findings of his researchers. Resulting news releases described Cassidy's 1934 visit to Lander where he "was positively identified by officers who had known him in the heyday of his outlaw career," and summarized the Wyoming Writers Project investigations. Citing as supporting evidence the corroborating investigation of the Cheyenne Register of the United States land office, William Johnson, "personally acquainted with the 'Butch Cassidy' of 50 years ago," the widely carried news items concluded, "George (Butch) Cassidy, once head of a notorious train robber and bank robber and horse rustler gang in Wyoming, died of stomach cancer in Spokane, in December 1937, under an assumed name—William Phillips. . . . The investigations 'brought to life' a man thought shot down by soldiers who ambushed him after a South American mine pay roll robbery in 1909. His real name is believed to have been George LeRoy Parker."[9]

The news releases of Christensen's findings were not favorably received. Public reaction ranged from disbelief to outright anger. Astonishment within the Spokane community was reflected in a letter of rebuttal by a local attorney, Lucius G. Nash: "I knew William Phillips well and he had often visited in my home. As a lawyer, I have my own method of looking at this thing. Nobody can make me believe Phillips was Butch Cassidy."[10]

The brief furor ended in a stalemate. Wyoming pioneers were positive of their conclusions; Spokane residents generally rejected the whole thing as nonsense; and Arthur Chapman's version of Butch Cassidy's death continued in acceptance.

As time passed and memories blurred, the elusive truth seemed to dissolve in hearsay. Opinions are like navels, everybody has one.

Chapter II
William T. Phillips

IN 1969, 20th Century Fox released its box-office sensation, *Butch Cassidy and the Sundance Kid.* With national attention focused on the activities of the Wild Bunch outlaw gang, the smoldering Butch Cassidy–William T. Phillips identity controversy once again was fanned into an inferno. People wanted to know what really became of this rogue of the bygone frontier.

In the little Utah farming community of Circleville, reporters located the family of Robert LeRoy Parker, the Mormon cowboy who became the notorious bandit leader Butch Cassidy. Cassidy's youngest sister, Mrs. Lula Parker Betenson, was still living.

When interviewed in 1970 the spritely eighty-six-year-old Mrs. Betenson made the startling revelation that Butch Cassidy had returned to visit his Utah family in 1925, some sixteen years after his reported death in San Vicente. "The law thought he was dead and he was happy to leave it that way. He made us promise not to tell anyone that he was alive. And we never did. It was the tightest family secret. He died peacefully in Spokane in 1937."[1]

When pressed for details, Mrs. Betenson demurred, saying only that "Butch Cassidy spent the rest of his life as a trapper and prospector in Alaska, Wyoming and Washington State."[2]

Lula Betenson's statements recalled the earlier claims of her brother's visits to Wyoming. In Lander, where the controversy was first generated some four decades before, my wife Pat and I began our investigation into the challenging puzzle.

Old-timers of the Lander area recalled Cassidy as an outgoing, happy-go-lucky cowboy who had sided with the small homesteaders in the land struggle with the cattle barons during the early settlement of the West. His own attempts at ranching, using the reverse E, box E brand ($\boxed{\exists}$E),[3] had placed him in conflict with the powerful stock growers association. Once on the association's infamous blacklist, Cassidy had retaliated by stealing horses and cattle from the large land holders, and after serving a two-year term in the territorial prison for rustling, he took up the life of banditry with a vengeance.

Locally, Cassidy was remembered not so much for his lawlessness as for his friendliness and generosity to the small settlers. It was with noticeable pride that old-timers spoke of their friendship with the bandit. One old fellow even boasted, "If he rode in here tomorrow, I'd hide him up again."

When we broached the subject of Cassidy's return to Wyoming, many pioneers were steadfast in their conviction that William Phillips, the mysterious visitor from Spokane, was their old outlaw friend, Butch Cassidy. Other, less numerous, old-timers put no stock in the stories, believing, like Charles Kelly, that William T. Phillips might have been an impostor.

Attempting to determine, once and for all, the final fate of Butch Cassidy, we wrote to the American Embassy in Bolivia. Surely the Bolivian government could answer the question of Cassidy's death at San Vicente. Cultural Attaché Graham K. French responded:

> We have attempted to find out from several sources any information that might be available here about these now famous outlaws, and we have drawn blanks everywhere. There appears to be no newspaper accounts of their activities in Bolivia, and Cnl. Julio Diaz, historian of the Bolivian Army, tells us that he knows of no military action against the two American bandits in Bolivia. They could have been here, he says, but he doubts that the military forces were concerned with them. There are, however, reports that one or both of the two men are buried several kilometers from Tupiza in southern Bolivia.[4]

There was no official record of Butch Cassidy's death in Bolivia! If not the Bolivian government, then perhaps the Pinkerton National Detective Agency—perennial pursuers of the Wild Bunch and vociferous proponents of Arthur Chapman's story—might have documentation of Cassidy's death. Again, exhaustive research in the Pinkerton Archives failed to produce a single verification of the legendary shootout. Instead, the files contained divergent memoranda based on rumor and hearsay.

A San Francisco informant, identified only as number 85, in 1909 reported that Cassidy had returned to the United States in 1905. "The last I heard from him by letter was from Baggs, Wyo. and he said he wanted Longabaugh to sell his part [of a South American ranching venture], and send him the money as he was going to the northwest territories. I have heard since, from a pretty good source, that . . . he was filled full of holes on the bridge at Green River, Wyo. . . . in the winter of 1905–6."[5]

Another report, from operative Frank Dimaio, who was assigned to track Cassidy and Longabaugh in Argentina in 1903, contained information obtained in a Detroit Italian restaurant in 1912, from a Mr. Steele, traveling agent at Buenos Aires: "I was in Mercedes [Argentina] last year visiting my trade. When I returned to the hotel one of the guests said to me 'Lift up the tarpaulin on the piazza.' Upon doing so I saw the bodies of Place [Longabaugh], his wife, and Ryan [Cassidy]. They had been shot to death while holding up a bank in a nearby village."[6]

Yet a third memorandum stated, "As late as 1913 we received information, through an informant, to the effect that at the Pen. in the City of Antofagasta, Chile, was a North American bandit, supposedly Butch Cassidy. . . . However, we never could verify the story."[7]

With no official record, and only confusion among the detectives who sought Cassidy, where, then, had Arthur Chapman gotten his information on the demise of the bandit leader? In his article, Chapman himself supplied the answer, "Through Mr. Percy A. Seibert, now an attorney at Santiago, Chile, who, as mine manager, had given employment to Cassidy, the writer of this article is able to relate the circumstances of the bandit's last fight. . . ."[8]

Each report of the San Vicente shootout has been traced to Percy Seibert as its original source. Regarding Seibert's importance in initiating these stories, Lula Betenson quoted her brother as telling the family in 1925, "I guess the heat turned off with the shooting when Sundance and I were supposed to have been killed. . . . I heard they got Percy Seibert from the Concordia Tin Mines to identify a couple of bodies as Butch Cassidy and the Sundance Kid all right. I wondered why Mr. Seibert did that. Then it dawned on me that he would know this was the only way we could go straight. I'd been close to Seibert—we'd talked a lot, and he knew how sick of the life

I was. He knew I'd be hounded as long as I lived. Well, I'm sure he saw this as a way for me to bury my past along with somebody else's body so I could start over. I'd saved his and Mr. Glass's lives on a couple of occasions, and I guess he figured this was how he could pay me back."[9]

In this light Mart Christensen's controversial Wyoming Writers Project findings commanded a closer inspection. Had Butch Cassidy escaped his pursuers in South America to return to the United States as William Phillips? Hoping to find some clue to this fascinating riddle, Pat and I traveled to southern Utah in 1973 to interview the outlaw's sister.

Although Lula admitted Cassidy did, at times, use the alias, Phillips, she did not concur with Christensen's claims.[10] In words later recorded in her book, *Butch Cassidy, My Brother,* Mrs. Betenson emphasized her intent to keep secret the final fate of her brother: "Robert LeRoy Parker died in the Northwest in the fall of 1937, a year before Dad died. He was not the man known as William Phillips, reported to be Butch Cassidy. . . . Where he is buried and under what name is still our secret. Dad said, 'All his life he was chased. Now he has a chance to rest in peace, and that's the way it must be.' Revealing his burial place would furnish clues for the curious to crack that secret. I wouldn't be a Parker if I broke my word. . . . If I were to reveal his burial place, someone would be sure to disturb it under some pretext and my brother is entitled to rest in peace."[11]

If William Phillips and Cassidy were not the same man, then who was this mysterious Spokane man, taken by so many Wyoming pioneers as Butch Cassidy, and said by his widow to have known the notorious bandit "very, very well?"

Where Charles Kelly's research ended, ours had to begin. William Phillips' death record placed his birth as June 22, 1865, in Michigan. His father was listed as L. J. Phillips; his mother's maiden name as Celia Mudge.[12] Records in the Spokane Elks and Masonic lodges further listed his birthplace as Sandusky, Michigan, and his father's name as Laddie J. Phillips.

Research in Michigan census records failed to produce a Laddie J. Phillips. Sandusky records did show a Celia Mudge, born in Sanilac County on November 19, 1852, but she would have been twelve years old in 1865, the year of Phillips' listed birth date. At age twenty-two, in February 1875, Celia Mudge was married at Minden, Michigan, to Hezakiah Snell. The couple's descendents know little of their grandparents and nothing of William Phillips.

Sandusky, Michigan was not formed until 1870, and birth certificates were not issued in Sanilac County until 1867. There is, then, no documentation of the birth of "William Thadeus Phillips."[13]

In her letter to Charles Kelly, the man's widow said they had lived in Arizona for a year before moving to Spokane, where city directories first listed the couple in 1911. Gertrude Phillips said that previous to their marriage her husband "did mural decorating in New York City for two or three years; at one time had a machine shop in Des Moines, Iowa, for about seven or eight years."

Neither Des Moines nor New York City records support Mrs. Phillips' contention.[14] Before May 14, 1908, the date of his marriage to Gertrude Livesay in Adrian, Michigan, there is no documentary evidence William T. Phillips ever existed.

If William Phillips' first proven presence was in May of 1908, when was the last substantiated report of the outlaw Butch Cassidy's whereabouts in South America?

Records of Cassidy's activities in South America were found to be scarce. His presence in Argentina is first documented by a letter written by the outlaw from the interior province of Chubut, to an Ashley Valley, Utah woman in August 1902.[15] The letter, now in the Utah State Historical Society Archives, was written to Mrs. Mathilda Davis, mother-in-law of Wild Bunch member Elzy Lay. In it Cassidy described the Patagonian frontier location of his newly established ranching operation.

Research in provincial archives by Buenos Aires journalist Justo Piernes revealed that Cassidy resumed his life of banditry in 1905. Piernes' findings, corroborated by Pinkerton records, indicated that Cassidy, with Harry Longabaugh and his consort Etta Place, restricted their raids to Argentina until late 1906, when they shifted their operations to the rich mining districts of the remote mountainous areas of southern Bolivia.[16] From there the record was much less clear. Pinkerton files were scanty, and most of the information, again, could be traced to Percy Seibert, the mining engineer at the Concordia Tin Mines.

As with Arthur Chapman, our most concrete information on Cassidy's outlaw career in Bolivia initially rested with Percy Seibert. Although Seibert passed away before our investigation, among his surviving possessions was a scrapbook filled with mementoes from his Bolivian tour of duty.[17] Two letters were of special significance. The first, written from Santa Cruz, Argentina, to "The Boys at Concordia," was signed J. P. Maxwell, an alias the Pinkerton files revealed was commonly used by Cassidy in Bolivia.

The second letter, a short note in the same unmistakable handwriting, and signed only "Gilly," was written from Tres Cruces, Argentina, on February 16, 1908. This brief letter was the last documented evidence of Butch Cassidy's presence in South America.

This left a three-month void before the mysterious William T. Phillips bound himself in matrimony to Gertrude M. Livesay in southern Michigan. Could it be that William Phillips really was Butch Cassidy?

Our continued investigation revealed that not all members of the Utah Parker family were in agreement with Lula Betenson in her dismissal of the William T. Phillips stories. Dan Parker, Cassidy's next younger brother, was living with his son, Max Parker, and daughter-in-law Ellnor, in Milford, Utah, when Butch Cassidy came to visit during 1930. Cassidy, with two unidentified men, talked with Dan for several hours. Ellnor Parker especially remembered the reunion because Butch rocked and sang to her newborn son, Max, Jr.

Following Cassidy's visit to Milford, Dan regularly received letters and money from his brother. He was careful to destroy all correspondence, but did confide to his daughter-in-law that Butch Cassidy was living in Spokane, Washington, under the alias, William Phillips. Ellnor remembered Dan's sadness in 1937 when he received word of Phillips' death. Poor health prevented his attending the funeral.

In 1970, following Mrs. Betenson's news releases, Ellnor Parker said she wrote to the outlaw's sister, relaying Dan Parker's knowledge of his brother's death, and the alias Dan told her Cassidy had used. Lula wrote back, Ellnor said, asking her not to share the information with anyone else.[18]

Did Lula Betenson reject the story as without basis, or had Ellnor

Parker stumbled across the well-guarded family secret? In Spokane a newspaper feature story further polarized the issue.

Intrigued by the raging debate over William T. Phillips' identity, in 1973 the *Spokane Daily Chronicle* assigned reporter Jim Dullenty to write an in-depth series on the controversial Spokane man.[19] Dullenty found that William R. Phillips, an adopted son, still resided in the community. The reporter also was contacted by an area woman, Mrs. Blanche Glasgow, who with her first husband, William Lundstrom, had been close friends with Phillips.

As Dullenty was writing his newspaper series, the leads developed in Wyoming put Pat and me in contact with the Spokane reporter, and with Blanche Lundstrom Glasgow and William R. Phillips. Both the younger Phillips and Blanche Glasgow had photographs of William T. Phillips. When compared to the few existing authentic photographs of Butch Cassidy, the resemblance was immediately apparent. It was no wonder Wyoming pioneers thought Phillips was the notorious leader of the Hole-in-the-Wall Gang.

For a professional comparison of the Phillips and Cassidy photographs, internationally renowned realist sculptor Harry Jackson was prevailed upon. Jackson believed the pictures were of the same man, pointing to basic bone structure patterns. The sculptor also expressed the opinion that the man very well could have undergone a face lift, noting the ears, especially, appeared altered.[20]

In Wyoming we located two nephews of Will Boyd, the man Charles Kelly said took Phillips into the Wind River Mountains in 1934. When shown the photographs of William Phillips, both men, Roy Jones and Herman LaJeunesse, who had gone with their uncle on the 1934 pack trip, were positive of their identification of the Spokane man.[21]

The two men said Butch Cassidy and Will Boyd had been close friends when Cassidy first came into the Lander area as a cowboy, and that Will's sister, Mary Boyd, had been Cassidy's sweetheart during those early years. Will also had told his nephews that Cassidy often found refuge in the Boyd home during his later years as an outlaw. To Roy Jones and Herman LaJeunesse there never had been any doubt that their summer guest was Butch Cassidy. Jones, who was raised by Will and his wife Minnie, said the family kept the information secret for several years after Phillips' visit.

Roy Jones said that when Phillips arrived in 1934 and asked Will Boyd to organize a pack trip into the Wind River Mountains, the former outlaw was accompanied by a Spokane woman, Ellen Harris, and her grown son who lived in Hollywood. Mrs. Harris and her late husband had been close friends with Phillips in Spokane. Ellen Harris often wrote the Boyds after her visit that summer and Roy still had her letters. From her correspondence it also was apparent that both she and the Boyds believed Phillips to have been Butch Cassidy.[22]

Will's sister, Mary Boyd Rhodes, was a widow and living in Riverton, Wyoming, at the time of Phillips' visit. Roy said his uncle had him take Mary up to their camp in the mountains. Mary's recognition of her old sweetheart was immediate, and both Roy and Herman related pleasant memories of the emotional reunion.

After Phillips left Wyoming that fall, Roy said that Mary received letters from the Spokane man, and it was the family's understanding that not long before he died Phillips sent Mrs. Rhodes his ring as a keepsake.

Roy Jones' story opened an entirely new area for investigation. If Mrs. Harris believed Phillips to have been Cassidy, were there other Spokane residents who shared her belief? What had become of Mary Boyd? Did the ring still exist? Like the letters of Ellen Harris preserved by Roy Jones, had any of William Phillips' correspondence survivied? Dizzy with the prospects, we took up the search with renewed vigor.

In Spokane William R. Phillips told us the fact that his father was Butch Cassidy was accepted in their home. He had never been told otherwise, by either William or Gertrude Phillips. It was, however, a well-guarded family secret. The younger Phillips, adopted by the couple shortly after his birth in 1919, today is puzzled at his father's national fame. When Charles Kelly wrote to his mother, he remembers that she purposely camouflaged her husband's background: "She just didn't want the notoriety."[23]

Bill Lundstrom had known Phillips as Butch Cassidy during the 1890s in Wyoming and Montana, where Lundstrom was a bartender. His wife Blanche met Phillips in Spokane through her husband in 1914.[24] Once Phillips became acquainted with her, Blanche said he took her into his confidence. She recalled the parties they at-

tended and the evenings she and Bill Lundstrom spent listening to
Phillips talk of his outlaw days as Butch Cassidy. He told of robbing
banks and trains, of hiding with the Indians to evade pursuing
posses, and of his adventures in South America.

Only a few of Phillips' inner circle of friends heard him tell of his
outlaw past. He never seemed to talk about it around Gertrude,
Blanche recalled. She and her husband kept it secret, "because we
just figured he never wanted it told. He told it to us in secret."

William Phillips died a man of few earthly possessions. The old
gentleman's most prized mementoes fell into the hands of his most
steadfast friends. Among the treasures the Lundstroms saved were
some handguns such as were used in the West at the turn of the
century, and a copy of a manuscript he had written in 1934.
Blanche's daughter showed us Phillips' two Colt revolvers and a
small .22 derringer. Carved into the pistol grip of one revolver was
Butch Cassidy's unmistakable brand, the reverse E, box E (ⲉⲉ).

The manuscript Blanche had saved would prove to be as intriguing as the mystery of Phillips' identity. The title of Phillips' manuscript: "The Bandit Invincible, the Story of Butch Cassidy."

In Wyoming we stepped up the pursuit of further information on
Mary Boyd. On the Wind River Reservation Esther Chamberlin,
whose husband Jesse had accompanied the Boyds and Phillips on
their pack trip, produced the first solid lead in our search. As she
related her husband's experiences in packing the former outlaw into
the back country of the Wind River range, Esther told of Cassidy's
relationship with the Boyd family, and his love affair with Mary
Boyd Rhodes. She also said a keepsake ring had been exchanged
between the two former lovers following Cassidy's visit. She understood that, although Mary's children had all passed away, a
granddaughter, Ione, was still living in Wyoming.[25]

After an intensive search, Ione, now Mrs. Carl Manning of
Casper, Wyoming, was located. Ione graciously consented to share
what she had. "Yes," she said, "I knew people were trying to find
out what happened to Butch Cassidy, and I knew I had proof. But I
figured if they dug deep enough they'd find me."[26]

Then Ione Manning produced the ring Phillips had given her
grandmother just before his death. Its beauty bedazzled; the Mexi-

can fire opal flashed an array of color. But the gem was not the ring's only distinction. Inside the band lay the evidence to William T. Phillips' identity:

Geo C to Mary B

George Cassidy to Mary Boyd! Here was the first documented proof that William T. Phillips claimed to be George "Butch" Cassidy.

Mrs. Manning then produced letters Phillips had written Mary Boyd Rhodes. The first, sent during the Christmas season of 1935, was mailed secretly: "One of my old friends from Montana came to see me the other day and is going to take me down town today to mail this as I never trust any one to mail my letters. I dont want them to know any thing of my affairs you understand."

That letter, written in 1935, was signed, "I am as always your old sweetheart   *Geo*

W. T. Phillips"

Phillips wrote those lines in secret. He did not expect the world to know what he had written. He was not staking a claim to the Cassidy name, but merely signing his outlaw name as unobtrusively as possible for the woman who had always known him as George Cassidy. He fully expected the secret he and Mary Boyd shared would die with them.

His last known letter was written April 8, 1937, just four months before his death. In that final letter Phillips told Mary of sending the ring Ione had shown us: "I am sending you under seperate cover my ring which I wore for over 35 years, as a Keepsake. I hope you will like it you will never see another like it."

When Phillips' letters ceased coming, Mary Boyd Rhodes began inquiring about the fate of her old sweetheart. On August 19, 1937, in a letter saved by Blanche Lundstrom Glasgow, Mary wrote William L. Fields, brother-in-law to Bill Lundstrom, and a Spokane contact for Phillips' correspondence:

Mr. W Fields

I am writing you a few lines asking you to give me a little information   would you answer the questions i want to [k]now   you [k]now i received letters from Mr. W. T. Phillips

all the time   i want received a letter from Mr. Phillips about a
month ago send me his ring he wore 55 years ago for a keepsake
      is he dead   i heard he was   if he is i want to [k]now   their is
something i want to find out   he had some thing of mine   you
[k]now i was his common laws wife while he was in Wyoming
         you please write and let me [k]now   i want to look into
things   he had a tie pin of mine i would like to have and did he
have any thing   i have been talking to a lawyer now let me here
from you right away   if you dont i will have some one from
Riverton to find out.[27]

Fields turned the letter over to Bill Lundstrom, who responded,
telling the Riverton woman of Phillips' death on July 20, after a
prolonged illness "since he came back from Wyoming some three
years ago." In answer to Mrs. Rhodes other inquiries, Lundstrom
concluded his letter, saying, "He left no insurance and had no
personal property. He sent you the ring because he wanted you to
have it to remember him by. If you tried to get the pin it would
expose you and him, my advise forget it."[28]

    With these letters, it appeared the investigation had run its
course. Butch Cassidy was last known to have been in South America
in February 1908; William T. Phillips first appeared three months
later, apparently out of thin air. Interviews with those who had
known Cassidy best revealed that those who had seen Phillips during
his Wyoming visits believed him to be Butch Cassidy. Photographs
of the man gave credence to their claims. Phillips even admitted to
being Cassidy, and now, with the ring and letters in Ione Manning's
possession, documentation of those claims could be made.

    It was all there, except for one thing: legal proof. Since finger-
prints couldn't be produced, it appeared the research had fallen just
short of its ultimate goal—to prove William T. Phillips was, or was
not, Butch Cassidy. The closest we had come were the handwritten
letters.

    Handwritten letters! Mary Boyd Rhodes had saved the only ir-
refutable evidence to Phillips' identity: his handwriting.

    A copy of the authentic letter handwritten by Butch Cassidy from
Argentina in 1902 was obtained from the Utah State Historical
Society. The documents were then sent to a legally certified hand-

writing expert, Master Certified Graphoanalyst and Questioned Document Examiner, Jeannine Zimmerman, of Aurora, Colorado. After a detailed examination—with no prior information to bias her evaluation—Jeannine Zimmerman gave the following analysis:

At your request, I have examined and compared the following material:

(1) Copy of a letter addressed to Mrs. Davis, Ashley, Utah, dated August 10, 1902; and

(2) Copy of a letter signed, W. T. Phillips, and dated December 17, 1935.

Several hours were spent in examining the style, relative size and proportions of strokes, line quality, skill ability; the appearance of pick-up strokes, connectors, terminal strokes and all other writing habits characteristic of the writer, as demonstrated in the document (1) outlined above. A comparison was then made with the handwriting of the second letter, document (2) above. Although there is a time lapse of 33 years between the execution of the handwriting on these two documents, many identifying characteristics noted in document (1) above were also evident in the later writing, (2) above. It is therefore my opinion that both of these documents, (1) and (2) outlined above, were executed by the same individual. I have made many notes on stroke comparisons in the examination of these two documents and would be glad to demonstrate these comparisons to you personally, as well as any other interested party.

If you have any questions, or wish to discuss this matter further, please let me know.

Sincerely,

Jeannine Zimmerman
Document Examiner[29]

There can no longer be any question. With the handwriting analysis performed by Jeannine Zimmerman, the Butch Cassidy puzzle has been pieced together and the picture emerges clearly: William T. Phillips was Butch Cassidy, "The Bandit Invincible."

Robert LeRoy Parker, alias Butch Cassidy,
1894.

Courtesy Duane Shillinger, Assistant Warden, Wyoming State
Penitentiary. Print by Ted's Photo, Lander, Wyo.

26

William T. Phillips, *c* 1930.

Courtesy William R. Phillips.

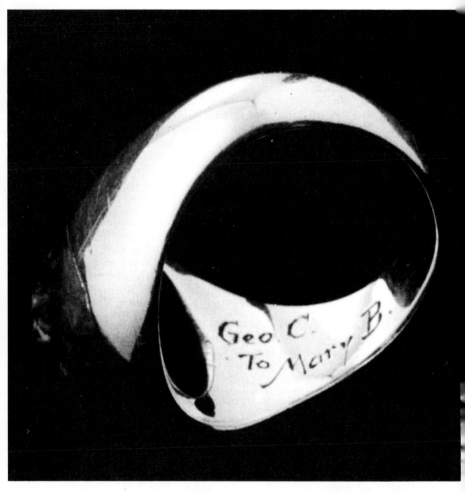

"Geo C to Mary B," the Mexican Fire Opal ring given Mary Boyd Rhodes
by William T. Phillips.

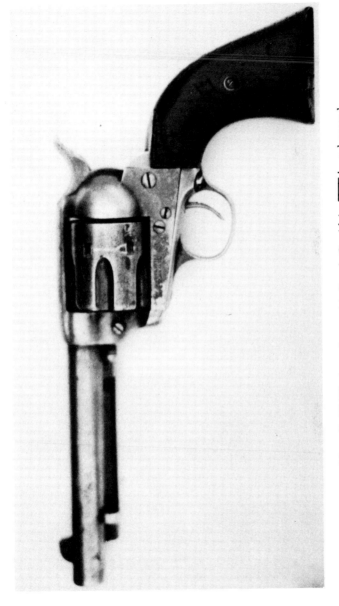

William T. Phillips' revolver, with Butch Cassidy's ⌶⌶ brand carved into the pistol grip.

Ellen Harris, during 1934 pack trip with William Phillips into the
Wind River Mountains of Wyoming.

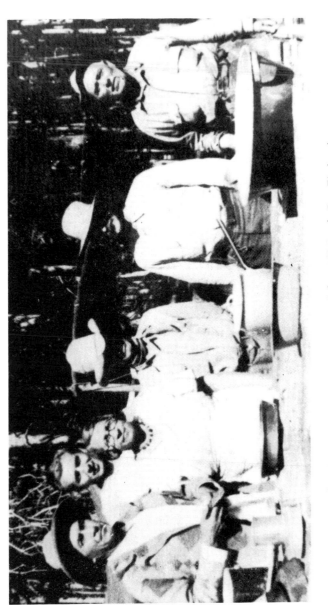

1934 pack trip group photograph. From left, Will Boyd, Ben Fitzharris, Mary Boyd Rhodes, John Boyd, Dan Boyd, and Bert Chamberlin.

Courtesy Ben Fitzharris.

Will Boyd.

Courtesy Herman LaJeunesse. Print by Ted's Photo, Lander, Wyo.

Mary Boyd Rhodes, with daughter Hazel (left), and granddaughter Ione
(right), c1935.

Courtesy Ione Manning. Print by Ted's Photo, Lander, Wyo.

William and Blanche Lundstrom, *c*1930.

34

Chapter III

The Bandit Invincible

"The Bandit Invincible, the Story of Butch Cassidy" was written by
William T. Phillips in 1934, following his visit to Wyoming. The
manuscript, written in third person, was William T. Phillips' attempt to set the record straight on the life of Butch Cassidy. It was
this narrative to which Gertrude Phillips had referred when she
wrote author Charles Kelly in 1938, "I have his account of Cassidy
in which he makes no mention of himself." It was this writing, also,
that Bill Lundstrom's widow brought to light in 1973 after forty
years of storage in an attic trunk.

Phillips' manuscript apparently had its beginnings in conversation around the campfire during his pack trip into the Wind River
Mountains. As he recounted episodes from his outlaw past, Phillips
was encouraged by Ellen Harris and her son Ben to write the authentic story of Butch Cassidy and his Wild Bunch. Mrs. Harris volunteered to type the manuscript, and Ben, who was working in Hollywood as a bit actor and prop man, offered to help market the
completed book.

When he returned to Spokane, Phillips began hand writing "The
Bandit Invincible." Completed sections were forwarded to Ellen
Harris, then living in California, for typing. Mrs. Harris, in turn,
typed the manuscript exactly as Phillips had written it, including
errors in punctuation, spelling, and grammar. Once finished, the
typescript was given to Ben for marketing, and a copy was returned
to Phillips in Spokane.

Although Ben knew Phillips was Butch Cassidy, he was not aware
of the former outlaw's career in South America. When he reached
the chapters dealing with Cassidy's adventures in Argentina and
Bolivia, he rejected the material, believing the concept of western
bandits in South America was too preposterous to merit serious
consideration. He refused to help place the manuscript and returned
his copy to his mother.[1]

Phillips next turned to the magazine market, but after receiving several rejection slips, including one from *Sunset Magazine,* he finally abandoned the manuscript as a failure.

Although neither Ellen Harris' copy of "The Bandit Invincible" nor the copy in Gertrude Phillips' possession in 1938 is in existence today, the manuscript was not destined for extinction. Phillips once had shown Bill and Blanche Lundstrom his copy of the manuscript. They were fascinated by the account, and some time after Phillips' death Blanche Lundstrom wrote to Ellen Harris requesting the opportunity to read again the former outlaw's biography.

The Lundstroms had been extremely close to Phillips during his Spokane years, and the "Bandit Invincible" manuscript held special significance for them. With Ellen Harris' copy of the biography in hand Blanche Lundstrom solicited the help of her daughters, Cleo and Veryl, and her sister, Madge Fields, in transcribing the manuscript.

Each was given a spiral-bound notebook and a handful of pages to laboriously hand copy. As each batch was completed more pages were distributed, with notations made to track the manuscript's continuity. Because the transcribing was done piecemeal the sequence of the original material was transferred several times among the notebooks. When completed Blanche's copy totalled 188 pages and nearly filled all four notebooks.[2]

When in late 1973 the *Spokane Daily Chronicle* ran its series by reporter Jim Dullenty, exploring the controversy over William T. Phillips' identity, Blanche, now Mrs. Mike Glasgow, remembered the manuscript she and her family had hand copied over forty years before, and contacted the reporter. Although Bill Lundstrom had passed away and Blanche had remarried and settled in nearby Medical Lake, Washington, the Lundstroms' copy of "The Bandit Invincible" had been saved. Mice had chewed the corner of one notebook, and the pencilled words were badly faded, but the manuscript had survived.

Resurrection of Phillips' manuscript as originally transcribed by the Lundstrom family has been a monumental, but vastly rewarding, task. Although the document lacked Phillips' handwriting, our continued exchanges with graphoanalyst Jeannine Zimmerman had alerted us to the continuity in the man's writing pattern—many

sentences began with "and," for example—in all the correspondence
we had found. As we restored William T. Phillips' misspellings,
punctuation patterns, and idiosyncrasies of grammar, there emerged
the same prose style that had characterized his letters. Indeed, the
man's unique peculiarities in writing were the very proof of the
manuscript's authenticity.

Phillips wrote in an unadorned, homely style. With straightfor-
ward conversational prose, he brought to life the colorful people and
times of the bygone frontier. And he wrote it as he recollected it,
with only the loosest organization, and often without chronological
order. He spelled the names of people and locations by ear, and paid
little regard to dates. His picturesque accounts of the escapades of
Butch Cassidy and his Wild Bunch allow the reader the rare
privilege of intimate glimpses into the life of the horseback outlaw.

But William Phillips was not spinning reminiscences for the mere
sake of entertainment. Financially broken by the Depression, in
1934 the man was sixty-eight, unable to support his family, and,
most important, dying of cancer.

The disappointments of his recent trip to Wyoming are reflected
in the bittersweet nostalgia of his poem included in the manuscript
prelude:

> *Back to old Wyoming where I roamed in the days of your,*
> *Searching for the faces of my pals, of long ago.*
> *Gone, are they, forever, from the mountain and the dales;*
> *Ne'er, again I'll see them, midst the hills I love so well.*

For twenty-six years he had lived a charade, a man without a past,
unable to share with any but a trusted few the memories of his
dramatic part in the epic of the American frontier. Beginning in
1930 with Arthur Chapman's article, Phillips had seen Butch Cassidy depicted as everything from a western Robin Hood to a monster
of criminal depravity, in a literal flood of newspaper dailies,
magazines, and pulp publications of the *National Police Gazette* variety, each purporting to give a true account of the bandit's exploits.
It was to this absurd tangle of fact and fantasy that Phillips addressed the "Forword" of his manuscript:

Many descriptions have been written of Butch "Cassidy" by

various men, some of which were fairly accurate, but as a whole, seemed more or less conjectures.

It has been my pleasure to have known "Butch" Cassidy since his early boyhood, and I am happy to say, that I have never known a more courageous and kinder hearted man in my life time. his reputation for varacity and intigrity in all his dealings, aside from holdups, is unquestioned. I have known him on several occasions to suffer both cold and hunger, in order to help some one whom he thought needed food and shelter more than he. The mystery of "Butch's" evasion of capture for so many years is very simple, "Friends" He had many friends in all walks of life. I knew of only one man, either in North or South of America, who might have been any enemy to him and eaven he respected his truthfulness. . . .

Cassidy did not rob for the lust of gain, nor was it his natural trend. He had as he thought, every good reason for his first holdup, and after the first, there was no place to stop.

i cannot feel he was entirely a victim of circumstances; and that, in a way he was goaded on to become the most dreaded, most hunted and surely the most illusive outlaw that either North or South America have had to contend with as yet.

Unwilling to risk exposure of his true identity, Phillips used the third-person narrative in relating the life of Butch Cassidy. In the entire manuscript, only twice did he slip into the first person. The ploy also gave him more latitude in justification of Cassidy's criminal career. From the advantaged perspective of a close friend of the outlaw "since his early boyhood," Phillips was best able to cultivate the Robin Hood image he felt Butch Cassidy deserved. His "crusade" in crime for the sake of the oppressed is intimated in the manuscript's dedication:

> to the old settler who built his nest among the foothills, and in the broad valleys of central Wyoming, During the years between eighteen eighty five and eighteen ninety five, many of whom forfited their lives, or their liberty, in their fight for settlers rights, as citizens of the united States of America, against the old time cattle baron.

Viewing his certain death, Phillips had to believe his life was not lived in vain. He had to justify his existence. He had to demonstrate how his sometimes nefarious actions had tried to make a point. Over half of his manuscript is devoted to details of Butch Cassidy's deeds of human kindness and to rationalization of his outlaw career.

In short, "The Bandit Invincible" is the last testament of a man who did wrong, who knew he did wrong, and who felt a need to tell others why he did wrong. It was Butch Cassidy's peace with his Maker.

Verifying the manuscript's authenticity of detail has involved thousands of miles of travel in locating hideouts and following trails described by the former Wild Bunch leader. Countless hours have been spent in libraries, courthouses, and newspaper offices in comparing historical accounts with Phillips' narrative of the gang's exploits. Voluminous notes were compiled from interviews and correspondence in tracing the people and places central to his story.

Haunting our efforts was the realization that the manuscript was written nearly forty years after the events had taken place. As with all such "histories" the truths contained were certain to be biased by the author's subjective viewpoint and the distortions of his memory.

To these problems of verifying details in the manuscript was added yet another complication. In launching his narrative William T. Phillips included the following words of admonishment:

> As all the characters depicted in this book have taken an actual part, I find it essential to substitute some of the real names of both persons and places which I shall mention. Also, some places of the holdups have been changed.

Despite these complications, careful scrutiny has proven the Phillips' narrative often to bear more truth than recorded history itself. This manuscript written in 1934 described people and places at the turn of the century with an accuracy attainable only through firsthand experience. Only a person who had actually been in the places described and had known the people discussed would have been able to provide such intimate detail. What discrepancies occur can be attributed either to distortions of memory or to Phillips' qualifying preface in protection of those who took an actual part.

Although Phillips avoided discussion of Cassidy's criminal career before his 1894–96 term in the Wyoming Territorial Prison, of the seven major robberies commonly attributed to Cassidy and his Wild

Bunch thereafter, all but one are related in intimate detail. Only the April 21, 1897 holdup of the Pleasant Valley Coal Company mine payroll at Castle Gate, Utah, was not described.

Central to Phillips' story of Cassidy's activities in the Lander area were two peace officers, Sheriff Orson Grimmett and his deputy Jim Baldwin. Grimmett also was described as being the proprietor of a Lander saloon. Fremont County Sheriffs' records revealed Grimmett served two terms as County Sheriff: 1895 through 1897, and again from 1899 to 1901.[3] The records did not list the various deputies over the years, but Jim Baldwin's activities as deputy under Grimmett were given detailed discussion in contemporary issues of Lander's newspaper, the *Fremont Clipper*. The 1896 Lander directory listed the "Free Silver Saloon, Grimmett and Davis proprietors,"[4] and continued research even turned up a photograph of Grimmett and Baldwin in the very saloon referred to in the Phillips manuscript.[5]

In one passage Phillips mentioned "Lone Bear's village, a little above the Big Bend" of Wind River in Fremont County, Wyoming. Esther Chamberlin, whose husband had helped Will Boyd pack Phillips into the Wind River Mountains in 1934, said Lone Bear had been chief of the Arapahoes when the tribe was moved to the Wind River Reservation. She said the chief's descendents had taken the name "Brown," and directed us to Vincent Brown, the chief's son.[6] We located Vincent Brown at his home directly across the Wind River from present-day Riverton, Wyoming, a little above the "Big Bend." He verified Mrs. Chamberlin's information, adding that his home was in the very location of the village Phillips had described.[7] Lone Bear had died in 1920, some fourteen years before Phillips' manuscript was written, and the town of Riverton had been in existence since 1906. Only a person who had visited Lone Bear's village before this date could have described the Arapaho camp.

Phillips also wrote that in Pueblo, Colorado, "Butch's source of information was through a man named Mike Moran. Moran run a salon in Pueblo and was always well posted. Mike acted for information bureau for the gang." A check with the Pueblo library revealed there was, indeed, a Moran Saloon in Pueblo. City directories for 1901 and 1902 show a "Moran Brothers billiards hall, Mark A. Moran proprietor," and thereafter, through the 1913 directory, the business was listed as a saloon.

The examples shown are but a few of those researched. William T. Phillips' manuscript is authentic. It is the autobiography of Butch Cassidy. The personal emotions and details from the outlaw's life could have been related by none other. The errors present are those inherent in the subjective view of a person's own life.

With "The Bandit Invincible, the Story of Butch Cassidy"; with information gathered from archives, contemporary newspaper accounts, personal testimony and correspondence; and with details of the man's years in Spokane as William Thadeus Phillips, we are now able to piece together the true—and most fascinating—life story of the man known in western history as Butch Cassidy.

Chapter IV

Robert LeRoy Parker

BUTCH CASSIDY was born Robert LeRoy Parker in Beaver, Utah, on Friday, April 13, 1866.[1] He was the first of thirteen children born to Maximillian and Ann Gillies Parker. It was a Mormon home, both parents having emigrated as children with their families— converted from England—during the first mass Mormon migration to Utah in 1856.[2]

Butch's namesake, grandfather Robert Parker, had been a weaver in the textile mills of Lancashire, England. When Mormon missionaries reached England in 1836 Parker was among the first to be proselytized. His zeal in conversion was recognized by the Church and he was appointed Conference President of the newly organized followers of the Church of Jesus Christ of Latter-day Saints.

When Brigham Young appealed for expert tradesmen to help in establishing settlements in the American West, Robert Parker sold his holdings in England and moved his family to the new "Zion." Joining the MacArthur Company at Iowa City, the Parkers loaded all their possessions in a two-wheel handcart and trudged 1,300 grueling miles westward across the plains and mountains to the valley of the Great Salt Lake. Twelve-year-old Maximillian, or Maxi, helped his father roll the cart over the rough terrain.

The Parkers first located twenty-five miles south of Salt Lake City in the village of American Fork, where Robert Parker taught school, but soon moved again to Beaver, Utah, because Parker's skills were needed there in establishing a woolen mill. It was in Beaver that Maxi met his bride-to-be, Ann Gillies.

Ann was nine when her father Robert Gillies, also a Mormon convert from England, arrived at Iowa City to sign on with the William B. Hodgett wagon train traveling with the Martin Handcart Company. Gillies had been called by the Church to apply his carpentry and cabinetmaking trade in the "promised land."

The caravan had a late start and was caught by winter storms in early November in the upper Sweetwater Valley in Wyoming, just short of South Pass. Before a rescue expedition could reach the assemblage nearly 150 of the 576 emigrants had lost their lives. The Gillies family, however, came through unscathed.

The family settled in Woods Cross, north of Salt Lake City, where they remained until Robert Gillies was called to Beaver, where he could better put his trade to use.

Maxi Parker married Ann Gillies on July 12, 1865, her nineteenth birthday. Robert LeRoy, called Bob, or Roy, to distinguish him from his grandfather, was born the following spring.

To support his family Maxi contracted to carry mail south from Beaver to the Sevier valley. Then, impressed with the Circle Valley along his mail route, in 1879 Maxi bought a homestead from a Mr. James, and moved his family—now including six children—into the vacated two-room log cabin on the property. Young Roy, then thirteen, hired out for the season to the Pat Ryan ranch at Hay Springs, near Milford.

While employed at the Ryan ranch Roy Parker had his first run-in with the law. He had ridden to town to buy a pair of overalls. The local general store was closed when he arrived, and rather than make a return trip, Roy let himself into the building, took a pair of jeans, and left a note promising to return later to pay his debt. The storekeeper took exception to Roy's approach to the problem and swore out a complaint.[3]

Roy Parker had been raised with the frontier ethic that a man's word was his bond. The IOU was an inviolate pledge. The merchant's distrust was an unfamiliar response and, before the matter was settled, the humiliated youth was having mixed emotions over legal process and blind justice.

In Circle Valley Roy's parents' first season on the new homestead was devastated with reversals. Spring gales forced Maxi to resow his wheat crop three times, and a summer drought followed, parching the land and withering the crops. The following spring, after a prolonged frigid winter, the family herd was reduced to two cows.

In an attempt to broaden their living base the Parkers homesteaded additional acreage, but rights to the property were contested by another settler in the valley. As was the custom in pioneer Utah Mormon communities, the case was heard by the local church bishop. The land was awarded to the other homesteader, and Maxi Parker was furious. The harsh realities of nature he could accept, but the bishop's decision was considered a personal affront.

Although Ann Parker was a staunch member of the church, Maxi was what was commonly referred to as a "jack-Mormon," not totally living up to the church's precepts. As a child he had detested his assigned task of polishing the boots of missionary guests in his father's Lancashire home. When Robert Parker apprenticed him to work in the mills he ran away and adamantly refused to return to the job. Later, as a grown man, Maxi developed the smoking habit—a definite taboo—and his church attendance was sporadic. Religious training of the children was relegated to Ann.

The land judgment nearly severed Maxi's relationship with the local "righteous." He believed the bishop's decision in taking the land was hypocritical punishment for his lax religious ways.

Unable to subsist on their 160-acre homestead, the family was forced to find other work to help overcome their debts. Maxi found work cutting ties and hauling timber for charcoal at the mining town of Frisco, to the west. Ann hired out to run the dairy at the Jim Marshall ranch twelve miles to the south, and Roy Parker also worked for Marshall as a ranch hand.

Of the children, Roy especially had viewed the bishop's land judgment with resentment. He felt religion had been misused to play a part in cheating the family out of their land. Like his father, Roy was less than devout, and would go to great lengths to avoid weekly religion classes. As his sister Lula later noted, "If he could find some chore—any chore—that needed attention, he stayed home to take care of it. Any excuse was convenient."[4] The Mormon Church was too confining for Roy Parker's restless spirit.

The younger Parker children looked up to Roy almost in worship. The younger brothers, especially Dan, emulated him in all their mannerisms. Lula's mother told her that Roy "made a fuss over kids, and they loved him, whether they were our own, our relatives', or neighbors'. There was always room on his horse for as many as could scramble up. If they were little, he'd put them all on and lead the horse."[5]

During Roy's second season at the Marshall ranch, an amiable drifter named Mike Cassidy went to work for the ranch. Roy took an immediate liking to the easy-going cowboy and it wasn't long before Cassidy took the youth in tow and trained him in skills with horses, cattle, and guns—and rustling.

Together with a pair of shady ranchers in the valley, Mike Cassidy was engaged in stealing cattle and horses from the western Utah ranges and trailing them east across the badlands to ready markets in the thriving mining communities of Colorado's western slope. To Roy Parker, Mike Cassidy offered a life filled with excitement, an escape from the confines of weekly religion classes and hard work for little pay. It took little for him to rationalize Cassidy's rustling as retribution for the transgressions of religious hypocrites and greedy land barons. In later years Roy would adopt the name of his wayward hero—partly in admiration and partly to protect the Parker family from embarrassment and shame over his own outlaw career.

In June 1884 Roy Parker's contribution to rustling efforts in the valley came to the attention of the law and he was forced to skip the country. The conditions surrounding his hasty departure were described by a family friend:

> Ann became suspicious when a herd of range cattle was driven into the corral. Leaving her churn, she found her son helping several neighboring ranchers brand the cattle. But the men hushed her, claiming that the cattle were theirs. The same cattle drifted back over the mountains and their Parowan owners took exception to fresh brands on their animals' ribs. They came over to Circleville to press charges against the registered owners of the misplaced brands.
>
> Robert LeRoy's branding cronies, in addition to being established ranchers, were family men. They persuaded the footloose boy to go to the marshal who—with Maxi away—must have been in connivance. Roy signed an affidavit claiming he had sold the cattle to the others.
>
> That done, he threw a saddle on the fastest piece of horseflesh in the country, one of Jim Kittleman's blooded mares.
>
> "Don't go," pleaded Ann. "We'll send for your father; he'll make things right."
>
> But Roy rode away.[6]

In looking back over the events leading up to her brother's outlaw beginnings, Lula Betenson reflected, "At thirteen, he had assumed the work and the responsibilities of a man; as he grew older, he watched both our father and mother leave home for periods of time to scratch out enough money to keep our family subsisting; he had smarted under the realization that a 'righteous Saint' had taken away from us our hard-homesteaded piece of land; he had admired an outlaw's skill with cattle, horses, and guns; he had sympathized with the small homesteader who had 'mavericked' cattle from land-usurping cattle barons—had even accepted the blame for the actions of two of them; and he had craved a freedom he could never experience at our little ranch in Circle Valley."[7]

In his travels eastward into Colorado in 1884 Roy Parker crossed the remote Robbers Roost country, an area long notorious as a hideout for men on the lam. The maze of water-etched canyons and wind-sculptured mesas even today confuses all but the experienced. Intimate knowledge of this dry, eroded wasteland gave an outlaw the edge over unprepared pursuers in the game of life and death he played. It is difficult to say who first discovered the dependable water seeps and plotted the trails through Robbers Roost. During the 1870s a notorious horse thief named Cap Brown used them to supply a ready western Colorado market with stolen Utah horseflesh, and by the time Parker trailed across the expanse a band of horse thieves including Tom McCarty was frequenting the area. It would only be a matter of time until Parker's path would cross that of the veteran McCarty.

Roy Parker first settled in Telluride, Colorado, and worked a pack train of mules hauling ore from the rich Telluride mines down the talus slopes to the processing mill in the San Miguel Valley below. While in Telluride, according to the Parker family, Roy got into a dispute with a local rancher over ownership of a colt he had taken with him when he left Circle Valley. The rancher filed charges and had the youth jailed in Montrose. Lula recalled that Maxi Parker traveled to Colorado to obtain his son's release. Once cleared of charges Roy left Telluride and took up the life of a ranch hand, drifting from one range outfit to another.

In the "Bandit Invincible" manuscript, Cassidy, as William Phillips, was unwilling to divulge his true origin. Instead, he skipped over his early years, saying only,

At the Age of fourteen we find him living on the ranch of a George Parker, in Southern Utah, a few miles below Green river city.

It was here that he adopted the name of Parker. His real name has always been concealed since he ran away from his childhood home. Soon after leaving the Parker ranch, He took the name of Cassidy and was Known in the north as George or Butch Cassidy.

The ten or eleven years which he lived in utah were employed in hearding cattle for Various cow outfits. He was an adapt With a rope, and an expert in the saddle and a hard worker.

As a matter of course he had no education, except three or four years in a country grade school. His greatest ambition was to learn   He was constantly studying. One of his hobbies was the study of human nature, or beings he could never become reconciled to the Variciousness of most people whome he met   as for him self, he was always happiest, when giving to others. This trait more than any other kept him broke the greater part of his life.

It was no effort for Cassidy to be kind to other people and to animals. for it was the most natural thing in his life. I never knew a child who did not take to him at sight   Dogs instead of barking at him would greet him with a friendly Wag of their tails. . . .

His physical description at the age of Twenty, was slightly above the average height, or about five foot ten and one half inches and well built. Weighing about one hundred seventy pounds. He had a frank open face, clear sharp eyes of gray blue, rather square set jaw and light hair. In his early Years he seamed to have a habitual smile and a glad hand for every one.

The physical features described were typical of the Parker family. The only deviation from recorded accounts of the man's appearance is his height, given as "five foot ten and one half inches," the exact stature of William Phillips. Most published descriptions of Cassidy are taken from the Wyoming Territorial Prison's Bertillion Book, which gave his height at age twenty-seven in 1894 as five feet nine inches. Regarding this record, the manuscript was later to say, "the description was good, except for higth. . . ." One other contemporary description of the outlaw, following the 1900 Union Pacific train holdup at Tipton, listed him as "five feet ten inches in height."[8] Continued comparisons of Bertillion records with known physical descriptions of other inmates revealed other discrepancies. One outlaw, William Donely, alias Lasso Bill, or Kid Donley, is known from other photographs to have been nearly six feet tall, yet his prison record lists his height as five feet four and three quarter inches.

Most of what is known about Roy Parker's early cowboy career comes from reminiscences of old-time cowpunchers who shared the various chuck wagons with him. One such veteran, John F. Kelly, related the following to author James D. Horan: "I worked with Butch on the Coad Brothers Cattle Ranch . . . on the North Platte in western Nebraska in the years 1882–84 [?]. I met Butch again in Miles City, Montana, in 1886. We both went to work for cow outfits opposite Forsythe, Montana, on the Yellowstone River for two months. Then we both went back to Miles City."

"I returned to Forsythe to work for a cow outfit. Shortly after Butch rode up. He asked for a loan of $25 to help him get to Butte, Montana. In the fall of 1887, I received a letter from him. When I opened it one hundred dollars in cash fell out. The letter said simply, 'If you don't know how I got this, you will soon learn someday.'"[9]

Wyoming sheepherder James Regan related that he first saw Cassidy at Henry's Fork in southwestern Wyoming: "His father and mother were the Parkers and they used to come to Burnt Fork where my mother-in-law lived. He was about 20 years, bore the name of LeRoy Parker, and was raised at Circleville, Utah." Regan recalled that Cassidy spent the winter of 1884–85 at Burnt Fork with several other young cowboys.[10]

Roy Parker also worked for the huge Swan Land and Cattle Company sometime between 1884 and 1886. Commonly called the Two Bar, after its brand, the ranch occupied most of the open rangeland in Wyoming, with more than 160,000 head of cattle.

One Two Bar cowboy who recollected Butch Cassidy well was George C. Streeter, who shared a bedroll with Cassidy off and on for two years. He described how Butch could ride around a tree at full tilt and drill every bullet from his revolver into a three-inch circle. He also was impressed with Cassidy's personality, "Butch was the best natured man I ever saw and he would never stand for anyone molesting me."[11] Friends such as John Kelly and George Streeter were to prove invaluable to Roy Parker during the ensuing years. He could not afford to have enemies in the territory. With a price on his head his very friendliness and generosity were his salvation, as he unabashedly pointed out in the foreword to his manuscript:

> The mystery of "Butch's" evasion of capture for so many years is very simple, "Friends" He had many friends in all walks of life. I know of only one man, either in North or South America, who might have been any enemy to him and eaven he respected his truthfulness.

Chapter V

Telluride

IN TRACING ANY OUTLAW, it is difficult to detail his whereabouts
and activities with certainty, but it is especially true of the outlaw
on horseback before the turn of the century. Distances were too
great, terrain too rugged, and hideouts too remote. Communica-
tions systems were virtually nonexistent. As historian Eugene Cunningham so aptly noted, "Because of the conditions of those days,
because of the efficient speed with which the outlaws moved and
struck, because of the secrecy with which they managed to clothe
their activities, no such thing as a chronological record of Butch
Cassidy's forays can ever be written. Even the Pinkertons who were
steadily on the trail of men terrorizing the railroads, worked for
months to discover which known outlaws had done a particular job.
Doubtless, Cassidy . . . and other outstanding leaders, got credit for
jobs they knew nothing of. And doubtless, too, they struck blows
never charged to them."[1]

The first major crime history has attributed to Butch Cassidy was
the June 24, 1889 robbery of the Telluride, Colorado bank. Report
of the holdup was contained in a Denver news item, three days later:

> The robbery of the San Miguel Valley bank of Telluride on
> Monday by four daring cowboys of the Stockton outfit on the
> Mancos is one of the boldest affairs of the kind ever known in
> southern Colorado. The robbers secured about $20,000. . . . They
> came to Telluride two or three days prior to the robbery, put their
> horses in Searle's stable and proceeded to take in the town, drink-
> ing and spending money freely. In this way they secured the
> information they desired and acted accordingly. The bank em-
> ploys one clerk as assistant to the cashier. During the morning the
> robbers took their horses from the stable, paid their bill and then
> visited two or three saloons, watching the bank in the meantime.
> Soon cashier Painter stepped out to do some collecting and the
> four rode over to the bank, and leaving their horses in charge of

one of the number, two remained on the sidewalk and the fourth entered the bank and presented a check to the clerk.

As the latter was bending over the desk examining the check this party grabbed him around the neck, pulling his face down on the desk, at the same time admonishing the surprised official to keep quiet on pain of instant death. He then called to his partners on the sidewalk, saying, "Come on, boys, it's all right." The boys came in and cleaned up all available cash amounting to $20,750, while their comrade held the trembling clerk over the desk by the neck. When their work was complete the clerk was released and fell in a heap on the floor. Surveying the quaking mass of humanity the robber said he had a notion to shoot him anyway for being such a coward, and then joining his comrades they mounted their horses and rode leisurely away.

When they had ridden a couple of blocks they spurred their horses into a gallop, gave a yell, discharged their revolvers and dashed away. It was fifteen minutes after this demonstration, of which little notice was taken, that Mr. Painter, on returning to his bank, found his clerk Shee too agitated to give a correct account of the affair.

His greeting to the cashier was, "It's all gone, all gone," and such proved to be the case.[2]

In conflict with this newspaper report, historical records have credited the robbery to three, not four, bandits. Involved with Cassidy in the robbery were outlaw Tom McCarty and his thick-set brother-in-law, Willard Christiansen, who used the alias Matt Warner.[3]

The three were assisted in staking their relays by Bert Charter, a young cowboy from Baggs, Wyoming, Bill Madden, a Texan who was tending bar in the late Ike Stockton's stronghold of Mancos, Colorado, and Daniel Sinclair Parker, Roy's next younger brother.

Following the holdup the bandits ran their horses down the San Miguel Valley and made their way up Keystone Hill to the first relay of horses, manned by Charter. The impromptu posse following Sheriff J. A. Beattie which took up pursuit was conspicuously missing its town marshall Jim Clark, who had "pressing business" out of town that day.

The chase was close and the outlaws were in danger of being overtaken before they could reach the summit. A few warning shots were fired in hopes of discouraging the front riders of the posse. One of the pursuers, upon discovering he was uncomfortably close to his quarry and dangerously outdistancing his comrades, dismounted and answered a pressing call of nature, giving time for the "cops and robbers" game to get in better perspective.[4]

While Parker and company swapped saddles onto the relay horses, Bert Charter tied a windfall to the tail of another horse and spooked it down the slope toward the approaching posse. The bandits made their escape while the thoroughly confused posse tried to regain control of their own stampeding animals, frightened at the advancing racket.[5] All the posse got for their heroics that day were four well-used horses and some wild tales for their grandchildren.

Jim Clark, the absentee town constable, had a more profitable day, as he later confided to Gunnison County Sheriff, Doc Shores, "The fellers who held up the bank were friends of mine. They told me their plans and said that if I made a point of being out of town at the time of the robbery they would give me a fair share of the take. They agreed to hide it under a big log along the trail on which they planned to make their getaway. They were true to their word and left me this roll of bills amounting to about $2,200."[6]

Following a circuitous route the Telluride robbers made their way to the northwestern Colorado juncture with Wyoming and Utah, the secluded Green River valley of Brown's Park, long a stronghold of horse thieves, rustlers, and highwaymen.

Here Roy Parker, now using the alias George Cassidy, and his companions felt safe. Few land officers dared venture across the treacherous trails into the distant park, and those who did, whether from Colorado, Wyoming, or Utah, were faced with the frustration of finding their quarry just out of reach across the state line. The outlaws who haunted the region knew their geography well in this unusual patchwork of state territories and easily managed to elude their pursuers.

The fugitives made their camp at a cabin hidden in the cedars on Diamond Mountain above the Brown's Park ranch of Charley Crouse, a long-time friend of Matt Warner. Cassidy divided his time between the cabin retreat and the ranch of Herb Bassett across the Park, alternating his attention from Bassett's library to the rancher's oldest daughter, Josie. The Bassett home was the social hub of Brown's Park and Cassidy became the main attraction with his open friendliness and keen sense of humor.

Barn dances and horse racing constituted the main diversion for the settlers. Charley Crouse was especially proud of his blooded race horses, and matched them against all comers. Cassidy, who had ridden Matt Warner's racehorse Babe—originally obtained from Crouse—in matches throughout the Colorado western slope before the Telluride heist, was in constant demand as a jockey in the Brown's Park matches, more often winning than not.[7]

Cassidy readily made friends with the local cowboys and often would ride with them into Vernal, Utah and Baggs and Green River, Wyoming in search of more varied excitement.

In the "Bandit Invincible" manuscript the Telluride bank robbery is conspicuous in its absence. Restricting all discussion of Cassidy's criminal activities to the period following his imprisonment from 1894 through January 1896, the narrative instead begins with an anecdote set in Green River following the fall roundup:

It was October of the year 1891 and 2, the town of Green River, Wyoming, was a busy place. Several of the larger cow out fits were shiping their beef cattle from this point for many of the big out fits in north western Colorado, north eastern Utah, and western Wyoming. and at this time, there was a large Gathering of cow punchers from a radius of one hundred miles.

The saloons were doing a big business, as usual at this time of year. and the boys were pretty much liquored up both day and night One might say they took relays to make more room. It was in one of the bunches that we find young Cassidy as he was known in the U- (U Bar) out fit. One of the camp cooks in this out fit that jokingly nicknamed him Butch as he was dedicated several times to furnish the meat for the camp.[8] A few of the boys were standing out side the saloone when a small boy came along riding a wall eyed poney, looked to see who was calling him

"Hey kid come over here." and bet that there wasn't a man in the bunch who could ride the pinto straight up bare back, with out a bridle. A big puncher John burns steped up to the poney examined the pintos back and said "Well, we might as Well drink on Jim" and made a jump for the poneys back A couple of good jumps from the pinto and John was piled and the drinks were on him. The others were anxious to try their skill. Butch

> tried his skill which didnt prove any different than the others.
> next, Pet Brennen a big puncher tried his luck and lost as the
> others did. The secret was the poney did not like the feel of
> shapps.
>   Brennen was a surley chap and was verry quarlesome when
> drinking. He was the nephew of a large cow rancher in that
> country and was educated in collage and was quite an
> athlete   was a bully and most men did not like him   had taken a
> dis like to Butch Cassidy and had started a querrell with butch
> and it wound up in a fight, with pete drawing a gun on butch.
> Butch was quicker on the draw and ordered pete to lay the gun
> down & he did like wise. and ended the fight bare handed of
> [illegible] Butch won out. and they shook hands after words
> Butch bought the drinks for the bunch.

Although the incident described more probably took place in
October 1889, the anecdote is most accurate in revealing the mettle
of the man known as Butch Cassidy. The outlaw was widely known
for his masterful self control. Not only did Cassidy hold his liquor
well, but he acted quickly with an ever-cool head under conditions
of clear danger. His ability to avoid bloodshed, as exemplified in
this story, would repeatedly be demonstrated in the years to come.
That he was able to pull off some of the most daring robberies in
history without having to rely on the reaction of his trigger finger
speaks much in behalf of the controversial rogue.

Following the discussion of Cassidy's scrape in Green River with
the surly Pete Brennen, "The Bandit Invincible" continues:

> Butch and some of the boys stayed in Green river, and injoyed the
> sale of the shipment of cattle. as it got close to Winter the boys
> scattered out for Winter quarters. Butch had some friends along
> the sweet Water river and near split rock also Lander. A friend
> from Elk Bason, Al Hinton, was some what of Butches tipe a
> fellow with which he had known Cassidy by the name of Parker.
> so Butch had to explain why he had changed the name, by saying
> he wanted to loose him self by going in to a new country. Butch
> and Hinton went to lander to gether by the way of the South Pass.

Al Hinton, who accompanied Cassidy to Lander in the fall of
1889, was Albert Hainer, a cowboy Cassidy possibly met in Brown's

Park. Hainer's past remains a mystery. Elk Basin may have been the Elk River area directly east of the Park, or the basin country around Rangely, to the south. Nowhere in the manuscript is Brown's Park mentioned.

Continuing, Phillips accurately describes the Lander area of the time:

> Lander was a happy friendly little town & Verry beautifull. every one knew every one around the country   there wasnt Verry many Killings in Lander or Verry many marriages as there was not many women and if either happened the Dr. Biship Talbot of the episcopal church was Welcomed. There was plenty of hard men in Lander but Verry few bad ones.
>
> There was no public dance Halls in Lander. Dances were all private and if any trouble arose the women were invited out and the fight went to a finish. It was stock raising and grain farm country and Lander was the center location. Fort Washakie was 15 miles from Lander and the Soldiers spent most of their money there.
>
> Lander was the country seat of Fremont County and their sheriffs took second place to none in that state. Court was held once a year and then one or two Civil Cases often a few days in Lander. Cassidy and hinton decided to Winter there. Butch soon became Verry popular there with whom he meet especially the children. He always had a smile and a Kindly word for them. He always bought candy for them and would always have a lot of them around him. He was always a gentleman with old and young, & never atended dances or associated with women or seldom atended parties, felt Verry much out of place at dances, but was a lover of music. He worked around Wyoming a lot.

Ethelbert Talbot was Episcopal Bishop of Wyoming and Idaho from 1887 to 1897. Regarding Talbot, Wyoming pioneer C. A. Guernsey once wrote, "The Bishop was very popular throughout the state and when he visited a town, especially the little interior places, all business took a moratorium, including the saloons, to give him the glad hand and attend his services. He made a visit to the saloons and proprietors and patrons were his staunch friends and all were liberal contributors to his cause."[9]

The respect Talbot commanded from Cassidy and settlers

throughout Wyoming and Idaho was a tribute to a unique man of the cloth. Talbot's compassion for the people of the territory is reflected in his own observation, "To do men good they must be met on their own ground. It is not a loss of dignity, but the truest dignity, to identify one's self with the sorrows, anxieties, and even the joys of those whom it is an honor to serve just because they are men. . ."[10] Cassidy would have more to say of Bishop Talbot later in the manuscript.

That Cassidy's arrival in the Lander area was noticed is born out in an April 1892 article in the local newspaper:

> Geo. Cassidy and Al Hainer made their first appearance here about two years ago, hailing from Nevada, and bringing with them some fine horses and a considerable amount of money.
> They established a ranch on Horse Creek, tributary of Wind River, about 65 miles from Ft. Washakie where they made the appearance of going into the horse raising business. They frequently visited Lander and Ft. Washakie where they spent their money freely and were classed as sports. It is estimated that during the time their money lasted, which was about a year, they spent in the neighborhood of ten thousand dollars, which seems to us a little over drawn. But it is certain that they lost heavily and went through with about all the ready money they had.[11]

The cabin Cassidy and Hainer moved into that winter on Horse Creek, the present site of Dubois, Wyoming, had only recently been constructed by two local bachelors, Hughie Yeoman and Charlie Peterson. The boys stocked up on staples and cigars from J. K. Moore's general store at Fort Washakie, agency for the Wind River Reservation, and laid in for the winter months.[12] Their nearest neighbors were Eugene Amoretti Jr., and the John C. Simpson family on Jakey's Fork.

Amoretti's EA Ranch on Horse Creek was adjacent to the Cassidy and Hainer cabin. Gene Amoretti had the distinction of being the first child born at South Pass, Wyoming, during the gold rush of 1868. His father, a former aide to Napoleon, later moved to Lander, founding a bank where young Gene was establishing himself as a junior partner.[13] The younger Amoretti started his EA Ranch from scratch as a teenager, working the roundups like any other hand. Cassidy hired out to his enterprising neighbor and the two struck up a lasting friendship. Amoretti was probably the only banker in the West who could later say Butch Cassidy was his friend. His bank in Lander was never robbed during the entire outlaw era.

Cassidy and Hainer spent Christmas 1889 with the Simpson family at the mouth of Jakey's Fork on Wind River, four miles downstream from their own cabin. Of that holiday one Wyoming historian wrote, "It cannot be said that anyone brightened up at the sight of Al Hainer, but Cassidy brought the spirit of frolic with him. Before dinner was on the table, those who grinned in silence were beginning to laugh out loud. The children hovered close about him. In the afternoon there was eggnog and then they had games. There are old-timers who tell to this day how the cowboys of the Wind River roared with laughter and the children shrieked with mirth and how Butch Cassidy set the pace, with his tow-colored hair in wild disorder and his puckered blue eyes blazing."[14]

Later that same winter Cassidy had occasion to return the Simpsons' kindness. When one of the Simpson children was stricken with influenza Cassidy saddled up and in blizzard conditions rode for medicine from the doctor posted at Fort Washakie. He covered the 120 mile round trip non-stop.[15]

In Lander the congenial Cassidy also left indelible memories. Deputy sheriff Harry Logue vividly remembered one of Cassidy's contributions to local excitement:

"Butch Cassidy with his partner Al Hainer and a man by the name of Whitney came to town with some blooded horses. They were staying at the old Cottage Home Hotel. They decided they would take a ride and talked John Lee into letting them use a buckboard. They went on up the street to the old livery barn which stood on the bank of Dick Creek. Well, they got the horses hooked up OK and Whitney and Butch got in. The team started to run down Main Street until it ran afoul of a hitching rack in front of Coalter's Saloon. Butch didn't stop when the team did and he landed on the sidewalk; Whitney in the middle of the street. The buckboard was a total wreck. Butch called to John Lee, who was standing in front of the Noble and Lane Store, 'John, come and get your buckboard.'"[16]

Town marshal Hank Boedeker also recalled Cassidy's presence at the time, noting the control he held over the group of hard cases already gathering about him:

"Once Al Hayner, Jakie Snyder, Butch Cassidy and several others rode into Lander and I saw them coming up the street. I knew where they were going to tie their saddle horses and I hurried over there, getting there ahead of them."

"I faced the gang before they got off their horses. I greeted them in a nice way, but I didn't intend taking anything off them. 'Fellows,' I said, 'I want your guns. I won't have you getting someone into trouble and getting yourselves into a mess here in town. If I have possession of your guns I know that won't happen.'"

"'Who do you think you are asking us to hand over our guns?' flared up Snyder."

"But Cassidy smiled, 'It's all right boys,' he said. 'We're giving him our guns.' And unbuckling his cartridge belt, to which his guns swung, he handed them to me. All but Snyder did the same. Then Cassidy gave Snyder one of those hard looks he could pass out when he felt that way, and Snyder unbuckled his guns."[17]

Among Cassidy's Lander friends was French-Canadian Emery Burnaugh, a freighter running mail from Lander over the Owl Creek Mountains to the isolated settlements in the Big Horn Basin. From the time Emery and Cassidy met in 1889 they were frequent companions.

Burnaugh was engaged to Alice Stagner, the pretty half-blood Cheyenne daughter of an Owl Creek settler, and while he devoted his attention to Alice, Cassidy divided his time between her two friends, Dora Lamorreaux and Mary Boyd, also half-blood daughters of Lander area pioneers. At first Cassidy was attracted to the French-Cheyenne Dora, squiring her to local social affairs and taking her on horseback rides around Lander and Fort Washakie. The attraction was short-lived, however, as Cassidy came to spend increasing amounts of time with the vivacious Mary Boyd.[18]

Mary's Shoshone mother had met her father, Bill Boyd, in his hometown of Platte City, Missouri. After their marriage the couple settled among her people on the Wind River Reservation, where Boyd supplemented his ranch income as a freighter and Indian trader. Mary was born in 1868, the second girl in a family of six children.

Old-timers recall Mary and Cassidy were sweethearts, and indica-

tions were that Butch had intentions of settling down and establishing a home for Mary. For a time they may even have lived
together—she later told of being his "common laws wife"—but their
moments together mostly were in fleeting clandestine meetings.[19]
Cassidy was to be a fugitive for the rest of his outlaw life.

Chapter VI

Alias Tom Ricketts

ON THE AFTERNOON of December 29, 1889, Abraham Coon was driving his stagecoach north from Muddy Station on the Dixon to Rawlins run. He had picked up the U.S. mail at Dixon and Baggs. One passenger, a Mr. Allen, was on board.[1]

Four miles north of Muddy Station the driver saw two horsemen approaching. "They rode towards me and when they got right to the horses' heads they rode out of the road on the left hand side of the coach, and leveling their revolvers at me told me to stop. 'Stop boys, and throw up.' I wound the lines around the front of the dash board of the coach."

" 'Throw up your hand, young fellow, or I will kill you. Get out of the coach boys.' We got out and got down side of the coach by the front wheel."

" 'Walk away from the coach entirely. Now boys, stand with your backs towards us and stand close together.' "

Each highwayman wore a dark suit of clothes, a large heavy overcoat, and "had a little piece of buffalo rope put on to represent false whiskers and mustache . . . fastened on with a little small string around his ear on each side."

As the younger man leveled his six-shooter at Coon and Allen, the older bandit saw a wagon approaching from the south.

"He rode out with his six-shooter. . . . he stopped them and talked to them for a few minutes, and rode on down, and the team drove past. . . ."

The outlaw "sat on his horse with his six-shooter in his hand. Mr. Elliot, the driver [of the wagon], waved his hand at us as the team was going by."

The bandit returned "and took the mail sack out of the coach and cut the strap and dumped the mail out on the ground . . . and got down on one of his knees and opened the letters. He first took the registered mail and opened the package and took the contents of the letters and put it in his pockets, and cut open quite a lot of other letters, threw them on the right; after he had got through with them he gathered up the mail in his hands and tucked it back in the sack and threw the sack into the coach, he walked up to the passenger and leveled his six-shooter on him and says, 'How much money have you got, partner?' The passenger handed him his pocket book, a buckskin pouch. 'Is that all you have got?' and the passenger said yes, and he says, 'Are you sure that is all?' and the passenger said yes."

"'How much money have you got, young fellow?' and I said, 'Four bits.' He said, 'Is that all?' I said yes, he said "Are you sure that's all?' I said yes, here I am, you can search me if you think I have got any more. He said, 'No, you can keep that, and when you get into Rawlins drink to the health of Frank Jackson.'"

The robber then mounted his horse and ordered Coon and Allen back into the stage, telling them "to go north and not turn back." The younger bandit, who had been standing guard, then "fired two or three shots under the horses, and we started." Coon headed the horses up the road toward Willow Springs, catching up with Elliot, who had stopped his team over the next rise.

Arriving in Rawlins, the men reported the robbery and the identities of the highwaymen were determined. The older man was known in the territory as William Brown and his young companion was going by the name of Tom Ricketts. Search of the immediate area failed to turn up either of the suspects.

The first breakthrough lead in the case came the following May. At a dance in Moab, Utah, Joe Murr struck up a conversation with the man known as Brown. "Frank Rogers was his first name, and Doc Lutz. We got to talking about what we had went through, and he got to telling me about his travels. Said he had to skip out of the northern country; he had robbed a stage up there." Ricketts also was at the dance and was introduced to Murr.

Officers followed the lead and in September 1890 Sheriff George Bush arrested Ricketts in Moab. Brown was captured in Johnson County, Wyoming, by Sheriff Frank Canton, while attending a dance at the Murphy ranch on Piney Creek.

Carbon County Deputy T. J. Carr transported Ricketts to the Wyoming Territorial Penitentiary at Laramie to await trial.

"He positively said his name was Ricketts for quite a long time. When I brought him to the penitentiary . . . I said, I am going to

take your description and name, and want the truth, I don't want
any lies; I want to make a record of it in the books of the office and
asked him his name. At the penitentiary he said Dan Parker. I said
'of the Parker family of southern Utah?' and he said yes. 'Then you
lied about your name being Ricketts?' I said, and he said yes."

On October 19, 1890, Dan S. Parker was checked into the territorial prison. In the Bertillion book his nativity was listed as Nevada.
His parents were registered as Maxi and Anna Parker of Circleville,
Piute County, Utah, and four brothers—William, Ebb, Mark, and
Arthur—and four sisters—Jimcie, Nell, Blanche, and Lula—are
cited. Robert LeRoy's name was among the brothers and sisters
absent in the listing.[2]

Dan was described as five feet nine and one half inches; complexion, fair with freckles; hair, tow, dark; eyes, grey. His physical
description placed his weight at 145 pounds and described a small
cut scar high upon the left eye, wide back jaws, upper lip projecting
some over the lower lip, a rather sharp pointed nose and a mouth
that draws in a little—all features typical of the Parker family.

The Bertillion record revealed that he was held in default of
$3,000 bail.

William Brown was not so easily identified. "He said he went by
the names of John Day, Doc Lutz, Frank Rogers . . . Jim Moore and
some other names." Brown also was said to have used the name,
Dolph Lusk.

On April 7, 1891, the men were taken to the U.S. District Court
in Cheyenne, where they were charged with "robbing a mail carrier
of the United States Mail and for putting the life of the carrier in
jeopardy in effecting such robbery by use of dangerous weapons."

After hearing testimony the jury returned on April 18 with the
verdict of guilty. Judge John A. Riner sentenced the men to the
Detroit House of Correction for the term of their natural lives, at
hard labor. They were delivered to Warden Joseph Nicholson at
Detroit on April 30, 1891.

Dan Parker remained in the Detroit House of Correction until
1894, when the Wyoming Governor, in response to the Parker
family's persistent pleadings, pardoned him.[3] He was never again
convicted of a felony.

Chapter VII

The Hole-in-the-Wall

WHILE DAN PARKER was basking in his short-lived glory as a desperate road agent, his elder brother Roy, as George Cassidy, was aligning himself with the small Wyoming homesteader "who built his nest among the foothills, and in the broad valleys of central Wyoming. . . . many of whom forfited their lives, or their liberty, in their fight for settlers rights, as citizens of the united States of America against the old time cattle baron."

The Phillips manuscript, written more than forty years after the fact, gives Cassidy's personal perspective on the conditions which led to the bitter conflict between the haves and the have-nots over rights to the vast territory. Although historically inaccurate, as reminiscences often are, the narrative does give a unique insight into the personal emotions and frustrations felt by the small settlers:

> During the years of 1890s, it was the settlers who gave the cattle men worries. the land had been thrown open to the Homesteaders. The stock men did any thing in their Power to keep the settlers out and finding the wide open ranges. Wyoming was made a state in 189[0] 4 of July, during president Cleveland's administration. Govener barber was made acting govenor over the stockmans association, and in 1892 the stock mans troubles were finaly brought to a head. one could never be sure of one's friends in Wyoming and Butch was one to find this out.

The compounded sins of mismanagement in the large cattle enterprises of the American West were dealt complete retribution with the winter of 1886–87, the worst in recorded western history. The changes that winter effected on the people of the frontier also shaped the future of Robert LeRoy Parker, alias Butch Cassidy.

The summer of 1886 had been uncommonly dry. The overgrazed range yielded sparse forage to carry the cattle into winter. In November the country was shadowed by a slate-blanketed sky, a sight that would become depressingly monotonous during the months that followed. By December the mercury plummeted to forty degrees below zero and failed to bounce back. Whole herds were buried alive, frozen on their feet like statues as the snow continued to fall. Those animals remaining turned to each others' tails for nourishment. There was no hay to feed the starving animals.

Hopes bounded upward when the chinooks of late January promised reprieve to the besieged landscape, melting some of the drifts. For a short time it seemed the cattle would be able to paw through the reduced cover and hang on until spring. The cold front that followed dashed the short-lived optimism. Snow, which so shortly before had been melting, froze into an impenetrable crust, sealing the livestock's doom from Canada to Colorado.[1]

The first day of spring was a day of reckoning for the financial magnates of the western cattle industry. There would be no more deceptive tally counts. The inflated profits paid the foreign investors were in the past. There was no more principal to rob.

Surviving cattle barons were quick to rationalize their losses, however, by laying blame on the doorstep of the johnny-come-lately, the homesteader. Struggling for a toehold in a once exclusive empire, the intruders were quick to capitalize on the ruins abandoned by the less persistent peers of the western realm. As one rancher put it, "Mavericking was good that spring."

There grew a smoldering resentment against these newcomers. More than ever, grass was gold and water priceless. The stage was set. The inevitable conflict between the haves and the have-nots was to prove a greater struggle than the conflict with nature itself.

The cattle barons created their quandary by offering a premium to their cowhands for every unbranded animal, or maverick, they brought off the range. Overzealous cowboys worked hard covering long distances to earn the extra windfall. After the catastrophe of the 1886–87 winter, competition between outfits gathering "motherless calves" got out of hand.

That disastrous winter also opened the eyes of many an ambitious hired hand. The range animals became fair game to anyone quick enough to lay his own brand on them.

Surviving barons tried to forestall their doom by expanding their empires and by driving off the settlers who popped up at every waterhole and on every fertile river bottom. They controlled the

Wyoming Territorial Legislature which enacted laws banning new-comers to the ranching business by governing the disposition of mavericks and by setting up commissions to rule on new brand applications. The landholders banded together in the Wyoming Stock Growers Association and excluded non-members from partici-pation in spring branding roundups. Any cowboy in their employ who had a brand or cattle of his own was summarily dismissed and placed on the Association's blacklist, unable to find work. Sympa-thetic to the cattlemen's cause was Amos W. Barber, Wyoming's acting governor from November 1890 through 1892.

The hottest news of the summer before Cassidy's winter on upper Wind River was the hanging of Jim Averell and Ella Watson, nicknamed "Cattle Kate," over on the Sweetwater. Averell had been waging a journalistic campaign against the large Sweetwater land-holders who were attempting to discourage settlement of the fertile valleys. A short distance up the valley from Averell, Ella Watson plied the world's oldest profession, bartering her favors for whatever the young cowboys had to swap.

Animosities came to a head when a vigilante party, all prominent ranchers, tried to scare the two into leaving the area. Averell and Watson didn't scare; hot emotions overrode intelligence: each was strangled at the end of a lariat looped over the branch of a limber pine.[2] The rift between settler and cattle baron was completed with that rash act.

It was into this conflict that Cassidy rode as he departed the Wind River country in the spring of 1890. His destination, as related in "The Bandit Invincible" manuscript, was the infamous Hole-in-the-Wall:

> Butch and Hinton started to powder river from Lander. stayed first night at Sub-Station with a John Burnett. Started down Wind river to the three quarter circle ranch. Tom Osborn owned the ranch. Tom was a friend of the to boys. went to the Cary Ranch. Divine the manager welcomed them.
>
> Butch and Al had a friend by the name of Tom Ohday, had a small ranch in the Whole in the Wall. Tom was considered as a cattle russler but was a Verry poor one but was a good natured Irishman.

All of the details in the narrative of Cassidy's journey check out.

John C. Burnet operated the Arapaho sub-agency and a road ranch at the location described. Tom Osborne's ranch, a portion of the Quien Sabe operation vacated by the Englishmen Berry, Pickles, and Jevens following the disastrous winter of 1886–87, was located along the Badwater drainage on the south flank of Copper Mountain. Bob Divine was foreman of Carey's CY outfit with headquarters near the present site of Casper, Wyoming. This ranch, the former Goose Egg, was the setting for episodes in Owen Wister's classic western novel, *The Virginian*.

Of the small-time Wyoming badman Tom O'Day, prominent Big Horn Basin rancher George "Bear" McClellan once observed, "Tom ain't a bad fellow when you get to know him. He's just a big, good-natured kid that thinks he is having a good time."[3] The Pennsylvania-born Irishman divided his time between a dugout home near Tom Osborne's ranch and the Hole-in-the-Wall area across the Big Horn range to the east. He later operated a saloon with John Nolan, whose KC Ranch near the Hole-in-the-Wall was to become the site of the beginning of the infamous Johnson County War of 1892.[4] Less benevolent than "Bear" McClellan, Johnson County's newspaper, the *Buffalo Bulletin*, referred to Tom as a "Montgomery Ward" badman.

The manuscript's description of the Hole-in-the-Wall valley also is accurate:

> He was invited to Whole-in-the-Wall by Ohday and then his troubles began.
> The Whole in the Wall is a beauty spot with the Wall straight up and only two outlets. A doz men could defend in against 100 men. A few settlers lived there and their chief work was raising hay for the few heads they owned. George Curry was another settler.

Located about sixty miles as the crow flies northwest of Casper, Wyoming in the north central part of the state, Hole-in-the-Wall is relatively isolated even today. The nearest community of any size is Kaycee, to the northeast, named for John Nolan's ranch brand.

The spur of the Rocky Mountains known as the Big Horn Range rises in a magnificant pyramid, reaching to the very clouds at its peak and tapering to dissipated points at its extremes north and

south. Far out into the prairie to the east and into the Big Horn
Basin to the west, hogback ridges rise in succession and face the
main peaks in humble homage. The first in this series of ridges is the
vermilion-hued Chugwater formation of sandstone. At the southern
tip of the Big Horns, the red beds to the east form an abrupt
precipice, called the Red Wall, that extends relatively unbroken for
nearly fifty miles. Nestled against the canyon-carved limestone
flanks of the mountain, tucked safely behind the wall, is the beautiful valley of the Hole-in-the-Wall.

At the northern end of the valley Beaver Creek escapes to the east
through the largest rent in the wall, while the Middle Fork of
Powder River, joined by Buffalo Creek from the south, flows
through a split midway in the formation's span. Some seven miles
up Buffalo Creek is the true Hole-in-the Wall. At this point, the
Red Wall abruptly cuts back to the east, forming a V-notch in the
barricade. Over the rim and down the steep talus slope of the cleft of
the notch courses a game trail that became the infamous "Hole."

The first rustler to use the unusual natural gateway in the Red
Wall was Sanford "Sang" Thompson, a midnight cattle dealer with a
misshapen foot. Sang, with Flat Nose George Currie, Black Henry
Smith, Walt Punteney, and Tom O'Day, discovered that by sliding
a large triangular gypsum boulder across the notch in the wall's
cleft, pursuers could not detect a trail at all, the slick red sandstone
never revealing a track. Concealed in the green ash grove up against
a sheer alabaster wall at the bend up Buffalo Creek, some two miles
across the valley, the rustlers constructed a makeshift corral of
windfalls and logs without the use of nails or wire.

Cattle were rustled, primarily from Carey's CY outfit, in small
groups along the shortgrass benchlands at the heads of Murphy and
Willow creeks to the east and driven over the V-notch into the valley
below. The boulder was lodged in the track and the cattle were then
trailed to the corral across the valley floor. For years stock detectives
could not figure out how they were losing cattle, and believed the
outlaws were using some concealed hole, or tunnel, through the red
sandstone wall.

Among the outlaws located in the valley when Cassidy arrived in
1890 were O'Day, George Currie, Walt Punteney, and Nate Champion.

Nathan D. Champion was a lanky, dark-complexioned Texan. A quiet man with strong determination, Champion was destined to play a critical role in the impending range war. His leadership in the opposition to the large landholders was recognized throughout the territory.

George Currie, later to figure prominently in Cassidy's escapades, was born in Charlottetown, Prince Edward Island, Canada, on March 20, 1871. His Scottish father was a stern, demanding Presbyterian, and George chafed under his religious restriction. Currie's family had settled in Chadron, Nebraska, when fifteen-year-old George "got fed up as it were, and decided it was best to run away."[5]

Regarding Currie's "Flat Nose" sobriquet, lawman Joe LeFors noted, "George's nose was so flat between his eyes that standing at his side, one could see his eyelids standing higher than the bridge of his nose."[6]

Like Cassidy, Currie was well liked by local settlers and was considered a pleasant man who was scrupulous in his dealings with his friends. Once when asked why he led the outlaw life, Currie laughed in reply, "Oh, I don't know, just for the fun of it I guess, just the fun."[7]

Walt Punteney, another of Currie's associates, was four years Butch Cassidy's junior. At age fourteen he and his brother Veed ran away from their Frankfort (Kansas) home to seek their fortunes in the West. While Veed took up a homestead near Thermopolis, Wyoming, and worked for the Embar Ranch for a grubstake, the husky, blond Walt turned to rustling.[8]

Men such as George Currie and his cohorts operated at one end of a wide spectrum of people who populated Wyoming's shortgrass empire. Some would divide the factions into "good guys" and "bad guys," but the lines often were blurred and it was difficult to tell who ranched and rustled a little from those who rustled and ranched a little. No side had a corner on virtue in those tense years leading up to the explosion known as the Johnson County War.

Cassidy settled in the valley a few miles to the northwest of Sang Thompson, taking a "squatter's claim" on Blue Creek, a tributary of Beaver Creek.

His stay at the Blue Creek ranch, however, was brief. Just before Christmas 1890 he was given word that law officers were closing in on him. Under the cover of darkness he rode over to Beaver Creek where a barn dance was in progress. Outside, he approached a youth going into the dance and offered him fifty cents to deliver a message:

"Go inside and tell Jim Stubbs there's a man outside want's to see him. And don't let anyone see you."

Stubbs, a respected settler who tended to his own affairs, purchased Cassidy's Blue Creek holdings with a handshake and an exchange of gold.[9] Cassidy promised to send the necessary papers the next spring, and rode west over the Big Horn, his next experiences to be the most bitter in his entire life, as intimated in the "Bandit Invincible" manuscript:

It was known that Cassidy and Hinton had recently came from the Whole in the Wall. and they were then considered members of the Whole in the Wall. and the Wild Bunch, and rustlers by the Stock men. and were placed on the black ball list. This always meant trouble. It meant that they were to be traped or Killed.

Chapter VIII

Prison Walls

CASSIDY'S discreet withdrawal from the Hole-in-the-Wall was well-considered. The large landholders, frustrated in their attempts to secure convictions in the courts, determined to solve their problems outside the law. Montana ranchers had earlier formed vigilance committees to purge the range of the rustler element, and within the Wyoming Stock Growers Association influential voices were urging a similar course of action in exterminating such "Knights of the Road and Rope" as Currie and Cassidy. Not a few were in favor of making a clean sweep, eliminating rustlers, squatters, and their sympathizers alike.

On June 4, 1891, northern Wyoming nester Tom Waggoner was left swinging from a rope. Words had turned to action; the exterminations had begun.[1]

At dawn on the first of November four armed men attacked Nate Champion in his winter quarters at the Hall cabin just up the Middle Fork of Powder River from the Hole-in-the-Wall. After a desperate battle the attackers withdrew, their mission unaccomplished. But Champion knew they would return. It was the beginning of the Johnson County Cattle War.

On November 28 Orley "Ranger" Jones pulled out of Buffalo, Wyoming, with a wagon full of lumber for his bride-to-be's new cabin. As he eased across the Muddy Creek bridge fifteen miles down the road, three bullets checked him off the blacklist.

Three days later John A. Tisdale headed home from Buffalo with Christmas toys for his kids safely tucked away behind the wagon seat. He made it only eight miles.

Over in the Big Horn Basin the struggle also had broken into open conflict. A loose-knit band of thieves led by Jack Bliss was preying on the large cattle and horse herds in the basin, from their base in the Owl Creek Mountains. During roundup Dab Burch and

Jack Bedford, two cowboys on the fringe of the rustling society, were arrested and charged with grand larceny involving three saddle horses. They were remanded to the custody of three "stock detectives" in the employ of rancher Otto Franc. The detectives, using the names Joe Rogers, John Peaveler, and John Wickham, bound the two men and tied their feet together under their horses in preparation for transporting them to the Buffalo jail. Once out of sight the three detectives executed the two helpless men and vanished from the country.[2]

After leaving the Hole-in-the-Wall, Cassidy again returned to the Wind River Basin where he and Hainer split their time between their cabin on Horse Creek and the Quien Sabe Ranch quarters abandoned by Berry, Pickles, and Jevens.[3] In their travels between their two operations the two stopped over at the Mail Camp road ranch along the south flank of the Owl Creeks, where Emery Burnaugh had located following his marriage to Alice Stagner.

Sometime late in August 1891, while Cassidy was staying at Mail Camp, Billy Nutcher, one of the Jack Bliss gang, rode in trailing three saddle horses, "one brown horse, one sorrel horse and one grey horse."[4] Nutcher put the horses in the corral and joined Burnaugh and his guests.

Cassidy was attracted to Nutcher's string and discussion of a sale followed. Nutcher told him "that he had traded cattle for the horses in Johnson County, and that the title was all right and that he would warrant it. . . . he had been out of the use of them all summer and was just returning home from a hunt for them." Nutcher then indicated that "he could not keep them at home," and "that the horses were of no use to him."

A deal was made and Cassidy became owner of the three saddle horses. Little attention was paid to paperwork in the transaction, which proved to be a grim oversight for Cassidy.

Big Horn Basin ranchers were paying close attention to Nutcher's shady dealings and when some of their finest saddle horses disappeared they soon learned Cassidy and Hainer had the stolen animals. A complaint was sworn out on August 28, 1891 by Otto Franc, one of the largest landholders in the basin. The complaint cited one horse owned by Richard Ashworth, whose spread bordered Franc's

Pitchfork ranch on the Greybull River. Ashworth, an Englishman, was one of the absentee ranchmen so common at the time and was not in the vicinity when the horses were stolen.

John Chapman, one of the earliest settlers in the basin, volunteered to track Cassidy and the stolen horses. Chapman found his first solid lead when he chanced upon one James Thomas in the Owl Creek Mountains. Thomas recollected seeing the horses in question in the possession of George Cassidy. Upon further prodding of his memory, Thomas recalled Cassidy shoeing the horses and mentioning a planned trip to the Evanston country.

At Fort Washakie, Chapman received further assistance from Rorick, the clerk at the Shoshone tribal agency, who told him Cassidy and Hainer had only recently departed for Evanston.

Upon reaching Evanston, Chapman stopped by the sheriff's office and Deputy Bob Calverly was assigned to accompany him on his mission. Search for their quarry proved futile until the next spring.

In April 1892 Calverly and Chapman got word Cassidy and Hainer were hiding on a ranch near Auburn, Wyoming. They further found that the two fugitives had an errand girl, Kate Davis, whom they persuaded to lead them to the ranch. Cassidy was resting on a cot inside a cabin and Hainer was some distance away at a sawmill. Calverly got the drop on Hainer and apprehended him without much fuss. It took longer to subdue Cassidy, as reported in the Lander paper:

> Two men, Cassidy and Hainer, well known in this locality, were arrested in the 8th of this month, in Star Valley, this state, on a charge of horse stealing. Cassidy offered considerable resistance, saying when ordered to throw up his hands, "Never to you damned sons of b____'s." At which one of the arresting party, Bob Calverly, grappled with him and after a desperate struggle in which the desperado was beaten senseless, and the cuffs and shackles were applied to his limbs, he was conveyed to prison at Evanston.[5]

Bob Calverly, in a letter some years later, was a bit more precise in his description of the tussle with Cassidy:

> I arrested Cassidy on April 11, 1892. . . . I told him I had a warrant for him and he said: "Well get to shooting," and with

that we both pulled our guns. I put the barrel of my revolver almost to his stomach, but it missed three times but owing to the fact that there was another man between us, he failed to hit me. The fourth time I snapped the gun it went off and the bullet hit him in the upper part of the forehead and felled him. I then had him and he made no further resistance.[6]

Fremont County Sheriff Charles Stough transported Cassidy and Hainer from the Uinta County jail at Evanston to Lander for trial. They remained in the Fremont County facility until July 16, 1892, when they were brought before Judge Jesse Knight's district court and formally charged with a single count of grand larceny. Obtaining Douglas A. Preston and C. F. Rathbone, two of the best criminal attorneys available, Cassidy and Hainer pleaded not guilty. Bond was set at $400.

The very week Deputy Calverly closed in on George Cassidy, another tense drama unfolded not twenty miles from Cassidy's old Blue Creek ranch in the Hole-in-the-Wall. Nate Champion again had unexpected company.

With Champion at John Nolan's KC Ranch cabin was Nick Rae, a husky homesteader from nearby Pine Ridge, and Billy Walker and Ben Jones, two cowboys out of work during the slack winter season.

An army of ranchmen and their hired Texas gunslingers, fifty in all, surrounded the cabin in the predawn hours, taking advantage of what cover was available. First Jones, then Walker, was captured when he stepped outside the cabin door. Nick Rae was first to draw gunfire when he walked out to see what was keeping the two cowboys. Champion dragged the mortally wounded Rae back inside the cabin and waited out the gunmen, coolly noting the day's activities in his diary. When the invaders set fire to the cabin, Champion made a run for it and was cut down in a hail of gunfire. On his vest they pinned a card reading, "Cattle thieves, beware!"[7]

Champion's diary, recovered from his body by news correspondent Sam T. Clover, who accompanied the invaders, was later published in the *Chicago Herald.* Its dramatic moment-by-moment account of the siege has become the most damning of historical evidence in condemning the ill-advised "invasion." As his attackers set fire to the cabin, Champion pencilled in the final entry, "The house is all fired. Goodbye boys, if I never see you again. Nathan D. Champion"[8]

There is a strong similarity in the ways Cassidy and Champion separately fought for their freedom. There also is an uncanny parallel between Champion's death and Arthur Chapman's scenario of Butch Cassidy's death in San Vicente, Bolivia. Both Rae and Longabaugh were described as venturing out of the shelter of a building to be cut down in a barrage of gunfire from a near army of opposing forces; both Champion and Cassidy daringly rescued their dying companions at no small risk to themselves; both leaders died bravely.

In Lander it took Cassidy until July 30 to raise the bail. He was released on a surety bond to Fred Whitney and Leonard Short, both local businessmen, while Hainer's bond was held by saloonkeeper Ed Lannigan's two sons, Bill and Ed, Jr. In the meantime the prosecution requested and received continuance until the July 1893 court term—a full year away—because witnesses John Chapman and John Thomas were not available.

On June 20, 1893, Fremont County District Court convened to hear the case. The defendents presented a motion for continuance and submitted to Judge Jesse Knight an affidavit claiming that J. S. Green and C. F. Willis, two witnesses to the transaction between Cassidy and Billy Nutcher, could not be located. The motion was denied.

After hearing the evidence Judge Knight charged the jury: "Whoever steals any horse, mule or neat cattle at the value of $5 or upwards, or receives, buys or conceals any such horse which shall have been stolen shall be imprisoned in the penitentiary not more than ten years. . . ." The rest is recorded in Lander's *Fremont Clipper* of June 23, 1893:

> The case of the State against George Cassidy and Albert Hainer . . . was submitted to the jury after a short argument on the part of the prosecution, represented by Judge M. C. Brown, he having been substituted in place of Simpson. The defense, represented by Preston and Rathbone, believing that no case had been made by the State, offered no argument. The jury was out about two hours when a verdict of not guilty was returned and the jury dismissed . . . the evidence showed that they were innocent purchasers and hence not guilty as charged in the information.

Three days before the verdict was to be rendered, on June 19, 1893, rancher Otto Franc again registered a complaint with Sheriff Stough, charging Cassidy and Hainer with grand larceny. The initiation of this case was based on a second horse of the three Cassidy had obtained from Billy Nutcher. Cassidy was released on another $400 surety bond posted by Eli Signor and Leonard Short, who also posted bond for Hainer.

At this time, as revealed in the "Bandit Invincible" manuscript, Cassidy began to suspect his companion, Hainer. Otto Franc was the man suspected of hiring the stock detectives who murdered Burch and Bedford the previous year, and Cassidy feared Hainer might have his own connections with the determined cattle baron:

> Butch was double crossed by hinton and arrested for the theft of a Veal. Hinton was arrested too. but was able to furnish Bail. Butch could not furnish Bail which was $2000 each. Butch layed in Jail about too weeks before he could get bonds man. couldnt figure out [illegible] Hinton got bonds man so easily. but that was all fixed with the sherif and stock men. Butch didnt believe his friend of several years had double crosed him. eaven tho he had been told of the suspicious warnings by his friends. They seperated tho. Hinton staying in Lander, while Butch went wondering around the Country till the trial could be heard 6 mo later. He went to Milk river country, Billings and Miles City where he spent most of the Winter. He went back to Lander to face Trial July 12.

Unable to bear the stigma of being branded a horse thief, the "bandit invincible" related the charge as theft of a veal, or "mavericking," both in the manuscript and in conversations with his Spokane friends in later years. Evidence that Cassidy and Hainer were separated after release from jail, however, is found in the reminiscences of Lander pioneer Harry Logue:

> The man Hainer, Butch Cassidy's partner, had a ranch up Wind River and Butch and he stole a bunch of horses. Charley Stough . . . had a warrant to serve on Hainer. Butch was not at the ranch when he went up to arrest them. Charley served the warrant and told Hainer to get ready to go to Lander. When he went to mount his horse, Charley told him he would have to give him his gun. Hainer said, "No, Charley, I won't give you the gun until we get to Lander. You will have no trouble with me." Charley

said, "Well, let's get going." When they got to the courthouse, Hainer said, "Well, Charley, here is the gun. Now the reason I didn't give you the gun was because there were some men laying for me and I wanted a chance which I would not have had if you had all the guns." Charley often said that Hainer could have killed him a dozen times on the trip down, as he was behind him time after time.[9]

Once court was in session, both sides called forth a battery of witnesses. Their testimony, unfortunately, was not recorded as full court transcriptions were not made at the time. On July 3 the jury retired to deliberate the evidence and returned on July 4, 1894, with the verdict: "We the jury find the above named defendent George Cassidy guilty of horse stealing as charged in the information and we find the value of the property stolen to be $5.00. And we find the above named defendant, Al Hainer, not guilty and the jury recommend the said Cassidy to the mercy of the court."

It was immaterial to Cassidy that the horses he had bought from Nutcher were stolen. It's a safe bet he knew Nutcher was a horse thief and that the horses in question were stolen. What did matter was that he felt the situation had been created by the large ranchmen as a trap and that Hainer was an instrument in the affair. In the Phillips manuscript Cassidy's shock and deep bitterness are revealed as he presents his side of the story:

[Butch] was convicted of cattle theft and Hinton never was tried and was set free for some reason. but it was soon learned that it was Judge Brenton's money that went Hinton's bail. And it was him who planted the sleepers as bait at trout creek. Hinton had asked for a separate trial and was granted one. Cassidys trial came first. and a special Jury was picked. and no one was intitled to a maverack unless they owned ten head of cattle or more and Cassidy had none of course. Judge Blake who was preciding Judge gave him two years in the state penetentary at Laramie City. and Hintons case was dismissed for lack of evidence. As Butch was the goat in that deal and inocent of the trap he was placed in.

The judge of the Third District Court was Jesse Knight, not J. W. Blake of the Second District Court in Laramie. There was a Justice of the Peace named Blakesley in Lander, but no connection to Cassidy could be found. No Judge Brenton could be found in Fremont County court records. Trout Creek flows through Fort Washakie, and the sleepers mentioned were stolen livestock.

Cassidy's lawyers filed for a new trial, but the motion was denied. On July 10, 1894, Judge Knight sentenced him "to the Wyoming State Penitentiary at, or near, Laramie City . . . for the term of two years at hard labor."

An intriguing sidelight to the trial is found in the court record. The same day Cassidy was sentenced to prison Al Hainer was also sentenced—but on a different charge. Judge Knight declared that Hainer had "abused, indued and otherwise injured David Blanchard, witness for the prosecution," and sentenced him to a term of thirty days and a fine of twenty-five dollars, for contempt of court.

The long trip to the prison at Laramie is detailed in Cassidy's biography:

> The sheriff was a friend of Butch along with many others and Butch went willingly with out chaines along with Sherif Orson. the sherif treated Butch as a companion travelor. and no one suspected him of being the Hole in the Wall leader of the Wild bunch, who had been captured and sentenced to prison as they had nothing in the papers. Orson recommended Butch Verry highly to the Warden at the pen. Warden Adams.

The sheriff at the time of Cassidy's trip to prison was Charles Stough, not "Sherif Orson." Grimmett was not elected to the sheriff's position until 1895. Accompanying Stough were Lander constable Henry Boedeker and Stough's deputy, Harry Logue. Grimmett could also have been present, however, as Cassidy was not the only prisoner on the trip.

In the entourage were Willie Nichols and Harry Gilchrist, two young cowboys from the Big Horn Basin country, being sent up for three years for stealing "neat cattle." Charley Brown, a Dubois area friend of Cassidy's, was on his way to a three-year sentence for rustling. At thirty-nine, the oldest prisoner in the group was Isaac Winkle, a surly, cross-eyed fellow who had been caught in the act of butchering a beef belonging to the Embar Ranch in the Basin. The sixth prisoner was William Wheaton, a young man with the unpleasant prospect of an eight-year stretch for manslaughter.[10]

Constable Boedeker recalled that when the prisoners arrived at the stone prison, now used as a dairy barn by the University of Wyoming, Warden W. H. Adams was aghast at seeing Cassidy without shackles. When Adams demanded an explanation, Boedeker said Cassidy dryly retorted, "Honor among thieves, I guess."[11]

On July 15, 1894, the following information was entered in the prison's Bertillion book:

> Wyoming State Prison number 187; Name, George "Butch" Cassidy; Received 7-15-94; Age, 27; Nativity, New York City; Occupation, cowboy; Height, 5'9"; Complexion, light; Hair, dark flaxen; Eyes, blue; Wife, no; Parents, not known; Children, no; Religion, none; Habits of life, intemperate; Education, common school; Relations address, not known; Weight, 165 pounds; Marks scars: features, regular, small deep set eyes, 2 cut scars on back of head, small red scar under left eye, red mark on left side of back, small brown mole on calf of left leg, good build.[12]

By stating his nativity as New York City, a story he also had told the Simpson family on Jakey's Fork, Cassidy directed attention away from the Parker family in Utah. He was not their first son to make the facility his temporary abode.

Following his entry into the prison record book Cassidy was seated for his mug shot. In the harsh light of the photographer, Cassidy looks disheveled, even injured. Of this photograph he was to later write in his biography,

> There had never been a photograph taken of him, except the one taken when he entered the penatentiary, and this was rather distorted & looked little like him so the best of the authorities had to go on was a description of his, excepting those who knew him personally.

Cassidy's imprisonment was the lowest moment of his life. His manuscript gives a haunting glimpse into his feelings of total despair:

> It was not until the cell door closed on Butch that he realized that he was realy in prison. He was then completly Broken. He was alowed a cell mate in a few days. and after was taken to the yards for exercise. he was always an obedent prisoner and gave no trouble to any one. He had money and was alowed to buy books, papers, but candy, or tobacco any thing he wanted.

There is no record of who shared Cassidy's cell. During his stay at the Laramie penitentiary 170 prisoners, including three blacks, three of Oriental descent, and one woman, passed through its gloomy corridors. They came from all walks of life. The most common charge was grand larceny with 88 offenders; the least common was rape, with only one offender. Burglary, forgery, murder, and manslaughter were common crimes, reflecting the violent growing pains of the West.[13]

Two of Cassidy's friends also were in prison: Abraham "Rocky" Stoner, from Cokeville, and Thomas Osborne Shepheard, the Tom Osborne at whose ranch Cassidy and Hainer had stopped on their way to the Hole-in-the-Wall.[14]

Stoner, fifty-one, entered the prison in 1893 on a four-year sentence for grand larceny of livestock. After his release "Rocky" Stoner was to provide sanctuary for Cassidy in his travels through southwestern Wyoming.

The story of Tom Osborne bears repeating. While drinking at his ranch with a saddle tramp named Thorn the inebriated Osborne was persuaded to sign a paper the tramp said concerned a transaction involving a saddle. When Tom sobered up Thorn showed him he had just signed over his ranch, and drove him off the property at gunpoint. Osborne later cornered Thorn in Lannigan's Saloon in Lander and hastened the rounder to his just reward. He was arraigned in November 1893, and on December 1 began a fifteen-year sentence at the Wyoming penitentiary for manslaughter. Public sentiment influenced Governor W. A. Richards to pardon him on August 9, 1896, and Tom returned to his Badwater ranch at age fifty-four, after serving two and one-half years.[15]

During the month of April, 1895, Cassidy's friend Charley Brown, with his cellmate Tom Morrison, escaped by digging through the wall of their cell diagonally down into the cellar and through the foundation of the prison building's east main wall. Two days later, Brown was captured and returned, eventually to be freed on February 24, 1899.[16]

According to the prison Bertillion book, Cassidy was discharged on January 19, 1896, by a pardon order from Governor W. A. Richards. The record stands in marked conflict with the outlaw's own recollections of his release:

About the 15 of Feb. 1895 a guard came and sumened Cassidy to the office. His caller was Judge Brent whose fault it was that Cassidy was there. The Judge offered his apology and wanted to shake hands and told Butch he would talk with the govener to release him. Butch refused the handshake also told the Judge he would get eaven with him if it is the last act I ever do. And when I shake hands with a Man, he must be a gentleman. This was new to the Judge for he was used to people begging him for favors. the Judge and Govener Richardson being good friends and stock men, Cassidy was released from prison April 1st, 1895. Cassidy had served 7 mo of his sentence and He was pardoned. The shock was almost as bad as when the Prison door closed on him. He was alowed to bid the other prisoners good by as well as the guards and Warden. They had all been good to him and respected his straight forwardness.

Other historical accounts have discussed a meeting between Cassidy and officials wherein the outlaw was offered his freedom if he would promise no further depredations within the state, but Cassidy's early release, as claimed in his biography, cannot be verified. There were no recorded prison releases on April 1, 1895.

About one thing there can be no question. When Cassidy left the Wyoming penitentiary his mind was set. If Butch Cassidy was going to be an outlaw, he would be "the most dreaded, most hunted and surely the most illusive outlaw that either North or South America have had to contend with as yet."

Maxi Parker homestead, Circle Valley, Utah, 1973.

Photograph by author.

Robert LeRoy Parker, *c*1883.

Courtesy Denver Public Library Western History Collection.

Telluride, Colorado, *c* 1890. The bank is the steepled building, middle left.

Bishop Ethelbert Talbot, *c*1906.

From Ethelbert Talbot: *My People of the Plains*. New York, Harper & Row, 1906.

Horse Creek cabin group photograph. From left, Al Hainer (?), Eugene
Amoretti, Jr., Hughie Yeoman, Bill Donely, Butch Cassidy.

Courtesy Frankie Moriarty. Original Photograph by H. C. Wadsworth, Lander, Wyo., c1889–1890.

Emery Burnaugh, 1892.

Alice Burnaugh, 1892.

Tom Osborne, 1893.

Tom O'Day, 1904.

Nathan D. Champion, 1891.

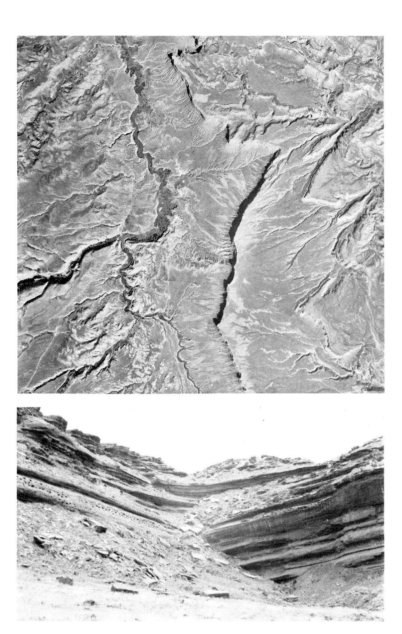

Hole-in-the-Wall, Wyoming. The game trail coursing down the V-notch
in the Red Wall was used by outlaws to drive stolen livestock to a brush
corral in the green ash grove at the bend in Buffalo Creek, center left.

Douglas Preston.

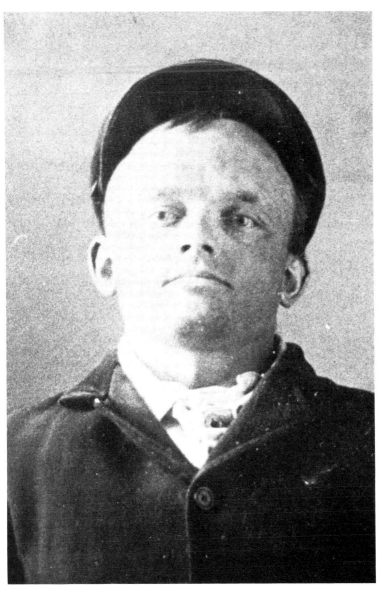

Charles Brown, 1894.

Harry Gilchrist, 1894.

Courtesy Duane Shillinger, Assistant Warden, Wyoming State Penitentiary.

William Nichol, 1894.

Courtesy Duane Shillinger, Assistant Warden, Wyoming State Penitentiary.

93

Isaac Winkle, 1894.

Courtesy Duane Shillinger, Assistant Warden, Wyoming State Penitentiary.

William Wheaton, 1894.

Courtesy Duane Shillinger, Assistant Warden, Wyoming State Penitentiary.

Abraham "Rocky" Stoner, 1893.

Courtesy Duane Shillinger, Assistant Warden, Wyoming State Penitentiary.

96

Chapter IX

The Wild Bunch

If you call a man a thief, treat him like a thief, and deprive him of all chance to earn a living honestly, the chances are he will oblige you by becoming a thief.—HELENA HUNTINGTON SMITH[1]

OF the "Bandit Invincible" narrative, the most moving passage is Cassidy's depiction of the days following his prison release. A churning undercurrent of apprehension, bitterness, frustration, and despair is powerfully communicated in his unpretentious, homely prose. Forty years had not deadened the agony of that recollection:

> He went to Lander and found his friends had lost no respect for him and confidence in him and showed him the best of time. Hinton was not in town but was nicely located on a stock farm and was Verry friendly with the stock men. Butchs old friend the sherif asked him what he wanted to do and he said I want to go straight if they will let me. It is the stock mans move and if they move in the wrong direction I will give them plenty to chase me for. He went to lost cabin and then to powder river and he soon found he was on the black list right in earnest. every place he went, there was no hands wanted. He then went to bad water country and found out there by a friend who had just came from Lander that a certain man in the sweet water country had sworn out a warrent for his arest for stealing 50 head of horses about 5 years previous to his release from the pen. Butch was not through that part of the country for a long time after the time the man had said the horses was stolen. It was just another excuse to tangle Butch with the law again. This man was enstrumental in the former arest and afraid that Butch might harber a grudge against him. He fansied another conviction would not be hard. That warrent had he but known would start all the hell that all the police officers in the United States were not able to stop.

Cassidy's enemy in the Sweetwater country is also discussed later in the manuscript, where he is given the name John Ainsley. An intensive search has failed to turn up a John Ainsley, nor record of any man in the area described who might have been Cassidy's enemy. From the context of Cassidy's trial record the man probably was Otto Franc, the Big Horn Basin rancher who signed both grand larceny complaints against Cassidy, on behalf of his neighbor, Richard Ashworth.

In retaliation Cassidy said he gathered fifty head of his persecutor's horses and "hearded them across the red desert down in to utah so far as the Lee's ferry Country where he scattered them all over as far as the breaks of the Colorado Canyon."

At this point Cassidy began to gather together his elite corps of horseback outlaws, the infamous Wild Bunch. The first of these recruits, as revealed in the Cassidy biography, was "Dick Maxwell, known in the north as Harvey Gratwick," a fictitious creation used to mask the participation of two men: Elzy Lay, who was still living at the time "The Bandit Invincible" was written, and Harry Longabaugh, the Sundance Kid.

Elzy Lay had been in Brown's Park at the time of Cassidy's arrival following the Telluride robbery. He was tall—about five feet eleven inches—dark-complexioned, and handsome. The quiet cowboy was an expert with horses, and with a gun.

Born William Ellsworth Lay on November 25, 1868, at McArthur, Ohio "Elzy" migrated west with his family, first to Iowa and finally to the northeastern Colorado communities of Laird and Wray, in 1887. There he befriended William McGinnis, a local boy whose name he would adopt as an alias in later years. Boredom had caused Lay to drift into Brown's Park in search of adventure.

During the period Cassidy was awaiting the July 1893 session of court Elzy Lay also was in Lander, getting into a minor scrape over ownership of a gun, but avoiding conviction.[2] While Cassidy was in prison Lay returned to the Brown's Park area, where he married Maud Davis of Ashley Valley, Utah, the year Cassidy was discharged from prison.

Harry Longabaugh obtained the sobriquet, "The Sundance Kid," after a term he spent in the Crook County jail at Sundance, Wyoming. Longabaugh was arrested on June 22, 1887, on three charges of grand larceny involving property, including a horse and revolver, belonging to Alonzo Craven, an area rancher. By August 4, the date of his trial, the charges were reduced to the theft of Craven's horse. After hearing testimony a jury returned a guilty verdict and Judge Scott sentenced him to eighteen months in the Wyoming Territorial Prison. But, since he was under twenty-one, the time was served in the Crook County jail. On February 4, 1889 he was released with full pardon because "his behavior has been good since confinement, showing an earnest desire to reform."[3]

Not much later, on May 18, the Crook County deputy sheriff was again packing a warrant for the "reformed" Longabaugh's arrest for threatening the life of one Jim Swisher. The warrant was never served. The Sundance Kid was gone.[4]

On the Sundance jailer's book Longabaugh listed his nativity as Pennsylvania. At other times he claimed he "was from a good New Jersey family and had a sister who was married to a Congressman from another state. After reading some thrilling novels on the West, he ran away from home and became a skilled cowboy and joined a hold-up or two, just for excitement and then joined Cassidy's gang."[5]

Harry Longabaugh was, in fact, the son of Josiah and Annie Longabaugh of Mont Clare, Lancaster County, Pennsylvania. His sister Sammana married Oliver E. Hallman, also of Mont Clare. Pinkerton files also listed a brother, Edward P. Longabaugh, and an unmarried sister, Emma, both later living in Boston, where Harry sought work before heading west in 1886. He also had a cousin, Seth Longabaugh, who worked in the mines at Eureka, Nevada.[6]

Longabaugh arrived in the Hole-in-the-Wall some time after the robbery of a Great Northern train on December 12, 1892, near Malta, Montana, with Bill Madden and Bert Charter, Cassidy's horse holders at Telluride, and a southwestern bandit named Harry Bass. Madden and Bass were captured shortly after the robbery and sentenced to ten and fourteen years, respectively, in the Montana State Penitentiary, at Deer Lodge.[7]

Longabaugh's personality is accurately portrayed in the "Bandit Invincible" manuscript:

Dick Maxwell was a man about Butchs size and build but was

slightly darker than Butch. He like Butch was quick as a steal trap in his movements and a dead shot.

Maxwell was a natural born gentle man and had all the earmarks of one. Always emaculate in appearance and the attitude of the perfect gentle man. He like Cassidy was the champion of the under dog. . . . Maxwell was not what one would call sullen, but he was Verry reserved & dispositioned to be distant except with his Verry closest friends and there were times when he held himself aloof from them. He was quick and active with a six shooter and if in a fit of temper or attacted he could shoot on the instant.

Another cowboy of the Brown's Park area to join Cassidy—but not mentioned in the biography—was Henry Wilbur "Bub" Meeks. Nearly the same age and size as Butch, the dusky Meeks also was a Utah Mormon drop-out. The son of Henry Meeks, one of the first midwestern Mormon converts to migrate with Brigham Young to Utah, Bub was reared near Wallsburg, Utah, where his father was a freighter. Moving to southwestern Wyoming range country near Robertson at the age of eighteen, Meeks had worked several years before with Cassidy in the Cokeville, Wyoming area.[8]

To round out his outlaw band Cassidy returned to the Hole-in-the-Wall where, in addition to George Currie, according to his manuscript,

He located three men he wanted. Kid Curry quick and fearless of no man or devil was his first man with a deadly shot. To Curry human life meant nothing. quite different from Cassidy. He did not look for trouble but did not wast time if it came his way. Cassidy would go a long way to avoid trouble not from fear but policy. Robing a bank meant nothing but Killing in cold blood was another, and which he did not aprove. Cassidy would rather out wit the persuers but Curry would kill if they followed to close. The second man was Dusty Bill Conner Odell and Killpatrick.

The features of Harvey Logan, or "Kid Curry," displayed an Indian heritage. Shorter and thinner than either Cassidy or Longabaugh, the dark-complexioned Logan had a steel nerve which quickly earned Cassidy's admiration as "the bravest man I ever knew." His soft drawl, deliberate movements, and extreme politeness belied the smouldering resentment he bore toward society.

Above his long, thin nose black eyes flashed a deadly warning when he was aroused.

The manuscript's detailed description of Logan, like that of Long-abaugh, reveals an intimate acquaintance with the outlaw:

Curry . . . who unlike either Cassidy or Maxwell in as much as he was rather inclined to be surly and appeared to resist new acquaintances regardless of who they were. He would not cause trouble but would resent the slightest insult or injury instantly. If a man did him wrong or attempted to injure him in any way, he never forgot it and at the first opportunity would eaven his score with him. His experiences in early life had been very bitter and he gradually arrived at the state of mind where he felt every one was against him and therefore did not hesitate to kill upon the least provacation. Cassidy was undoubtedly the only living man who had any control over him. Cassidy's very calmness seemed to put a chill of fear in him.

Logan arrived in the Hole-in-the-Wall following a shooting in which he killed Powell "Pike" Landusky in Montana during the Christmas season of 1894. Although Logan had been in the central Wyoming outlaw stronghold before, most of his time since 1884 had been spent in the Montana Little Rockies area engaged in ranching with his three brothers, all operating under the alias Curry. By 1896 Logan's older brother Henry died of pneumonia, and his next younger brother John had been dispatched with a shotgun blast following a feud with a neighbor over water rights. Only the youngest brother, Lonie (pronounced Lōne-ee), remained in Montana, operating a saloon at Harlem.

Before their arrival in Montana as the Curry boys, Logan and his brothers had lived with an aunt in Dodson, Missouri, just outside Kansas City. Although history records their nativity as Kentucky, in the 1894 Chouteau County voting records the boys stated their birthplace as Tama, Iowa.

"Killpatrick" was Ben Kilpatrick, known as the "Tall Texan." A soft-spoken cowboy from Knickerbocker, Texas, Ben weighed 180, had dark hair and light brown eyes. His left eye had a disfigured iris, which made it appear to have two pupils. His nickname came from his six feet, one inch height.[9]

Regarding Dusty Bill Conner Odell, Cassidy could have been

referring to any of a variety of men in the Hole. The Odell reference may have been O'Day, although there was a cowboy named Jim O'Dell in the area. There was a Bill Cruzan connected with the gang, a man named Conner who was thought to have been in the area at the time, and a "Dusty Jim" Hockett. Most likely, he was Bill, or Will, Carver.

Carver also was a Texan. When he joined Cassidy he had already served his apprenticeship with the notorious "Black Jack" Ketchum gang of the Southwest. The light-haired, sandy complexioned, five-foot, seven-inch outlaw was described by the *San Angelo Standard* as "a plain, unassuming, quiet sort of desperado, of a very retiring disposition, and rather shunned than courted notoriety. He was adverse to society and preferred to dwell in the solitudes of the great southwestern plains."[10]

When Cassidy returned to the Hole-in-the-Wall there was much news to learn. After a short duration of near martial law and occupation by black troops sent by President Benjamin Harrison following the ill-fated Johnson County War, nesters and ranchmen had settled into an uneasy, distrustful coexistence. The rustlers played the standoff to their advantage.

In mid-August 1895 law-abiding residents became alarmed when Albert "Slick" Nard, one of the Jack Bliss gang, severely wounded a sheepman named Schlicting in a botched highway robbery attempt in the Lost Cabin country. Captured, Nard was given a stiff sentence of fourteen years in the penitentiary.[11] Although not a member of the Hole-in-the-Wall Gang, Slick Nard's cold-blooded attack caused public attention to focus on the anarchy of the area.

At this same time it was discovered that the rustler faction had been especially active in moving stolen cattle out of the Big Horn Basin. The Keystone Ranch alone had lost 175 head in the season. In retaliation Fremont County sent deputy Jim Baldwin on a sortie into the outlaws' lair, as told by George Currie in the Phillips manuscript:

> George Curry was one of the settlers. Jim Baldwin was the sheriff and was to pay a Visit to the Whole in the Wall. Jim was a fine fellow said Curry but he had better not raid the Whole in the Wall for if they are looking for trouble they will get it. Well Jim

did raid, with twenty men but was taken back to Fremont on stretchers   The boys in the Whole were not eaven scratched.

Not one book on the history of the Hole-in-the-Wall has mentioned this confrontation. Yet research in the back files of Buffalo and Lander newspapers revealed that Fremont County deputy sheriff Jim Baldwin did, indeed, raid the Hole in late August 1895 with a posse of area ranchmen, upon whom the rustlers had been preying so effectively. Stretchers notwithstanding, the manuscript account of the unsuccessful raid is verified in detail by news reports of the affair.[12]

Set in the time frame immediately following his prison discharge, Cassidy led his newly formed band of desperadoes in his "first bank robbery" in southern Utah, as related in his memoirs:

> Butch was to look over a certain bank then make plans for a hold up. A bank in Central Utah was planed on. Horses & supplies enought to last 5 days in the foot hills of Wasatch mts 20 miles from the hold up. They set fire to an old abanded shack three miles from town to atract atention. It was 12 o'clock. Cassidy did the hold up. Maxwell stood gard. They got most of the Money. and were out of sight before a possie could be formed. They rested their horses that night and ate a cold meal and slept. after two days travel they stopped to rest in Wyoming. They found they had $7,000, They devided so they could have their share in case of a split up.[13]

Later in the manuscript, regarding this yet-to-be verified "first robbery," Cassidy justifies his actions by claiming the bank owner, a Mr. Kinney, had foreclosed on a widow, "Minnie Rathburn," as she was unable to repay a loan following the death of her husband. The deceased, John Rathburn, had been a miner in the Utah town where Kinney was also a pillar of the church. Rathburn and Cassidy had been close friends, and following the robbery Cassidy found the widow in Salt Lake City and persuaded her to take a portion of the robbery money, arguing,

> I consider that most of his money is blood money squeezed out of his mortage victims. . . . The only difference between him and myself is that he uses the law when he holds people up and I use a six shooter. The law says he can demand his pound of flesh I

admit but to me its not honest. No, I feel no remorce for doing this job. I feel that I have done a good deed. I am outlawed now so Ill devote the rest of my life taking money away from such sharks as Kinney and returning it to those who are honest and need it. . . . I suppose if you and your children had been turned out to freeze it would have been all right cause the law said so. Thats where the law and I disagree. There is one right. That is Charity toward your fellow man when he needs your help. I want you to take this money . . . try and make it do a little more cheerful work than Kinney would have done had I not persuaded him to turn it over to me.[14]

The Phillips manuscript is replete with such examples of Butch Cassidy's "Charity." More than half of the narrative is devoted to the rationalization of his acts of banditry. By placing this "first robery"—in retribution against the self-righteous and unscrupulous banker Kinney—immediately after his prison term, he bolsters his Robin Hood image and reinforces his claim that "he had as he thought every good reason for his first hold up, and after the first, there was no place to stop."

In detailing Cassidy's escape route following the Utah robbery the manuscript discusses a little-known hideout used by Butch Cassidy and his Wild Bunch: "They hid out in the Cook stove basin for a long time then they began to look around again. Butch went to the Whole in the Wall from big horne Canyon in three days distance of 80 miles as the Crow flies."

Cook Stove Basin lies at the extreme northeastern reach of the Big Horn Mountains, overlooking the rugged Big Horn Canyon. The basin was ideal as a hideout: well situated for water, grass, and wild game. A cabin in the basin, now used as a cow camp by Wyoming rancher Hiram Bischoff, was built by Sam Garvin, a rustler of Cassidy's era.

Southern Montana rancher Phil Boyd, whose summer range lies in the vicinity, said the area described was used by outlaws long before Cassidy took advantage of its benefits. Horse thieves used the basin as a stopping point in their travels between Oregon and the Dakotas during the 1870s and 1880s. At the time Cassidy was in the vicinity Jimmy Mogen operated a road ranch for the traffic in the adjacent Garvin Basin.[15]

Across the gorge, in the Pryor Mountains, yet another cabin had Kid Curry's name carved into one of the logs. The outlaws forded the Big Horn River at Chain Canyon, named for the barricade of chains the rustlers suspended from bolts driven into the canyon's sheer rock walls. This evidence of outlaw habitation now lies beneath the waters of Yellowtail Reservoir.

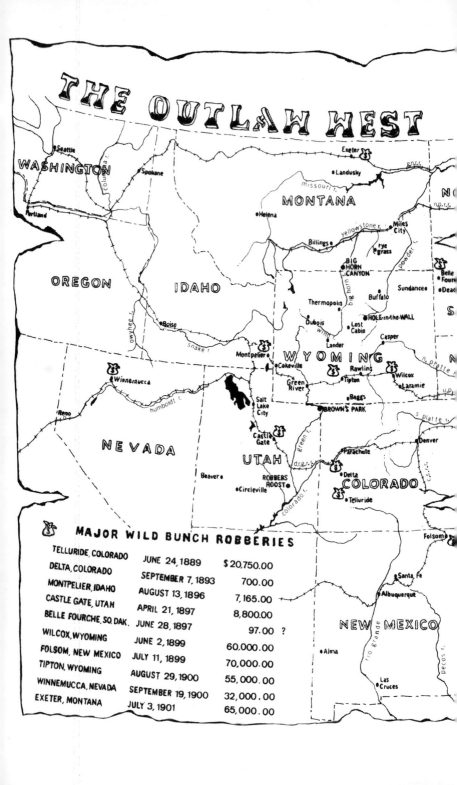

THE OUTLAW WEST

WASHINGTON
Seattle
Spokane
Portland

OREGON

IDAHO
Boise

NEVADA
Reno
Winnemucca

MONTANA
Exeter
Landusky
Helena
Billings
Miles City
rye grass
BIG HORN CANYON
Thermopolis
Buffalo
Sundance
HOLE-in-the-WALL
Dubois
Lost Cabin
Lander
Casper

Belle Fourche
Deadwood

WYOMING
Montpelier
Cokeville
Green River
Rawlins
Tipton
Baggs
BROWN'S PARK
Wilcox
Laramie

Salt Lake City
Castle Gate

UTAH
Beaver
Circleville
ROBBERS ROOST

Parachute
Delta
COLORADO
Telluride
Denver

NEW MEXICO
Santa Fe
Albuquerque
Alma
Las Cruces
Folsom

MAJOR WILD BUNCH ROBBERIES

TELLURIDE, COLORADO	JUNE 24, 1889	$ 20,750.00
DELTA, COLORADO	SEPTEMBER 7, 1893	700.00
MONTPELIER, IDAHO	AUGUST 13, 1896	7,165.00
CASTLE GATE, UTAH	APRIL 21, 1897	8,800.00
BELLE FOURCHE, SO. DAK.	JUNE 28, 1897	97.00 ?
WILCOX, WYOMING	JUNE 2, 1899	60,000.00
FOLSOM, NEW MEXICO	JULY 11, 1899	70,000.00
TIPTON, WYOMING	AUGUST 29, 1900	55,000.00
WINNEMUCCA, NEVADA	SEPTEMBER 19, 1900	32,000.00
EXETER, MONTANA	JULY 3, 1901	65,000.00

Chapter X

Montpelier

THE FIRST ROBBERY historically credited to Cassidy and his Wild Bunch following his release from the Wyoming penitentiary was the August 13, 1896 holdup of the Montpelier, Idaho bank. Although juxtapositioned to several later chapters in the narrative, the details of the robbery as told by Cassidy are verified in news accounts of the time. Assisting Cassidy in the holdup were Elzy Lay and Bub Meeks:

> He went as far north as Idaho Falls and then down to Blackfoot, Pocatello, and made his way over near Bear Lake. Of all prospects he had looked over he considered the best was a small thriving town near the head of Bear Lake. The chance of a get away from there appeared good and the bank seemed to carry plenty of money. He returned to the gang. They considered the trail they would take for their get away and studied landmarks for they would need plenty of land marks to make speed in a get away. They made camp at the point where they would leave the relay about fifteen miles out of town at the head of a creek where there was plenty of food and water for the horses. There was no fire built. In the morning they wrapped a light supper of food in their slickers and tied them behind the saddles. It was planned to stick together across the Green river valley, also across the Wind River range of mountains and down through the Sweet water country if possible.
>
> About one o'clock they rode leisurely into town. One stayed with the horses and Butch took the lead in the bank. It was a matter of a few seconds to line up the customers and bank employees. Maxwell stood at one end of the line while Butch transfered the cash to a sack he carried. First the money in the vault & then the cash behind the counter. Coming from behind the cage, he noticed that one man in the line up had a small boy on the floor beside him. He put the contents which was currency into the bag and then examined the customers and found two six shooters. He told them to hold their hands up. They made for the door and

their horses & were gone. The whole thing took about ten minutes.

The alarm was set off and a posse aranged emmediately. The delay gave the Wild bunch a three minute head start. They reached their relay Changed horses and were off again. Owing to the relay being a little way from the main trail, the possie did not discover a change of horses had been made and continued to follow until nearly dark and their horses played out. They were forced to abandon the search until the following morning. The bandits finally stopped to rest and divided the cash which was about 28 thousand dollars. They parted again to meet later.

A legend persists in Wyoming that Cassidy and Elzy Lay, being hard pressed by posses, buried some of the Montpelier loot in the Wind River Mountains. Cassidy dug a hole in the sand at the base of a large, lightning-struck stump with the butt of his revolver and deposited the money, figuring the snag to be a good enough landmark to guide them back to the cache. The same old-timers who tell the story talk in terms of $30,000, which is similar to the $28,000 figure claimed by Cassidy, but is substantially larger than the $7,165 reported by A. N. MacIntosh, the Montpelier bank's teller.[1]

At this point the manuscript describes a visit Cassidy made to his "Lander sweetheart," thought to have been Mary Boyd. Before departing, Cassidy was given a gold chain and cross by the girl "to wear in memory of her." Cassidy's secretive meeting with Mary Boyd, according to Lander pioneers, was but one of many throughout his outlaw career.

A man like George Cassidy, who played fast and loose with the law, did not present the most secure picture of domestic tranquility to a young girl. Mary's situation was complicated further in that she was a half-blood. In May 1892 Mary gave birth to a daughter. Unable to handle the responsibilities of an unwed mother, she gave the child up. Gray Hair, an old Arapahoe woman, took the baby and named her Mary B'Hat. The "B" stood for Boyd; the "Hat" was Gray Hair's family name.[2]

The father of Mary's daughter has never been fully established. Cassidy could have been her father—the child was conceived the previous August, when Cassidy left for Evanston with Billy Nutcher's stolen horses—but Mary B'Hat was told that Mary Boyd became infatuated with the son of a Lander businessman. When it became apparent Mary was pregnant the young man's family intervened and whisked the errant son out of the country. Mary bore her shame alone.[3]

When Cassidy was in prison Mary Boyd married a local cowboy, Ol. E. Rhodes, on July 31, 1895 in Dubois, Wyoming.[4] However, clandestine meetings continued once Cassidy was released from the penitentiary.

After leaving Lander, Cassidy's biography says the outlaw followed the Wind River drainage as far as Muskrat Creek, and the old stage station at Soda Springs (abandoned before the town of Shoshoni was formed in 1906), where he turned south, eventually crossing the Sweetwater River and continuing "on his way to an old friend of his, Jess Johnson on a willow creek ranch on the east side of the [Green] mts near whiskey gap."

Jesse Johnson was a tall, handsome, southern gentleman with ice blue eyes and jet black hair. He hunted buffalo in Kansas before migrating to Wyoming in 1879. At Green Mountain he built up a horse ranch and operated a sawmill with his sons. Johnson's ranch on Willow Creek, known as the Diamond Six, is now a part of the Matador Cattle Company holdings. That Johnson was a close friend of Butch Cassidy was, until our interviews, a well-kept secret among Sweetwater settlers.[5]

While Cassidy ate, Johnson related news of the movements of Grimmett's posse, combing the country east as far as the Rattlesnake Range, and the Rawlins posse under Lou Davis, scouting the Green Mountain area to "the main crossing of the Sweet water at Merrysville." From Johnson's report Cassidy decided his companions had safely made it to the gang's hideout in "Big Horn Canyon."

From Jesse Johnson's ranch the narrative describes Cassidy's continued flight. While horseback posses searched the western states the outlaw took an extended trip into the midwest, giving time for the pursuit to lose its fervor. Heretofore, it has always been assumed that the outlaw always made his escape on horseback, following a loosely braided network of trails extending from Mexico to the Canadian line. Now, with the Phillips manuscript, insight is given into the true resourcefulness of this remarkable rogue.

From Jesse Johnson's ranch near Whiskey Gap, Cassidy made his way east and south, across Shirley Basin, to the head of the Little Medicine Bow River, where he "found a sheltered hideout but left the horse saddled for a quick getaway if discovered." He then continued to his intermediate destination, "the ranch of his old trusted friend Frank Burns on the Medicine Bow river 15 miles from Hanna on the Union Pacific railroad."

Frank Burns was not identified, but the Weir Ranch near Medicine Bow, Wyoming, had a reputation of being a hangout for outlaws. Located on Rock Creek at its junction with the Medicine Bow River, the ranch was started in 1884 by a man named Wolf from Weir, Nebraska. Billy McCabe was ranch manager for several years. Of this ranch, one Wyoming historian wrote, "This is the ranch which has been known as the Robbers Roost Ranch for many years and purportedly was a hangout for the Cassidy gang on their trips from Brown's Hole and other points west to their rendezvous in the Hole-in-the-Wall country."[6]

While at Burns' ranch, according to the Phillips manuscript, "Butch was on dangerous grounds as he was 20 miles from the Union Pacific holdup at Wilcox." This mention of the Wilcox train robbery site is a clue that the described flight may not have taken place after the 1896 Montpelier bank robbery, but after some other strike following the 1899 Union Pacific train robbery at Wilcox. Further details in the narrative of Cassidy's flight also support this possibility.

After obtaining a new outfit of clothing from Frank Burns, "to change his appearance," Cassidy went into Hanna and boarded a passenger train which took him east as far as State Center, Iowa, "where he had friends on a farm there." State Center, and Zearing—also mentioned in the story—lie in near proximity to Tama, Iowa, the town Kid Curry had listed as his birthplace.

From central Iowa, Cassidy made his way to Chicago, where the manuscript says he went to the Ontario Theater and met a young girl "who worked on a percentage." Thinking "she wasn't the sort who belonged in that sort of place," Cassidy took pity on the lass and, after hearing the melodramatic story of how she had come to land in such a dive, offered to help her improve her lot in life. He bought the girl a train ticket for Seattle, where "would be the best place to get good honest work," gave her $500, and saw her off at the depot, saying "And if this little act of mine but proves to be the means of helping you back to the place you are entitled to in life, I am only to happy to have been able and the one to perform it."

Two days later, the narrative continues, Cassidy ran into a cowboy friend from Wyoming, "Buck Williams:"

> He had come to Chicago with a car load of stock. Told Butch of some of the things that had happened. also told him that he [Butch] and Bill Hays were reported to have been killed down in Elk Basin. As soon as the news reached rock springs, Preston your old friend the lawyer went down to claim your body and bring it back for burial. As soon as he saw the body he knew it was not you. and was he happy. He got drunk and stayed that way for a week. Say oldtimer maybe you think you haven't any friends in rock springs. I'll bet if you road in there tomorrow they would turn the town over to you. and put on a regular fourth of July celebration. They said old Grimmet had tears in his eyes when he road out of Lander with his posse to head you off after the Montpelier robery.

Early in the morning of May 13, 1898, a posse under Sheriff C. W. Allred of Price, Utah, gunned down two men, one of whom was tentatively identified as Butch Cassidy. Uinta County, Wyoming Sheriff John Ward and attorney Douglas Preston, Cassidy's defense attorney in Lander, were called and the body was positively recognized as that of Johnny Herring, a young cowboy who bore a striking resemblance to Cassidy. The other man was thought to have been Joe Walker, a minor Utah badman.[7] Again, in this context Cassidy's trip would not have taken place earlier than May 1898.

The conversation continues:

> Have you heard any thing of Kid Curry lately?
> You remember that fellow Howe that Mormon over in Star Valley? Well, him and one of his deputies got after old man Stoner arested him as an accomplice of you fellows. took him into town and just raised hell with him trying to get him to admit that he knowed something about you fellows but they couldn't get anything out of the old man so finally turned him loose.
> Well, it seamed Kid got wind of what they done to the old fellow so he went gunning. He trailed Howe and his deputie over into Star Valley and headed them off and they shot it out. When

it was all over, Howe and his deputie had moved on in the next world.

They lost all track of the Kid when he struck Green River valley. Too bad for Howe. He always wanted to kill somebody. and when he got a chance to kill a real hard man he forgot how to pull the triger and draw at the same time. That Kid sure is bad medicine when he gets a sore spot.

I am sorry the Kid got mixed up with Howe. but the damn fool had no business tieing into old Stoner. He had nothing to do with the holdup.

Stoner was Cassidy's old prison inmate friend, Abraham "Rocky" Stoner, of Cokeville. There also was a Sheriff Howell, not of Star Valley, but of Thompson, Utah, at that time. The incident involving Kid Curry was the murders not of Howell and one of his deputies, but the May 26, 1900, slayings of Moab Sheriff Jesse M. "Jack" Tyler and his deputy Sam Jenkins, in Post Canyon north of Thompson, Utah. The deaths were laid at Harvey "Kid Curry" Logan's doorstep.[8]

After bidding Williams goodbye Cassidy concluded that he had better leave Chicago, being "not so much afraid of Buck as he was of Jimmy Morgan," who, with "Toot Herford and Harry Long," had accompanied Buck Williams to Chicago with the fall shipment of cattle. He boarded the boat, *City of Petoskey,*[9] bound for Frankfort, Michigan. From Frankfort he took a train to Mancelona, "a small town cut out of a dense forest to make a junction," where he was given the last room in the town's only hotel:

> The furnishings of the room consisted of 2 cots, 1 dresser an old wash stand with bowl & pitcher of water a couple of chairs, and no rug on the floor. He pushed a chair against the door instead of locking it so if any one tried to enter it would knock the chair over and wake him up. He removed his shoes coat and hat only before retiring so He would be ready for a quick get away if necessary. blew out the oil lamp and was soon asleep. At one o'clock a rap came on the door.
>
> Who is there & what do you want?
>
> It is the land lord. I have a party I must ask you to share your room with.
>
> Butch removed the chair from the door and got back in bed

without lighting the lamp. The land lord lit the lamp. Butch keeping quite with his arm over his eyes or lower part of his face rather shading his eyes so he could see the fellow unobserved. As the fellow took of his coat Butch saw a sherif's Star and did not feel verry comfortable. But thot if he doesn't get funney neither would he but was ready for action if it Was necessary. He did not sleep well and was up in the morning before six.

He dressed verry quietly and went out the same way so's not to desturb the sherif's rest. Upon going to the office he inquired as to whom the room mate was. and was told he was a sherif from Manistee who was looking for some bandit by the name of Cassidy that he had been seen there the day before and by some way had made his get away before the officers could nail him.

After this close brush Cassidy caught a train for Saginaw, transferred to another train going to Bay City, where he then hired on as a crewman on the schooner *Eagle*, bound for "Sand Beach, about 12 or 14 hours run in fair weather." The *Eagle*, "a trim little schooner with fore and aft rigs with gafftopsails," was skippered by a Captain LaCroix:

> At 9 o'clock they arrived at Sand Beach and after an all night With rough Waters and verry rough coming in to dock and about 500 feet out from the Break Waters the captain ordered [illegible] to stand by to lower canvass. And at about one hundred feet from the break water, he gave the order to lower the mainsail; at the same time he veered her slightly to starboard, and as soon as the bow entered the opening in the break water, he brought her up quickly, to port, and she slipped into the harbor as though in a light summer breeze. Once inside the break water it was only a few minutes until she was located at her regular landing place.
>
> Captain LaCroix had performed a mighty clever bit of seamanship in bringing his little vessel through that narrow entrance of only one hundred and fifty feet, in a South east gale of wind.

Although there was no "Sand Beach" in the Michigan Thumb area, Port Sanilac and the inland town of Sandusky lie in the area described, and Sandusky is the very town "William Phillips" claimed as his birthplace. Cassidy found the people of "Sand Beach" to be "jolly and carefree." As recorded in the manuscript, his pleasant experiences there occasioned him to question the course his life had taken:

Cassidy sometimes regretted that he had ever made the start that was to exclude him from society for perhaps the remainder of his life, but it had been done and he was fully determined to continue until such time as he could safely hide himself in some isolated foreign country where he could be free from molestation, but there could be no thought of this until he had amassed a sufficient amount of money, with which to enter into some kind of business. . . .

In "Sand Beach" Cassidy was hired by a traveling circus to drive one of their wagons, "as good drivers of six-horse teams were not easily picked up in that part of the country." From Sand Beach the circus first played Bad Axe, then Cass City, where on the second day,

Butch came face to face with a former special deputy sheriff whom he had known well in western Wyoming.

This is a hell of a mess, he thought, to be bottled up in a country like this.

There was little chance of a get away, if this fellow was allowed to get to an officer or even spread the alarm on the circus grounds, so he instantly formed a plan which he thought might work out. It just happened that when he met the fellow, they were alone and back of the wagons. so he made a bold break, Always armed, Butch, after a quick glance around, made a quick step toward the man and at the same instant drew and pushed his six shooter against the fellow's belly, as he remarked, One word out of you, or even a look, and you will be coyote bait. Now turn around and walk slowly, down the street ahead, and don't forget that I have you covered. I'll direct you which way to go.

Butch took a position about a half step behind, and a little to the right of his man, and with his hand on the butt of his six shooter, he was ready for instant action, should the fellow make the [illegible] to make a run for it. After coming to a forest they continued for a distance of two hundred yards, they turned into a abandoned logging road. Then addressing his man in a mild voice he said, Walker, I hate to do this but I must tie you up for a few hours.

Walker had a good drink out of the creek & then Butch tied Walker with his own belt to a tree. Butch also took the man's handkerchief rolled some moss in it and made a gag which he stuffed in Walker's mouth.

116

IN SEARCH OF BUTCH CASSIDY

Butch then retraced his steps and made his way to the depot.
Found a passenger train was leaving at 7 so he returned to the
Circus ground and selected a few small articles which he wished to
take with him. Returning to the Depot, he wrote a short note
addressed to the Postmaster, describing Walker's Predicament
and how to find him.

Butch boarded a train bound for Pontiac, Michigan, figuring he
had a three-hour head start before Walker would be found. At the
outskirts of Pontiac he left the train and, in a nearby field, changed
clothes with a scarecrow "which entirely changed his appearance."
He then hired out to a local farmer for a week, giving time for
pursuit to die down, before making his way to St. Louis, where he
again obtained a new outfit of clothes.

In the context of this prolonged flight through the Midwestern
states Cassidy reveals some practical insights into his cunning in
avoidance of capture when so hotly pursued:

Habit is one of the most Potent factors which aid in the capture
of crimnals. realizing this, Butch has always made it a Point to
avoid forming a habit of any sort. He changed his walk, the
combing of his hair, how he wore his hat and the style of his
clothes. He often noticed that a change of hats was one of the
most effective disguises a man could affect and he never failed to
make use of it. no matter how rediculous a certain hat made him
look. he would unhesitatingly make the change.

Cassidy never over estimated his own ability, nor under estimated the ability of his pursuers, but, he at all times applied very
natural Psychology in all his actions, and avoided all the things
the other fellow would most naturally conclude that he would
also. So there was practically no way of getting a line on him
unless one was to meet him face to face, and then very few would
recognize him, unless they had been quite well acquainted with
him.

From St. Louis, Cassidy took the train westward. When he again
reached Wyoming he jumped the train on a heavy grade near
Medicine Bow, and walked to the ranch of his friend, Frank Burns:

Well, I'll be damned, Where'n hell did you blow from?
exclamed Burns when Butch showed up at the ranch. Butch
explained how he got there and then asked for some chuck.
I see by the Cheyenne Tribune that they come near nailing you

in Chicago. And followed you all around Michigan. That was a hell of a stunt you pulled on Walker there in Michigan, served him right though, he was a dirty skunk, anyhow. You know they always suspicioned him and Slick Nard of killing Birch and Bedford over there in the basin where they found them dead, after they had been shot through the head while tied to their horses and their hands tied behind their backs. in my mind that was no holdup as they said, but just a plain killing on their part. Or they might have been hired to do it by old man Loyd.

I haven't seen anything about that in the papers. What time did they find him? asked Butch.

Oh about midnight. they wouldn't have found him then if it hadn't been for the dog they took with them. He found him. He was a little stiff & weak but aside from having his feelings hurt, by 'skeeters' he was all right.

Well, I had to tie him up or go to jail. Do you know Burns, I think I'll have to go back to that neck of the woods some day & upset one of their little banks for them. They'd get an awful kick out of it. Their so damn slow in that country they can't stop quick. I even slept with the sherif one night in Mancelony when he was hunting for me. I'll bet they'd elect a new sherif if they knew that.

Have you heard any thing new in the Country since I've been gone?

Well not much. I heard that they have a standing Posse in Cheyenne, who are waiting for you to stick up another train, and I heard, too, that the Hawley boys are planning to stick up the First National Bank, in Lander.

Cassidy's extended trip has been researched in depth. "William Phillips" had to have written from a first-hand acquaintance with the areas described. The man "Walker" may have been one of the detectives—Rogers, Peaveler, and Wickham—who were suspected in the murders of Dab Burch and Jack Bedford in 1892. Slick Nard definitely was associated with the two in Jack Bliss's horse-thieving ventures.

Burns' reference to the special posse waiting for Cassidy "to stick up another train" would also lead to the belief that the trip described did not occur after the Montpelier robbery, but some time later, as Cassidy had not yet robbed a train. The Hawley boys creation may have been in reference either to the Whitney brothers near Cokeville

or to the Hardy brothers, who were minor outlaws in the Hole-in-
the-Wall country:

> So the Hawleys are figuring on sticking up old Emeretti, eh?
> Well, it ain't in the catalogue. Emeretti is too damn fine a man,
> and besides he's a friend of mine, so I'll just have to bust up their
> little game, in that direction.
>
> How's my old pal, Coally? Is he in shape to carry me a couple of
> hundred miles?
>
> Oh yes, he's in fine shape, and just rarin' to go.
>
> While Burns did some odd chores about the house Butch sat
> down & wrote three or four short letters. One was addressed to
> Kid Curry; one to Dick Maxwell, another to a certain ranchman
> in the Rosebud country, and lastly, a long one to his sweetheart in
> Lander in which he told her to look for him in their old hiding
> Place in about a week.

Returning to Lander, Cassidy met his sweetheart in their secret
meeting place:

> Oh, George, I'm so glad you're safe.
>
> Taking her arm, he led her to his horse. He told her all about
> himself leaving out nothing that he thought might be of interest
> to her. there were no secrets between he & this woman he loved so
> dearly and who, in turn, loved him to the point of idolatry. They
> sat on the soft grass and he took her in his arms, held her against
> his breast, telling her over & over how dearly he loved her.
>
> We are thinking of moving to California, but I can't bear the
> thought of leaving but I suppose I must, it is finally decided
> upon.
>
> That would be fine. I could Possibly see you oftener than I can
> while you are here. No one will be looking for me in that Part of
> the Country. If nothing happens to me within the next two years I
> think I'll leave this country and go to South America   And after I
> get settled I intend to return for you and then we shall always be
> together in a country no one will know us, and there will be no
> anxiety for either of us.
>
> If you do conclude to move to California, be sure our mutual
> friend, you know who I mean, has your exact address. Although
> she has no suspicion of our attachment, I shall find a way to learn
> your address from her, and when ever I write you I shall use
> sensitive ink, & write between the lines. You can do the same in
> writing to me. All that is necessary is to put a little soda into

some water, and use a tooth pick in writing. Just the same as you would use a pencil. As soon as the writing is dry, it can't be seen until after it has been subjected to heat or the fumes of amonia or smelling salts. Can you remember this? You Practice how to do this when you are alone then you will know how much soda to use in making it Properly.

As it was growing quite late, it was necessary that the lovers should part. As they kissed each other with fond good by, little did either of them realize the many long and tortuous years that would pass before they would see each other again. Deciding to return to town he led his horse quite close to her home, and after kissing her a final good by, he swung into the saddle, and was off.

By placing his secret meeting with his sweetheart in the Lander area, Cassidy again directs attention toward Mary Boyd Rhodes, who later admitted to being his "common laws wife." Mary, however, was not Cassidy's only lover. The meeting described bears a striking similarity to yet another of his recorded love affairs. Ardythe Kennelly, in her historical novel *Good Morning, Young Lady,* described a much similar scene between Cassidy and the heroine "Dorney Leaf," in Salt Lake City at the turn of the century, just before Cassidy's departure for South America. Dorney Leaf, whose family did move to California, actually existed—although not under that name—and the details of the novel parallel the Phillips account.[10]

After seeing his sweetheart, according to the manuscript, Cassidy rode to his Lander destination, Gene Amoretti's house:

Riding through the back streets of the little town and entering the yard of a small home, he made several light taps on the door.

Who's there? someone asked.

A friend, answered Butch. A light was switched on and a door was opened

My god, is that you or a Ghost? asked Mr. Emeretti, as he got a good look at his late visitor.

It's me, all right, answered Butch. I have a few words to say to you regarding the bank. He told him of the planned holdup of the Hawley boys. Mr. Emeretti thanked him for the information & while Butch ate they had a long visit.

Emeretti gave him a hearty hand shake and assured him that any time he could be of service to him he would be more than glad to extend it.

Chapter XI

Castle Gate

On April 21, 1897, the Denver & Rio Grande noon train arrived in Castle Gate, Utah, with the Pleasant Valley Coal Company payroll aboard. The crowd of miners barely noticed two horsemen ride up to the general store. Race horse trainers were not an uncommon sight, and Butch Cassidy and Elzy Lay looked the part, right down to the riding surcingles on their blooded animals.

Cassidy dismounted, walked to the building, and leaned against the outside staircase leading up to the coal company's office. As paymaster E. L. Carpenter and two assistants brought the payroll from the train Butch blocked their path and shoved his revolver into the paymaster's ribs, at the same time relieving him of his satchel. Before the astonished crowd could react Cassidy caught his nervous bay mare, and the two bandits were off in a cloud of dust, leaving pandemonium behind.

A station agent tried to telegraph Price, Utah, but the wires were cut. Carpenter had the train's engine uncoupled from the rest of the train while men grabbed all kinds of weapons and scrambled for a handhold on the moving machine. As it built up steam going down the narrow gorge of Price Canyon the engine whizzed past the unseen robbers changing horses behind a section house some distance down the track.[1]

Circling Price, the two bandits headed south while Sheriff Donant led his Price posse in the opposite direction toward Castle Gate. Muddled posses from Castle Gate and the small town of Huntington became so confused they ended up shooting at each other. Changing horses at relays manned by Bub Meeks, Bert Charter, and Joe Walker—a Utah recruit—Cassidy and Lay eluded the posse in the San Raphael desert, doubled back north, and rode into Brown's Park $8,000 richer.

With the daring Castle Gate robbery Cassidy perfected the technique developed by Tom McCarty in relaying horses along a planned escape route. Several weeks before a robbery Cassidy would gather, train, and harden the horses to be used in the getaway. Blooded animals were selected, grain-fed, and exercised rigorously. For the robbery sure-footed horses capable of fantastic speed over short distances up to fifteen miles were chosen. When the first relay was reached the saddles were switched to deep-chested, long-legged thoroughbreds able to maintain a man-killing pace, hour after hour. The unsaddled initial horses were driven ahead, able to keep up once relieved of their load. If necessary, a second, and even a third, relay of horses with stamina were stationed along the route. Fine horses were Cassidy's trademark; no impromptu posse could keep pace past the first relay.

Like the holdup of the San Miguel Valley Bank in Telluride, the Castle Gate robbery was not mentioned by name in the "Bandit Invincible" manuscript. The location most closely approximates that of Cassidy's "first bank robery," but neither the robbery amount nor the details of the affair match. These omissions are among the unexplained discrepancies found in the manuscript.

A few days following the Castle Gate holdup a rider leading a jaded grey pack horse rode into the yard of the Dan Hilman ranch, nestled in Wyoming's Little Goose Canyon on the east flank of the Big Horn Mountains, some seventy miles north of the Hole-in-the-Wall.

The stranger was invited in and, as Mrs. Hilman fixed him some food, he fell asleep in the chair he had straddled near the cook stove. Then, revived by the smell of cooking food, the trailworn visitor wolfed down his supper like a man who had missed several meals. The watching Hilmans kept their curiosity contained.

After he had eaten the stranger profusely thanked Mrs. Hilman for the generous meal. He was a man who spoke with conviction. Rubbing the red stubble on his chin he turned to Dan Hilman and looked directly at his host through steel-blue eyes, bloodshot from hours without sleep.

"I need a job."

"I'm sorry, I can't use you," replied Hilman. "I know your type. You cowboys just want to sit a horse and ride herd. I need someone who's willing to work. I've got fence to mend, hay to put up, and cows to milk. A cowboy's a luxury I can't afford."

"Oh, I know how to work, alright. And I'm not afraid to do what has to be done. Just give me a chance to show you."

Hilman gave the stranger a hard look. Somehow he didn't seem the saddle tramp he first appeared. Dan reached out his hand. The Hilmans had just taken on a new hired hand.

"My name's LeRoy Parker. I've been working for Bob Mock up toward the Montana line. I'd been there all winter without drawing any wages and when I asked to buy a new pair of overalls, he got mad. He said I was lucky to have a roof over my head when so many cowboys were out of work. Rather than have trouble, I left. Thought I'd cross the mountains into the Big Horn Basin, but the passes are still blocked with snow. Been bucking snow all day before I gave up and dropped in [on] you folks."[2]

LeRoy Parker proved to be Dan Hilman's best hand. When the early rising Hilman hollered, "hit the floor, boys," Parker was already out in the barn doing morning chores. Every menial task on the farm was attacked pleasantly with exuberance. To the paying guests on Hilman's budding guest ranch, Parker was a delight, and Dan's son Fred was captivated by the congenial cowboy.

On Sundays, Parker would take thirteen-year-old Fred and the neighbor boy, Joey Hurlbert, over the hill to put on dazzling displays of marksmanship. Spurring his horse along the fence he alternately shot at the fence posts, first with the pistol in his right hand, then in the left, never missing a post. Fred recalled that his own attempts to mock his cowboy hero met with only mediocre success. When the good-natured hired hand gave young Fred his .44 carbine for his very own, the young man nearly burst with pride.

One noteworthy incident from that summer took place during the haying season. While Fred handled the team from the front of the hay wagon Parker and neighbor Billy Sackett pitched hay up into the rack. Spying a rattlesnake in the field, Parker winked at Sackett and scooped the snake high into the air with his pitchfork. Up on the rack, when Fred saw the snake coming his way, all hell broke loose. Parker and Sackett laughed so hard they were too weak to stand.

One day far in the future, Fred Hilman would again be teased about that rattlesnake in the hayrack.

With all his good-natured banter there still was an air of aloofness, something deeply mysterious, about LeRoy Parker. Fred remembered that he seemed to keep a saddled horse picketed near wherever he was working. Relaxing around the table after dinner, he would set his chair backwards, elbows lightly resting on the chair's back, in a position commanding a view of the door and windows. His actions were quick, almost nervous. The Hilmans discreetly overlooked his mannerisms. He worked hard; that's all they cared.

Parker had a friend who often would come to visit, staying in the bunkhouse with the sandy-haired cowboy. The tall, dark stranger with the carefully trimmed mustache was polite but distant, his eyes shifty, almost embarrassed looking. The Hilmans thought they'd heard Parker call him Elzy. Fred believed the man said he was a bartender, possibly in Sheridan.

At times Parker would request a short leave, and would ride off with his mysterious visitor, sometimes for days at a time.

One morning towards fall Parker's smiling ruddy face was missing from the breakfast table. Fred remembered that he was sent to the bunkhouse after the hired hand. When he looked in the bunkhouse door he spied a scrap of paper tucked under the edge of a horse collar on the wall. On the paper was a note, worded simply:

"Sorry to be leaving you. The authorities are getting on to us. Best home I've ever had. *LeRoy Parker (Butch Cassidy)*"[3]

Chapter XII

Belle Fourche

THE SUMMER OF 1897 marked the arrest and trial of Bub Meeks for his part in the Montpelier bank robbery. While carousing in Cheyenne, Meeks aroused the suspicions of a railroad detective. The previous summer outlaws had failed in an attempt to hold up a Union Pacific train in Wyoming, and had fled to Jackson Hole, just before the Montpelier heist. The detective thought Meeks was one of those involved in the affair.

When Meeks returned from his trip to Cheyenne he was arrested upon detraining at Cokeville.[1] Upon interrogation his alibi for the previous summer held up, but Oregon Short Line Railway employee Joseph Jones suspected Meeks' involvement in the Idaho bank robbery, and alerted Uinta County Deputy Sheriff Bob Calverly.

Calverly, the same man who arrested Cassidy in 1892 near Auburn, Wyoming, wrote the Montpelier bank, and A. N. MacIntosh, the bank teller, made a positive identification. Bub had held the horses at Montpelier.

After a hectic trial in Montpelier before Judge D. W. Standard, Henry Wilbur Meeks was found guilty of robbery and was sentenced on September 7, 1897, to thirty-five years in the Idaho prison at Boise.[2]

The year 1897 also marked the apex of rustling activity in Wyoming. In Johnson County, Sheriff A. Sproal was operating under increasing pressure to take action in ridding the territory of the rustler element. He hired as deputy one Billy Deane, a young Texan. Early in April 1897 Deane rode out of Buffalo with the grandiose idea of capturing the entire Hole-in-the-Wall Gang single-handed. His first stop was at the Alfred Grigg home just north of the Hole. The Griggs operated a post office in their home, and often hosted the various members of the outlaw band.

Mrs. Millicent James, daughter of Alfred Grigg, was only six at the time of Deane's visit, but remembers well what happened:

Deane was with my dad in the post office and mother looked
out the window and saw these two men coming in. She sent us
children down in the cellar to stay but we could see what was
happening. They came in various doors of the post office. . . .
[One] raised his gun to shoot Bill Deane, but mother grabbed it
and it went off into the roof. They left after dad and Bill Deane
got their guns, but Deane said he'd leave so as not to put the life
of my folks in danger, that they might kill him. My folks begged
him not to go. . . . There were two men; one we definitely think
was Kid Curry.[3]

Deane's next encounter with the outlaws occurred on April 13
near Kaltenbach's sheep shearing sheds, in broad daylight, with
twenty sheep shearers as witnesses. One shearer saw it this way:
"Deane saw four men coming down the creek over the hill. . . . After
riding toward the four men Deane dismounted and began to shoot.
They also immediately opened fire. Deane's horse broke loose and as
he turned to catch it he received several shots in the back. The shots
must have taken effect immediately, for Deane was dead when first
reached."[4]

Subsequent reports trace the gang to the Lost Cabin country
where they robbed Charles Bader's road ranch, pilfered sheep camps,
and "borrowed" twenty-five head of saddle horses and mules from
the Swift Company sheep camp.[5]

A holdup of the Union Pacific apparently was plotted that spring,
but the plan evidently leaked out and was aborted. Walt Punteney
said they next looked as far north as Dickinson, North Dakota, for a
bank to strike before finally settling on the Butte County Bank at
Belle Fourche, South Dakota.[6] An account of the events leading up
to that robbery is given in "The Bandit Invincible:"

After leaving Lander, Butch, He continued riding until the
fifth day he made camp on the head of Grass creek, a short
distance east of Powder river. The third day of his stay on Rye
grass, Maxwell showed up. . . .
The fifth day brought Kid Curry to camp & the trio was
complete. Preparations were begun for the holdup of the Belle
Fourche bank in Dakota.
Kid Curry had accurate knowledge of this place & a getaway
looked good. Word was sent to Tom O'Day, and a young fellow

by the name of Woodward, to meet Butch and Curry near Sundance.

The Woodward in the manuscript could have been one of the two Woodard brothers, Charles and Clarence, who resided in the Thermopolis–Lost Cabin region of central Wyoming. Both brothers had continual brushes with the law. Charles later killed Natrona County law officer Charles Ricker, who was pursuing him after he escaped from the Natrona County jail, where he had been awaiting trial for burglarizing a Casper store. He was lynched by an angry mob of Casper citizens on March 28, 1902, before justice ran its course.[7]

Clarence Woodard was sentenced for his part in the burglary and spent the next two and a half years at the Rawlins penitentiary. It was not his first Wyoming imprisonment. From July 9, 1896 to January 31, 1899 he was in the old territorial prison at Laramie, finishing his term in the new Rawlins facility after it was opened in 1898. From Clarence's record it appears the "Woodward" mentioned would have been Charles.[8] The name, however, could have been a creation to avoid mention of Walt Punteney's complicity in the affair as, like Elzy Lay, he was still alive when the biography was written.

On Monday morning, June 28, 1897, Belle Fourche was recuperating from a weekend veterans celebration when hell broke loose, as described in Cassidy's memoirs:

It had been planned that all O'Day was to do was to act as lookout, before the bunch rode into town, but Tom, after a drink or two to many, managed to get himself arrested & Butch & the other three were compelled to put the job over without a lookout. Riding into town about one thirty, they made directly toward the bank, leaving Woodward with the horses. There were several People in the bank when they entered. making use of their usual tactics, one of them lined the Customers against the wall while the other forced the clerks and cashier from behind the wall of the tellers cage, where they soon lined up with the others. Curry held the bunch in line while Butch ransacked the tellers booth and the Vault. In less than 5 minutes the job was over, and after hearding the customers and bank employees into a small back room, which butch took the trouble to lock as they left, they were soon in their saddles and away.

There has been much confusion over the participants in the Belle Fourche bank robbery. The *Buffalo Bulletin* published information from a Butte County (South Dakota) wanted poster, which had a garbled description of the robbers:

George Currie—About 5 feet 10 inches, weight 175 pounds, age 27 years, light complexion, high cheek bones, flat forehead, flat pug nose, big hands and bones, stoops a little, long light mustache, probably clean shaven.

Harvey Ray—About 5 feet 8½ inches, weight 185 pounds, age 42 years, dark complexion, round full face, bald headed, heavy long dirty mustache, might have heavy beard, dark grey eyes, hair quite grey about ears, inclined to curl, bow-legged.

Roberts—About 5 feet 7½ inches, age 32 years, rather small, weight about 140, very dark complexion, possibly quarter breed Indian, formerly from Indian territory.

Roberts—Rather small man, about 5 feet 6 inches, weight 130 pounds, age 28 years, very dark, probably quarter breed Indian, large upper front teeth protruding from mouth.[9]

The George Currie description is only partly accurate; he was 26 in 1897, and not as tall as the report stated. Harvey Ray, also connected with a variety of Wyoming rustling escapades, has never been identified.[10] The first "Roberts" description approximates Harvey Logan, and the second possibly his brother, Lonie.

No sources confirm the manuscript's claim of Cassidy's participation in the Belle Fourche robbery. Cassidy definitely was in the area, working for the Hilman ranch along the Big Horn Mountains, and he did take extended trips away from the ranch with his friend "Elzy." But the possibility that Cassidy and Lay could have been involved in the Belle Fourche holdup is first raised with the discovery of the manuscript.

In corroboration of the manuscript, R. I. Martin, a witness to the holdup, said Tom O'Day arrived in town several hours earlier, stopping in the Sebastian Saloon. Instead of joining his cohorts inside the bank the inebriated O'Day remained outside with the horses.

When the robbers left the bank O'Day panicked and ran back into the crowd, while his horse followed the gang out of town. Joe Miller, the blacksmith, ran home to get his new .30–.40 Winchester and rode his horse bareback in pursuit. Frank Bennett, the flour mill owner, thought Miller was one of the fleeing robbers and fired on the rider, nicking Miller's ear and dropping his horse from beneath him.[11]

Realizing O'Day was missing, the outlaws temporarily reigned up near an artesian well two hundred yards up the hill from Main Street before continuing their flight. In the confusion, O'Day ran up to a citizen named Tracy, and "said his horse had run away from him. He went up along the sidewalk west until he came to the vacant lot between the saloon and printing office, then, he crossed the lot, and went into the water closet back of the saloon."

Rusaw Bowman, the butcher, also saw O'Day enter the outhouse. "He closed the door and was in there a very short time; came out . . . and I threw down on him, and told him to throw up his hands."

After a search of O'Day revealed only some cartridges and a pint bottle of whiskey, Bowman, "with three or four other men, turned the water closet over, got a rake, and pulled the gun and scabbard out of the hole."[12]

Since the Belle Fourche jail had only recently burned to the ground, O'Day was locked up in the remaining steel cage, out in the open. He was later removed to the Deadwood, South Dakota jail.

The Cassidy biography gives a detailed account of O'Day's companions' flight following the holdup:

> Leaving the town at as high a speed as their horses would travel, they rode for 18 miles to their relay of horses. Throwing their saddles upon the fresh horses, they turned the others loose to shift for themselves. As the chance for leaving a blind trail was good at a certain point they turned sharpley to the left, leaving no sign of trail whatsoever. They had calculated that any Possie that might be following them from either Belle Fourche or Spearfish, would probably reach this point about dark and there would be unable to Pick up their trail before morning, or perhaps not even then.
>
> Their judgement Proved correct. all trace of them was lost at this point and after a tiresome search the following morning, the possie disbanded and returned to town.

Riding until about Midnight, the bunch covered a distance of ninty miles & were back on the head of the Rye grass creek, where they were safe for the time being. After a rest of 3 or 4 hrs, they saddled their horses & were again on their way. their course for some distance lay through a rather rough territory after passing Lame Deer creek, they changed their course to northwest, where they followed the divide between Rosebud & Tongue river. They continued on their way toward Pryor Gap. That night they made a fireless Camp in the foothills of the big horn, and the following day continued their way to the Big Horn Canyon and their old hideout where there was a considerable amount of food stored. The food cache consisted mostly of bacon flour & beans, but it was very good with the addition of mountain sheep steaks. With the finest pasture for their horses, & plenty of good water & food for themselves, the boys were quite satisfied to remain in the Canyon for some time until the country quieted down again. Here they were absolutely safe. No one ever came near that Part of the Country, not even the indians.

As soon as they reached the hangout, they proceeded to divide the money from the holdup. They had nearly 30 thous. dollars. This they divided 5 ways. 1/5 set aside for the defense of Tom O'Day although he had taken no actual part in the holdup they felt he was entitled to it & would need it for his defense. After a two wks stay in the Canyon, Woodward, who was the least known of any of them was sent into Billings to gather all the news he could & bring [illegible] of few supplies. Woodward reported that O'Day was being held as an accomplice to the bank robbery. according to all the papers which Woodward brought from town everything had quieted down. Butch had been recognized & the entire force of officers in central Wyoming was paying close to the Hole-in-the-Wall. Consequently it meant almost instant capture for any of them to enter the Hole.

After the Belle Fourche robbery Wyoming citizens determined to wipe out the den of thieves in the Hole-in-the-Wall. Joe LeFors and CY ranch foreman Bob Divine led an attack force which clashed with three of the Hole-in-the-Wall community at the head of Buffalo Creek on July 22, leaving "rustler" Bob Smith dead and two men wounded.

Divine, with a crew of fifty-four, returned to the stronghold July

30 and rounded up nearly four hundred head of "stray" livestock. The impregnability of the Hole-in-the-Wall had been shattered.[13]

While Divine's roundup was progressing along Buffalo Creek the Wild Bunch was having a celebration in the small cowtowns along the southern Wyoming line. Starting at Dixon the gang literally took over the town, toasting their recent successes. When they became bored with Dixon they moved on to Baggs, where, before finally departing, they paid a silver dollar for every bullet hole they put in Jack Ryan's Bull Dog Saloon.[14]

Later that fall, on September 19 in Red Lodge, Montana, the city marshal, Byron St. Clair—recently from Fort Washakie—met Walt Punteney, Harvey Logan, and Harry Longabaugh on the town's main street. The three, who were well acquainted with St. Clair, indicated their intentions of robbing the Red Lodge bank, owned by none other than John Chapman, the man who helped Bob Calverly arrest Cassidy in 1892. The trio suggested St. Clair should take a long overdue fishing trip, in light of the circumstances. Byron failed to take the suggestion and alerted Sheriff John Dunn. A news bulletin from Billings, dated September 24, tells what happened:

> Sheriff Dunn of Red Lodge, and posse came in from north with the three men supposed to belong to the gang of robbers wanted for the raid on the Butte County bank at Belle Fourche. . . . The prisoners were in Red Lodge last Sunday and on Monday Sheriff Dunn learned sufficient to put him on alert. He started with a small posse after them and traced them by way of Absarokee to Columbus where he was joined by Stock Detectives W. D. Smith and Dick Hicks and Constable Calhoun. They followed hot on the trail to Lavina, on the Musselshell where they came upon the men just going into camp. Two men were getting water at a spring and the other was picketing his horse.
>
> On being summoned to surrender, the two men at the spring jumped over the bank and attempted to defend themselves, but whenever they showed their heads the officers fired and they surrendered. The one with the horse parlied, and getting behind the horse he drew his revolver, when a shot went through the horse's neck and the man's wrist, causing him to drop the revolver. He mounted and the horse ran a mile before it fell, shot dead. The man surrendered.[15]

Harvey "Kid Curry" Logan was the man shot through the wrist. This gunshot wound, which ripped his lower right arm and left deep scars, was later to be a major feature in identifying Logan. The unidentified blond with Logan was Walt Punteney, as he was soon to admit, but the exact identity of the other man has never been established. The men were transported to join Tom O'Day in the Deadwood jail.

On October 15, 1897, the State of South Dakota indicted Harve Ray and George Currie (both in absentia), Thomas O'Day, Walter Punteney, and "Thomas and Frank Jones" in the charge of first degree robbery.[16]

Then, on the evening of October 31 all of the captured Belle Fourche robbers escaped, gaining their freedom by overpowering the jailer and his wife, "beating the woman quite badly, on account of her resistance."[17]

There was more to the story than Deadwood authorities cared to release. The outlaws had the freedom of the outer jail corridor at the time of their escape, and five saddled horses had been secreted in Spearfish Canyon just before the break.

"Frank and Thomas Jones" borrowed horses all along their escape route, and indications are they never stopped until they crossed the Canadian line.

O'Day and Punteney weren't so successful. A Spearfish (South Dakota) boy out hunting rabbits at daybreak on November 2, fired a shot and flushed the two fugitives from their cover. By one o'clock that afternoon the posse tracked them down. O'Day had played out, unable to keep the man-killing pace set by the husky Punteney.[18]

Once recaptured, Punteney and O'Day faced almost certain conviction. Subsequent developments in their prosecution are given added perspective in the light of the following "Bandit Invincible" excerpt:

> "Boys," said Butch. "I think I have a scheme we can work. I'll ride to Hot Springs above Thermopolis where Bob McCoy is. I guess you all know him. I'll give bob a roll of money & have him go to Deadwood & fix things up for Tom. Bob is realiable. No one has anything on him & he is not known over there. What do you say?"

"Well weve got to get Tom out if we have to ride into Dead-wood and take him away from the jail house."

Butch rode into Thermopolis on the 3rd day. It was no trouble to locate Bob.

Bob was clever. he never got directly mixed up in any deal. He could always furnish a lot of information to anyone he knew & liked. He drank sparingly & talked less than he drank. He was reserved & from his expression gave one the idea he was a good man to leave alone. There was nothing bob wouldn't do for a friend. it was no trouble to induce him to undertake the mission that Butch asked of him. He liked O'Day.

Butch gave him 3 thous in cash 1 thous for the lawyer another thous if the lawyer wins & 1 thous for Tom O'Day. Butch promised to make it right with Bob.

Three days later Butch arrived back at the Canyon. and they all felt they had done all they could for the time being towards Tom's release.

That O'Day and Punteney had two of the best criminal lawyers available—Temple and McLaughlin—gives substance to the manuscript story that Cassidy sent money via Bob McCoy for O'Day's defense.[19] This contention also is supported by contemporary news accounts of the trail: "On behalf of the defense, Bob McCoy and Sam Brown of Big Horn basin testified that Putney took dinner at Brown's ranch near Thermopolis, Wyo., nearly 300 miles from Belle Fourche, the day before the bank robbery."[20]

The outcome of the trial was reported in the *Buffalo Bulletin* of April 7, 1898: "Walter Putney, one of the Belle Fourche bank robbers was acquitted at Deadwood week before last, and now Tom O'Day has also been acquitted. The *Deadwood Pioneer-Times* comments very severely on this miscarriage of justice, and states that the evidence left no doubt of O'Day's guilt."[21]

Evidence and miscarriage of justice notwithstanding, Tom O'Day and Walt Punteney were free men.

Wild Bunch group photograph, c 1896. From left, front row: (1) ?,
(2) Cleophas Dowd?, (3) Bill McCarty or Harry Longabaugh, (4) Butch
Cassidy, (5) Bert Charter, (6) Tom McCarty, (7) "Blue John" Griffith,
(8) Elzy Lay, (9) "Flat Nose" George Currie, (10) Ben "Tall Texan"
Kilpatrick; second row: (11) Jack Ryan, (12) Lonie "Curry" Logan, (13)
John "Curry" Logan?, (14) Harvey "Kid Curry" Logan, (15) Matt Warner;
top row: (16) ?, (17) John Henry, (18) Tom Vernon, (19) ?.

"Fort Worth Five," members of the Wild Bunch, *c*1900. From left, seated:
Harry "Sundance Kid" Longabaugh, Ben "Tall Texan" Kilpatrick, Butch
Cassidy; standing: Will Carver, Harvey "Kid Curry" Logan.

Henry Wilbur "Bub" Meeks, 1897.

Courtesy William C. Linn, Pinkertons. Original photograph by Idaho
State Correctional Institution, Boise, Idaho.

Albert "Slick" Nard, 1895.

Courtesy Duane Shillinger, Assistant Warden, Wyoming State
Penitentiary.

Big Horn Canyon. Cassidy's hideout was in Cook Stove Basin, middle left.

Oblique SKYLAB photograph, 1973. Courtesy United States Geological Survey, EROS Data Center, Sioux Falls, South Dakota.

Jesse Johnson's Willow Creek Ranch, Green Mountain, Wyoming.

Photograph by author.

137

Clarence Woodard, 1896.

Courtesy Duane Shillinger, Assistant Warden, Wyoming State
Penitentiary.

"Dorney Leaf."

Courtesy Ardythe Kennelly Ullman.

Harry Tracy, *c* 1901.

Grimmett's "Free Silver Saloon." Jim Baldwin, center; Orson Grimmett, behind bar, left.

Courtesy John Henry.

Chapter XIII

Handwriting on the Wall

On February 15, 1898, the U.S. Battleship *Maine* was blown up in Havana Harbor, sparking councils of war in the nation's capitol. For months Hispanic-American relations had escalated to their climax.

At that same time another war council was being held by ranchmen in Rawlins, Wyoming, over equally aggravating but more regional depredations. 1897 had been a bumper year for the lawless element, and the cattlemen decided it was time for action. Stock detectives were hired to ferret out the rustler hideouts, and a bounty was discussed as an incentive.

The cry was not without cause. Two weeks following the ranchmen's conference, the *Denver News* reported that "Harvey Ray and other escaped Belle Fourche bank robbers have been joined by a party of Powder Springs thieves and together they are driving everything before them to the Hole-in-the-Wall region."[1]

Action was sought from Governor W. A. Richards, himself a rancher. The stockmen were not alone in pressuring Richards. His files bulged with protest letters, suggested solutions, and proffered assistance.[2]

Richards conferred with sheriffs Lou Davis of Carbon County, John Ward of Uinta County, and O. A. Sproal of Johnson County. The sheriffs pledged their cooperation but were also quick to point out the magnitude of the task. Sproal later wrote the governor: "The whole country is up in arms, and every device is used to protect and conceal the parties he [the sheriff] is after, or desires to watch, and every obstacle is thrown in his way. He is powerless and if he goes into the country with sufficient force to carry out his plans, it sets the whole country by the ears, and seriously endangers the peace of the country and the lives of some of its citizens."[3]

Governor Richards also sought cooperation from his counterparts in neighboring states: Robert Smith of Montana, Heber Wells of Utah, Alva Adams of Colorado, and Frank Steunenberg of Idaho.

Each having come in for a share of embarrassment over the depredations of the Wild Bunch, a summit conference was set for mid-March.

The event which brought the cauldron to boil had nothing to do with Butch Cassidy, however. During the last week of February 1898 a tragic incident in Brown's Park and its bloody aftermath forever closed that area as a fugitive haven.

A local hard case named Patrick Johnson fatally shot Brown's Park teenager Willie Strang. In his flight Johnson joined two desperate Utah escaped convicts, Harry Tracy and David Lant. Posses from three states, organized under Routt County (Colorado) Sheriff Charles Neiman, cornered the three fugitives in the rimrocks at the base of Douglas Mountain, and in the ensuing gun battle Tracy killed rancher Valentine Hoy with a bullet through the heart.

The badmen at length were run to ground, and Johnson received a stiff prison sentence. Tracy and Lant, however, again were able to escape before they could be brought to trial.[4]

Once the law finally came to Brown's Park, ranchers wanted to eliminate the outlaw element entirely. J. S. Hoy, the murdered man's brother, wrote the *Denver News* on March 6:

> There is talk of sending militia to destroy or rid the country of criminals. . . . Might just as well send a lot of schoolboys to do the work, to get lost or killed themselves. Hunting men in a thickly settled country or on the plains or open country is one thing, but to hunt them in these mountains snowcapped in sections the year around, cut by impassable canyons, unfordable rivers, gulches, gullies and where nearly every section of land affords a hiding place, is another proposition. To round up the whole country is impossible, nor can any considerable number of men enter the country without their presence being known to the criminals. . . .
>
> One or two men on the trail of a criminal will succeed where 100 men will be sure to fail. They must be hunted like wild animals, once on their trail stay on it, camp on it, until the scoundrels are run down, and there are men who will do it, men just as brave, determined and cunning as the outlaws themselves.
>
> . . . the public in general is misled in regard to the habits of these desperadoes. They think and talk of a Robbers Roost as if they had a permanent stopping place from which as occasion or

inclination moved them, they sallied forth to rob and kill. In the very nature of things a permanent abode is impossible. If such were the case they could be easily surrounded and captured by sieges if in no other way.

Desperadoes who are now in New Mexico this winter may be in the wilds of Montana next winter, paying this section a visit on their way, terrorizing the people, robbing camps and stealing horses en route. They are migratory criminals, here today, there tomorrow, changing their names when they change locality. The names of these men, so far as known, should be sent to the different sections, giving a minute description of each by the authorities of every state from British Columbia to Mexico, so that the work of extermination would continue until they could find no resting place. $1,000 reward for the capture of every known member of the band will put an end to them and restore peace and security to many a long-suffering and terrorized community.[5]

On March 14, 1898, three days after Hoy's letter was published, Colorado Governor Adams and Wyoming Governor Richards met in Salt Lake City with Utah Governor Heber Wells. Following the meeting the Lander (Wyoming) *Fremont Clipper* reported its outcome, heralding that "a concerted action by the three states concerned will be made to break up the infamous 'Robber's Roost' gang which has been terrorizing portions of the three states for the past two years. In all probabilities the work will be done by special officers, sworn in for that purpose, and who will have the powers of deputies in each state. . . ."

"Determined men in each state will be selected who have nerve and who have been officers in their respective states when it was something serious to serve as a conservator of the peace. They know the country and also know nearly all the outlaws."

The optimistic editorial ended with the expressed hope that the extermination of the outlaws would "wipe out a blot upon the fair names of our young western states."[6]

Even during the governors' conference the outlaws stepped up their activities. On the day of the conference the Hoy ranch was raided in retaliation for J. S. Hoy's letter to the press. Cattle and horses were run off and camps looted of supplies. Further north, nearly five hundred head of CY Ranch cattle and many of the outfit's best saddle horses were reported driven off the range.[7]

But, as second-rate "Montgomery Ward hard cases" swaggered in their ignorance, cooler heads in the outlaw camp could see the writing on the wall.

Following the sinking of the *Maine* three regiments of volunteer cavalry were approved by Congress, and Colonel J. Torrey of Wyoming's Embar Ranch was named commander of the Second Volunteer Cavalry, dubbed the "Torrey Rough Riders." For recruits he picked volunteers from among the finest horsemen throughout Utah, Colorado, Montana, Idaho, and Wyoming.[8] For George Cassidy the call for volunteers presented a double opportunity. By joining the cavalry he could both avoid capture and redeem himself in the eyes of the law.

The outlaws were gathered at Steamboat Springs, Colorado, when Cassidy proposed his idea to his associates. The situation was described in a Wyoming Writers Project manuscript by A.F.C. Greene:

> In the early days of the Spanish-American War there was a brief period when the excitement over Cuba was almost overshadowed in several cities of the Rocky Mountain region by tidings that the Wild Bunch was gathering for a great foray. The train robbers and stock rustlers of Wyoming, Montana, Utah and Colorado were rendezvoused near Steamboat Springs. Some reports said there were 50 outlaws in the camp. . . . It was a situation to worry the most lymphatic peace officers, and as for the express companies, there was not one of their cars went through not that did carry two or more heavily armed guards, in addition to the messenger. The governors of Wyoming, Utah and Colorado gathered in Salt Lake City to discuss measures for protection. . . .
>
> Governor Richards of Wyoming got word from Sheriff John Ward, who had come to Salt Lake with him, that the latter was leaving town on a confidential errand, whose nature he could not divulge. The next day, the sheriff returned and told the story of his trip to Wyoming's governor. Butch Cassidy had sent for him. He got the message from a man who met him on the street. Complying with directions which the intermediary gave him, he took the Rio Grande eastbound train in the after noon and went to Soldier's Summit, which was as lonely a station as you could find

in all the western passes—a water tank, a little depot and some
coal sheds on the crest of a wind-blown divide, where the snow
hangs for nine months in the year. Here he waited for the coming
of the night. At the appointed hour, the sheriff struck out along
the ridge, and when he had gone more than a mile through the
darkness, he reached the rendezvous, an open space among
gnarled old trees. Here was a log. He seated himself upon it, and
Butch Cassidy came to him out of the darkness. The two shook
hands. They talked of bygones, of the old Wyoming days; of men
who had died with their boots on since they last saw each other.
And then the outlaw came down to business. He spoke of the
conference of the governors, and talked about the militia and the
guards on the express cars. "You can tell the companies," he said,
"to take their gunmen off the trains. They ain't going to need
them. Nothing is going to come off, and you've got my word for
that." So the sheriff told Wyoming's governor, and shortly afterwards the conference adjourned *sine die.* The outlaws had gathered
near Steamboat Springs to see if there were some way they could
enlist in Torrey's Rough Riders, then being recruited to go to
Cuba. That project of going to fight the Spaniards came to nothing.[9]

John Ward did confer with Governor Richards during the Salt
Lake meeting, and although there is no documented record that
Cassidy approached Ward, the incident has been an often repeated
legend. The meeting also is similar to one detailed in "The Bandit
Invincible," except the sheriff mentioned was Orson Grimmett, and
the setting was the cabin of a widower named "Joe," just outside
Lander:

> He asked his friend Joe if he would do something for him and
> Joe said Yes, you know I would do any thing in the world for you
> and you know it.
> Yes I know you would   you have proven that many times and
> I trust you. I am asking you if you are willing to bring [illegible]
> Orson Grimmet up here   I would like to have a talk with him
> before I leave.
> Sure Butch I'll go but for the life of me I can't see why you
> should see him. Are you thinking of giving your self up?
> No Joe not by a damn sight and I don't think Orson would
> make a move to arrest me if we were alone and no one but you

knows I am here and I have heard that he would like to have a talk with me alone and if you will go and get him I will take a chance once. You needent tell him who wants him. Just say a sick friend wants to see him and he will come.

Grimmet was a saloon properitor also, and Joe did not have any trouble of finding him. Orson had no idea who was waiting for him and was so surprised he was speechless for the moment. Then he hurried across the room. Taking Butch in his arms like he was his own son. And all he could say for the moment was Butch and held him at arms length and looked his face over carefully.

Well, Well, Butch, my old Friend I might have known you wouldn't truste me. We three are here alone and no one will ever know that we have met so no Butch tell me what I can do for you.

Nothing, my Friend I just wanted to see you once more and explain a few things that I wanted you to know. I knew you were my friend and I was not takin chances in sending for you. After I leave here, I expect you to take up my trail but if you will give me a few hours start I know you won't over take me this time at least.

After they had talked for a while Orson asked him if he wouldn't like to see his old deputy, Jim Baldwin.

I would give a lot to see Jim if you think it would be all right to let so many know of your seeing me.

Oh yes Butch. Jim, you know him You couldn't pull a secret out of him with a ball team and would love to see you just as [illegible] as I was.

So he asked Joe to go to the Fremont Bar and hunt Jim up and Bring a bottle of the best liquor with you. In a short While Joe was back and Jim Baldwin. Baldwin also was so Verry much surprised. To see Butch waiting for him.

Well I'll be damed if it isn't Butch   where in the hell did you come from? We all thought you were in Mexico. He stood holding both of Butches hand and a trace of tears could be seen. After having a drink around Butch explained in full what he had done and what he hadent done and why he had done what he did.

I didn't want to kill the man who swore out that last warrent for me but I did want to let him know I wasn't afraid of him. [illegible] I wanted to hurt him so I went and stole 50 head of his best horses and drove them out in the hills and turned them loose for any one that wanted them. I didn't want them and I gave him something to swear out a Warrent for. And I'll always continue to worry him at every opportunity.

Well Butch I don't blame you and it would serve the Cuss right if he lost ever horse he had. I heard you had threatened to kill him because he had sat on the Jury that convicted you.

He is a dam liar Orson I have never threatened to kill any man yet. If I had I would have made good. What I did say was to Judge Brent before my pardin that I would square account with him some day if it was the last thing I ever did. And afterwards I told him I was sorry I had said it and for him to forget it. There is no use shooting a rat like that. The best way to hurt them is through their pocket book. They will Holler louder than if you cut off both legs. I steal their money just to hear them holler. Then I pass it out among those who realy need it.

Well Butch I am sorry you realy feel that way but I guess you are partly right at that.

It was two o'clock before Grimmet & Baldwin left.

Cassidy's concern over his notoriety—both the earned and undeserved—was not without just cause. On March 28, 1898, Colorado Governor Adams wrote Governor Richards he had hired a bounty hunter, one James W. Catron, to "go to the land of the rustlers and arrest Cassidy if possible. I am inclined to the belief that he will either get Cassidy or Cassidy will get him, with the chances in favor of him getting Cassidy."[10]

By April 11, however, Richards received a less smug report from Adams: "This venture I must record as a failure. He [Catron] talked so much that he was more apt to give up his scalp than to get the scalp of the other fellow."[11]

Although Adams' plan failed, Cassidy's situation was not getting more secure. The release of Punteney and O'Day in mid-April 1898 only added to the resentment sweeping the land. On May 7 the harried Governor Richards received an urgent letter from the president of the Buffalo (Wyoming) First National Bank:

As representatives of the only large financial institution in this country and consequently as custodian of the funds of almost our entire population, we desire to call your attention to the severe danger which threatens both us and them from the lawless element which infests what is familiarly known as the Hole-in-the-Wall country. For a long time we have felt that we were constantly menaced with a danger that it was beyond our power to guard against or control and which it is not within the power of the county officers to reach. The Belle Fourche robbery was a surprise to us only in that it happened there instead of in Buffalo. . . . The gang has been recently reinforced by the addition of several desperate and reckless men—among them Tom O'Day and Putney of Belle Fourche fame—as soon as the grass is strong enough for them to make long rides and keep their horses in condition—then will be serious trouble in this section and very probably in this town.

We have asked our sheriff, Mr. Sproal to call on you and talk the matter over and we trust that you will see your way plain to have the state take this matter up. In our opinion nothing but an organization similar to the Texas rangers, who could go into that country and make it their headquarters til they had driven out or captured these men, will reach the case. We desire also to impress upon you our conviction that it is imperative that action should be taken at once, as trouble may be expected at any time.[12]

With the intense heat in the field Cassidy discreetly removed himself from the scene. That fall he and Elzy Lay, using the aliases Jim Lowe and William McGinnis, showed up at the WS Ranch of William French, near Alma, New Mexico. Soon other new hands drifted onto the ranch; the Wild Bunch had found a new sanctuary. As Jim Lowe, Cassidy kept the boys in line, and rustling which previously had devastated the WS herds miraculously ceased. William French prospered as never before.[13]

From this New Mexico haven the Wild Bunch set out in 1899 to begin a new chapter, expanding their activities to become, as hack writers would fancifully dub them, "The Train Robbers Syndicate."

Chapter XIV

Wilcox

THE OVERLAND FLYER belched its way out of Rock Creek station, building up steam for the steep grade ahead. Over the next eight miles westward to Wilcox, sidetrack for the passing eastbound and westbound Union Pacific trains, the engine would labor its cargo to a 350-foot higher level. At Wilcox an unscheduled stop would upset the punctual timetable of Section No. 1 during the early morning hours of Friday, June 2, 1899. Dark shadows darted about in the eerie light as a red lantern flashed the dreaded signal: Distress on the rails ahead. Mail clerk Robert Lawson tells what next transpired that eventful night:

> As soon as we came to a standstill, Conductor Storey went forward to see what was the matter and saw several men with guns, one of whom shouted that they were going to blow up the train with dynamite. The conductor understood the situation at once and, before meeting the bandits, turned and started back to warn the second section. The robbers mounted the engine and at the point of their guns forced the engineer and fireman to dismount, after beating the engineer over the head with their guns, claiming that he didn't move fast enough, and marched them back over to our car.
>
> In a few moments we heard voices outside our car calling for Sherman, and looking out saw Engineer Jones and his fireman accompanied by three masked men with guns.
>
> They evidently thought Clerk Sherman was aboard and were calling him to come out with the crew. Burt Bruce, clerk in charge, refused to open the door, and ordered all lights extinguished. There was much loud talk and threats to blow up the car were made, but the doors were kept shut. In about 15 minutes two shots were fired into the car, one of the balls passing through the water tank and on through the stanchions.
>
> Following close upon the shooting came a terrific explosion, and one of the doors was completely wrecked and most of the car

windows broken. The bandits then threatened to blow up the whole car if we didn't get out, so Bruce gave the word and we jumped down, and were immediately lined up and searched for weapons. They said it would not do us no good to make trouble, that they didn't want the mail—that they wanted what was in the express car and was going to have it, and that they had powder enough to blow the whole train off the track.

After searching us they started us back and we saw up the track the headlight of the second section. They asked what was on the train, and somebody said there were two cars of soldiers on the train. This scared them and they hastened back to the engine, driving us ahead. They forced us on the engine, and as Dietrick moved too slowly they assisted him with a few kicks. While on the engine, Dietrick, in the act of closing the furnace door, brushed a mask off one of the men, endeavoring to catch a glimpse of his face. The man quickly grasped his mask and threatened to "plug" Dietrick.

They then ran the train ahead across a gully and stopped. There were two extra cars on the train, a tourist sleeper and a private car. They were uncoupled, and while this was being done, others of the gang went to the bridge, attempting to destroy it with their giant powder, or dynamite, which they placed on the timbers. After the explosion at the bridge they boarded the engine with the baggage, express, and mail cars, went on for about two miles, leaving the extra cars.

Upon arriving at the stopping place they proceeded to business again and went to the express car and ordered the messenger, E. C. Woodcock, to open. He refused, and the outlaws proceeded to batter down the doors and blew a big hole in the side of the car. The explosion was so terrific that the messenger was stunned and had to be taken from the car. They then proceeded to the other mail car, occupied by Clerks O'Brien and Skidmore and threatened to blow it up, but the boys were advised to come out, which they did. The robbers then went after the safes in the express car with dynamite and soon succeeded in getting into them, but not before the car was torn to pieces by the force of the charges. They took everything from the safes and what they didn't carry away they destroyed. After finishing their work they started out in a northerly direction on foot.

[They] found behind a snowfence, blankets and quilts, as well as two sacks of giant powder, each about 50 pounds in weight.

The men all wore long masks reaching below their necks and of the three I observed, one looked to be six foot tall, the others being about ordinary sized men. The leader appeared to be about 50 years old and spoke with a squeaky voice, pitched very high.

They appeared not to want to hurt anyone and were quite sociable and asked one of the boys for a chew of tobacco. Our train was delayed altogether about 2 hours.[1]

The "Bandit Invincible" account of the Wilcox robbery parallels that of mail clerk Lawson, including mention of Kid Curry striking the engineer "because of his slowness to obey their orders." Lawson's fifty-year-old "leader" with the squeaky voice, however, fits none of the gang except possibly the unidentified Harvey Ray of the Belle Fourche bank robbery. According to Cassidy, his accomplices, besides Kid Curry, included "Maxwell, Killpatrick and Conner."[2]

In describing the robbers' flight Cassidy's biography only lightly touches on a tragic complication to an otherwise flawless robbery execution:

They left relays of horses at sheep creek, on the little medicine River, next to Bates creek. They missed judged the speed of the possies and was faced with each other. and the battle was on. There was 20 men in the possie to 6 of the Bandits. Cassidy began by droping the horses of the possie after they had fired on them. Curry killed the sheriff. When the leader was killed the rest of the possie loaded the sheriff on a horse and was on their way to Douglas and the hold up was a success. The loot was $48,000. They went back to the big whole Canyon after a while to settle down to normal life.

The bandits' retreat northward was first discovered by authorities when a Mr. Hudspeth rode into Casper after being driven from his range at gunpoint by three men fitting the outlaws' descriptions. A quickly formed posse under Sheriffs Oscar Hiestand of Casper and Joe Hazen of Douglas picked up the robbers' trail at "the old oil well on Casper Creek about six miles from town." Heavy rains which fell immediately after the robbery aided the posse in their pursuit, because the tracks of the outlaws' horses were readily visible in the mud.

Near the old horse ranch fifteen miles from Casper on the Salt Creek road the posse drew fire from the retreating bandits. One

horse was wounded as "all dismounted and sought cover waiting for
an opportunity to return the fire of the outlaws but owing to the
latter using smokeless powder it was impossible to locate them.
Sheriff Hiestand was standing alongside his horse with the bridle
rein thrown over his arm adjusting his rifle when a rifle ball struck
right in front of the horse who jumped away, breaking the rein and
immediately disappeared over a hill."[3]

This robbery saw the introduction of a formidable new weapon on
the part of Western outlaws, smokeless powder firearms. Not only
were the bandits given a long-range advantage over the law officers'
inferior weapons, but the absence of a telltale puff of smoke with
each shot made the bandits' advantage even more lethal.

"The nerves of our people were at a high pitch," the Casper paper
reported, "when Tom McDonald rode into Casper early Tuesday
morning with the information that the big-hearted, brave Joe Hazen
had been shot through the stomach and seriously wounded it seemed
as though all lost heart."

"While searching for the rendezvous of the robbers it seems the
posse had dismounted and were walking up a draw following the
tracks of the outlaws' horses. Dr. Leeper and Joe Hazen were together and the doctor started in an opposite direction in search of the
trail and was called by Hazen who had remarked that he had again
struck the trail. Dr. Leeper started toward Hazen and was within
five foot of him when, without a moment's warning, the robbers
opened fire, hitting Hazen in the stomach, the ball entering near the
navel and coming out 2 inches from the spine. Hazen, with heroic
courage, told Dr. Leeper that he had been struck and the doctor
immediately gave him such medical treatment as was possible under
the circumstances. Having no shelter of any kind, he was compelled
to lay out in the weather for several hours until after scouring the
country a spring wagon was obtained and the wounded man was
brought to town. . . . Genuine sorrow was depicted on the faces of
our residents when it was learned that Hazen had been wounded."[4]

The mortally wounded sheriff died in Douglas hours after being
taken there by special train. In the field the robbers continued their
flight on foot, stopping at David Kidd's sheep camp and procuring a
meal from the herder, John DeVore. In a page from a B movie
script, the fugitives were next reported "to have swum the Powder

River which at the present time is a raging torrent which none but desperate men who feared their lives would think of attempting to ford."[5]

By June 15 newspaper accounts told of the use of bloodhounds, the state militia, and the offer of an $18,000 reward for the capture of fugitives now identified as George Currie and "the two Roberts boys." Veteran stock detective Joe LeFors was now tracking the robbers for the posse.

LeFors picked up the outlaws' trail near the Hole-in-the-Wall and tracked them for nearly two hundred miles steadily for five days with only short night rests in dry camps with little food. The trail led from the Hole-in-the-Wall to the north end of EK Mountain, on to the Billy Hill ranch in the foothills of the Big Horns, where the outlaws were mounted with superior saddle horses, then west over the Big Horns, dropping into the Big Horn Basin on the No Water drainage, then west to Kirby Creek, finally hitting the road to Thermopolis, where Lander law officer Arthur Sparhawk put the posse on a wild goose chase by persuading them to make directly for the Wind River Canyon through the Owl Creek range at the south end of the Basin, rather than continue following a two-hour-old trail. LeFors later hinted Sparhawk may have misled the posse on purpose.[6]

The robbers continued in a southeasterly direction, crossing the Owl Creek range by climbing a well-hidden trail up a side canyon on the west side of the steep Wind River Canyon, and dropping down into the Wind River Basin to the south by way of Mexican Pass, a saddle in the range.

Once across the Owl creeks the robbers made their way directly to the isolated Muddy Creek road ranch that Emery Burnaugh had only recently located on the Casper to Lander, and Dubois stage road. The Burnaughs later recalled the outlaws numbered at least five men, including Cassidy. While the exhausted fugitives secreted themselves in a natural cave in a sandstone outcrop behind the Burnaugh ranch buildings, Alice Burnaugh made sandwiches and had her two boys, Carl and Claude, deliver them in a lard pail to the men at the cave.

One unsolved mystery surrounding this visit of the Wild Bunch to the Burnaugh ranch involves a lonely grave on the gravel point immediately above the hidden cave. Bud, the youngest of the Burnaugh children, understood that one of the outlaws had been badly wounded and died at the ranch a short time after their arrival. The identity of the dead robber is argued to this day.[7]

Having buried their dead companion, the outlaws pulled out, going in different directions. Three of them continued westward to the Wind River, turning up its course toward Dubois and drawing a short, but futile chase from Fremont County officers. They stopped at Will Boyd's ranch at the mouth of Crow Creek on Wind River, then apparently doubled back over the Owl Creek range, for they were next seen in old Thermopolis where they feted the little community in a style reminiscent of the 1897 Baggs (Wyoming) celebration.[8]

The bandits were last seen at A. G. Rupp's post office and general store at Welling, just south of the present town of Manderson, and in a direct line with the Big Horn Canyon destination mentioned in Cassidy's manuscript.

After a short stay at the secluded cabin in Cook Stove Basin, the manuscript indicates Cassidy crossed the Big Horn River to the Pryor Mountains, and out Pryor Gap to Laurel, Montana, where he first purchased new clothes and a "fedora" before boarding a train for Seattle.

From Seattle Cassidy "went as a crewman on the Elinor," through the Straight of Juan de Fuca and down the west coast, finally making harbor at San Pedro, the seaport by Los Angeles, heavily used in sea trade at the turn of the century. "He was glad for the new ideas," he wrote, "and had gotten away from cow punching lingo and eaven his walk was different, and if he found him self in a tight pinch he could use this experiance to a good advantage."

After saving the lives of his shipmates in a tangle with "strongarm men" outside "a notorious dive known as Bentlys" Cassidy went to Los Angeles, after first buying clothes of "a color that he had never wore before. With hat to match . . . [to] give him the apearance of an ordinary travelor."

Finding quarters in a Los Angeles sailors' hotel, Cassidy hid out, spending "the great part of the time in his room and contented himself with reading." He was amused to read that in his absence two robberies, one in Montana and one in central Colorado, in as many days, had been attributed to his Wild Bunch. "One thing plain," he commented, "the gang would have little time free from pursuit with every crime committed being laid at their door."

After helping a destitute widow, the mother of "a ragged little newsboy who begged him to buy a paper," he prepared to leave Los Angeles for a rendezvous with his outlaw band in "Albuquerque," ending the chapter with one final note of self-indulgence:

That mother thanked him and the grateful, happy kids furnished Cassidy more happiness than he had known in years. It made him forget for a few moments that he was a hunted outlaw and nearly every hand was against him. Little did he care about the law. The only fear he had was that some time he might be forced to kill to protect his own life. Aside from this, his conscience never bothered him. Such was this man Cassidy, a cool, calculating and fearless outlaw, a man of steel when engaged in a holdup, but gentle as a lamb whenever an opportunity presented itself whereby he might be of help to someone in distress.

Chapter XV

Diamonds or Shackles

THE Pinkerton National Detective Agency, hired by the Union
Pacific to capture the Wilcox robbers, placed two of their best
operatives, Charles Siringo and W. O. Sayles, on the assignment.

At Fort Duchesne, two hundred miles east of Salt Lake City, the
two operatives picked up the trail of Harvey Logan and one other
outlaw, headed south. After a ride of five hundred miles Siringo and
Sayles arrived at Dandy Crossing on the Colorado River, one week
behind Logan and his companion.

From Dandy Crossing the detectives trailed one of the outlaws up
White's Canyon to the top of a mesa where tracks of a band of horses
obliterated the outlaw's trail. Staying in the area, the operatives
went first to Bluff City, Utah, and finally to Mancos, Colorado, before
loading their horses on a train for Durango. Unsigned bank notes
passed off by the robbers there confirmed they were on the right
trail.

Several false leads were followed from Durango before the outlaws'
trail again was found, leading down the Arkansas River into Kansas.
Tipping the robbers' hand were two horses they were trailing, a
large dapple gray and a cream colored animal.

Sayles was called to Montana where other Wilcox bills had begun
to turn up, and Siringo was joined by Arthur Sparhawk, the former
Fremont Country (Wyoming) law officer. The men followed the bandits east across Kansas into Indian Territory and on to Hot Springs,
Arkansas, where again a false lead sent them on a futile chase to
Nashville, Tennessee, where Sparhawk had a malaria attack and had
to drop out of the chase.

Returning to Hot Springs, Siringo again found the trail, which
led down the Arkansas to its mouth. At Helena the bandits took a
boat across the Mississippi. There followed a game of cat-and-mouse
back and forth across the river until the outlaws separated, one going

up the Arkansas, the other taking a tramp steamer down the Mississippi. At that point Siringo was ordered to abandon the chase and
proceed to Montana.[1]

While Siringo has written of the sacrifices, hardships, and persis-
tence necessary in the thankless task of tracking the outlaws, the
fugitives' perspective also has been recorded. The harried existence
of members of Cassidy's Wild Bunch is graphically portrayed in an
excerpt from the memoirs of Cassidy's Telluride accomplice, Matt
Warner:

> It was hell proper. It wasn't a case of just one outfit of deputies
> trailing us, but posses was out scouring the whole country, and
> we was running into fresh outfits every little while and had to
> suddenly change our direction, or dodge into a rock or timber
> hideout, or backtrack, or follow long strips of bare sandstone
> where we wouldn't leave tracks, or wade up or down streams long
> distances so they would lose our tracks. We had to put into
> practice all the tricks we had learned as cowboys and learn all the
> new tricks outlaws had to know to stay alive.
>
> A big part of the time we didn't dare to build fires at night or
> even in the daytime. So when we did feel safe to build a fire we
> would cook up baking-powder pones, bacon, and beans enough to
> last several days. Then we would eat this cold, soggy, stale stuff
> without coffee in cold or dark camps.
>
> In the daytime we would sweat, fry, or sizzle under the hot
> desert sun, or ride for whole days with our clothes soaking wet in
> rainy weather, or sleep in wet clothes on cold nights under one
> saddle blanket. It didn't make any difference if one of us got sick,
> or nearly died with rheumatism or toothache, or got a leg broke;
> he had to grit his teeth and trail right along anyway. If he died he
> died just like a horse or dog along the trail and didn't receive any
> more burial than they would, and his body would be eaten by the
> coyotes.
>
> On hot days when we pushed, lickety-split, in desperate,
> cross-country flights over mountain and desert with pursuing
> deputies in sight part of the time, we would sweat like butchers.
> The sweat would roll down our bellies and backs, and the hard,
> heavy money belts would gall a raw ring clear around our bodies,
> and the money got heavier and heavier and the sore rawer and
> rawer every mile we rode, till we thought we couldn't stand it any

longer. More than once one or the other of us let loose and acted like a crazy man, swore like a trooper, pawed at his belt, and threatened to tear the damned thing off and throw it away.

While we was frying, freezing, starving, and depriving ourselves of every comfort and pleasure of existence, here was all that stolen money in our belts that would buy anything we wanted, and we couldn't go anywhere or contact anybody to spend it. We just had to leave it there making raw rings around us, weighting us down and wearing us out, while we was nearly perishing for the things it could buy for us.

That's what an outlaw had to face. That's the other side of the adventure and romance of outlaw life.[2]

In Montana, Pinkerton operative Sayles discovered Lonie Logan had sold his saloon in Harlem after a stranger had visited him shortly before the Wilcox affair. He then reappeared following the holdup and reentered the saloon business. His cousin Bob Lee also was seen frequently in the area thereafter, and by the time Sayles arrived the two were operating the Club Saloon, Curry Brothers, Proprietors.[3]

The outlaws' friends tipped them off when Sayles arrived and both quickly left town, Lonie seeking haven at his Aunt Lee's house in Dodson, Missouri, and Bob Lee returning to Cripple Creek, Colorado, where he took up dealing cards in a local saloon.[4]

On February 28, 1900, only six days after Lonie had arrived, a posse of Kansas City detectives and Pinkerton operatives surrounded the Lee farmhouse at dawn. Lonie saw them coming and slipped out the kitchen door, revolver in hand. He ran for a patch of woods, but a withering crossfire from the approaching officers stopped him 150 yards from the house.

The detectives entered the farmhouse and caught Mrs. Lee frantically trying to burn banknotes and correspondence from her son Bob. Seeing the Cripple Creek postmark on one signed envelope, detectives headed for the nearest Western Union office, and in about as much time as it took to send a telegram, Bob Lee was in custody in Colorado.[5] He was transported to Cheyenne, Wyoming, and arraigned before district court on mail robbery charges.

On April 17, 1900, Sheriff Preece of Vernal, Utah, while searching for a local rustler named Tom Dilly, caught sight of a man in camp on the opposite bank of the Green River. Preece thought he had found his man, and had his posse open fire. Returning their fire, the lone man took to a rocky slope, shielding himself behind a boulder. After a long period of silence from the outlaw's side of the river members of the posse circled behind the man and found him dead, shot through the head. It was thought that sheriff Tyler from Green River, Utah, had fired the fatal shot.

After discovering the man Tyler had killed was not Dilly the posse began to speculate as to the identity of their dead outlaw. Someone suggested he might have been one of the Union Pacific train robbers. Wyoming authorities were notified.

Sheriff John Ward and John DeVore, the herder who had fed the fugitives at the Kidd sheep camp during their flight after the Wilcox robbery, were sent for and they identified the dead outlaw as Flatnose George Currie. The dead man's father, John Currie, from Chadron, Nebraska, came to Thompson, Utah, and claimed the body, taking it back to Chadron for burial.[6]

As the excitement over George Currie's death abated, interest in the Wilcox robbery revived with the opening of Bob Lee's trial in Cheyenne, on May 25, 1900. Witnesses were called, several from Montana, to testify as to stolen bills found in his possession. More witnesses testified as to his presence in Montana and in Colorado following the robbery. No evidence actually linked him to the Wilcox robbery, although it was well established he had handled some of the stolen money, had used several aliases, and was connected with the Curry brothers. On May 28 the attorneys rested their cases. The next day the jury's decision was heralded in banner headlines:

LEE GUILTY![7]

Once convicted Robert E. Lee began a ten-year sentence at the Wyoming State Penitentiary in Rawlins, on May 31, 1900. He was thirty-five.[8]

In relating Butch Cassidy's activities following his trip from Seattle to Los Angeles on the *Elinor,* the Phillips manuscript mentions Lee's arrest:

Cassidy stayed in Los Angeles about four weeks allowing himself but a few days in which to meet the gang in Albuquerque. When he decided to leave, he called the city ticket office and made reservations for Mr. Jones to Albuquerque and engaged a compartment. The train left Los Angeles early in the evening, which would leave him undisturbed until morning. He made arangements with the porter to make up his birth early and slipped a dollar in his hand and told him he did not want to be disterbed the rest of the day. About 8 o'clock in the evening, he rang for the porter who made up his bed and he was left alone from then on until he arrived in Albuquerque.

Two days after, Maxwell arrived and the third day Kid Curry arrived into town. By mere accident they had all found different places to room. A meeting was aranged and they soon got together to discuss further plans of operation. It was learned that a short time pryer to their arrival, a Rio Grand train had been held up and the robery had been charged to them. so it was unsafe to remain longer than necessary. One of the men connected with the Union Pacific hold up had been picked up and was awaiting trial at that time. While he was considered staunch, some little slip might reveal their meeting place. After waiting several days for Conner, they decided to move on South to San Antonio where they would feel safer for the Winter.

The Rio Grand train robbery probably was that on July 11, 1899 of the Colorado and Southern near Folsom, New Mexico. Many did believe the Wild Bunch was involved; Elzy Lay had been identified as one of the robbers.

Lay, in the company of Black Jack Ketchum's brother Sam and a man known only as "G. W. Franks," was trailed to isolated Turkey Creek Canyon near Cimarron in northern New Mexico. The posse closed in and a grim battle ensued.

Elzy Lay was shot twice through the body in the initial volley from the surrounding posse as he was on his way to the creek with a canteen early in the morning of July 16. Sam Ketchum's left arm was shattered by another shot. From then on, the desperate Franks held off the entire posse.

Sheriff Ed Farr of Huerfano County was killed, and there is some evidence that Lay regained consciousness long enough to fire the shot which felled the officer. Henry Love, a member of the posse, later died of leg wounds he received in the bloody shootout.

With the death of Farr the battle diminished into a waiting game until nightfall. Lay, by then conscious, was helped to his feet by

Franks, and between the two of them they managed to boost Ketchum onto his horse and made their way out of the canyon.

Ketchum's shattered arm and loss of blood made riding too difficult, and Lay and Franks found refuge for him in a cabin not far from the battle scene before continuing their flight south. Four days after the fight Ketchum was captured and identified, but he soon died of blood poisoning.[9]

Elzy Lay and Franks successfully eluded posses until Lay was captured on August 16, 1899 at the V. H. Lusk ranch in Eddy County, New Mexico.[10]

After a lengthy trial in Raton, New Mexico, Elzy Lay, alias William McGinnis, rancher William French's "paladin amongst cow punchers," was sentenced on October 10, 1900 to life imprisonment at the New Mexico Penitentiary at Santa Fe. Events had taken an ill-boding turn for those who rode the outlaw trail.

Even as the law was closing in on Lonie Curry, Bob Lee, George Currie, and Elzy Lay, Pinkerton detectives were making yet another advance toward rectifying the Union Pacific's embarrassment over the Wilcox robbery. Working on information that bills with telltale burned corners were turning up in southwestern New Mexico, operative Frank Murray went to Alma. There he attempted to trace the bills to their origin.

Murray entered a saloon where Cassidy, as Jim Lowe, was tending bar. As the unsuspecting operative asked questions about the gang's whereabouts he was treated to a drink by the very man he was attempting to locate. Tipped off as to his precarious situation, Murray quickly departed the area, mentioning something about needing a cavalry regiment to carry out the order which had sent him there.[11]

Although the Cassidy memoirs do not mention the outlaws' retreat at the WS ranch, the narrative does place Cassidy in New Mexico at the same time. From there, the manuscript relates Cassidy's next move:

> They scattered going different ways to eventually meet in San Antonio a week later. There, they were fortunate to find suitable places to stop where there was little chance of being recognized and decided to spend the Winter there.

The actions of Maxwell and Curry were largely dictated by

Cassidy. At first they [illegible] Maxwell was a profesinal poker player. and Curry liked the society of women, and the dance hall life. But Cassidy was different. He insisted they lead the quiet life or go their own way without him. Having confidence in Cassidy's ability and realizing the importance of his judgement they finally agreed to his plan and thus spent a quiet Winter.

In contrast to the Phillips manuscript, Pinkerton operatives placed Cassidy and his gang in their "suitable place to stop" in San Antonio during 1900, a year later, when the outlaws made their headquarters at Fanny Porter's "sporting house" in the Hell's Half Acre district, a common refuge for men on the lam. Fanny Porter, a twenty-seven-year-old native of England, ran her bordello in a rented building at 505 South San Saba. Detectives interrogated Fanny's five female "boarders," ranging in age from nineteen to twenty-four. They described Cassidy as a handsome gentleman who performed acrobatic feats on a bicycle for their entertainment. Longabaugh and Logan were not given as flattering a buildup.[12]

While discussing the meeting in San Antonio during the winter of 1899–1900, the "Bandit Invincible" manuscript also mentions Harry Longabaugh's sweetheart Etta Place, giving her the name "Betty Price:"

Maxwell had a sweet heart who always seemed to know of his whereabouts and would occationally pay him a visit, but never for any length of time. She was a smart woman and beautiful to look at. What her early history was no one knew, she apparently loved Maxwell dearly, but was not the mushy type.

Maxwell was sure much in love with Betty Price and was extreamaly jealous in his respect for her. Unfortunate was any man who intentionally, or otherwise passed any disperoging remark about Betty in his presence. At one time he knocked a man cold for simply remarking that he'd give half his interest in heaven for that woman. . . .

Betty was a true match for Dick Maxwell. She at all times looked and carried herself like a lady attending to her own business and showed no interest in any one but Maxwell. When they first met I do not know, neither did I know whether they were married or not. Of one thing I am certain, they were truly devoted all through the years I knew them in the United States and South America.

Here, for the first time, "William T. Phillips" slips into the first person narrative, indicating his own involvement in the plot of his story and in the lives of the people described.

His praise reveals a deep respect for "Betty Price," whom the Pinkerton Detective Agency—naming her variously Eva, Emma, and Etta—had thought was either a school teacher from Denver or a prostitute from Texas. None of Fanny Porter's "boarders" had a name even remotely similar, and although Denver directories list a Gertrude E. Place, music teacher, who disappears from the record after 1900, no connection to the Wild Bunch has ever been established. Too, like "Betty Price," the name Etta Place could have been an alias. A detailed search of United States Census records, state by state, has failed as yet to produce any solid leads.[13]

Chapter XVI

Tipton and Winnemucca

By 1900 Butch Cassidy was thirty-four. He had been an outlaw for eleven years, nearly two of which were spent behind bars. For the past four years he had been intensely hunted by peace officers throughout the West as, one by one, the refuges for the gang were penetrated. Settlement of the frontier, with accompanying railroad networks and advancements in the telephone and telegraph, all but cut off the former routes of escape. The American frontier in which the horseback outlaw had so effectively thrived was fast becoming a page from a bygone century.

The reversals the gang had experienced by early 1900 drove George Cassidy to one last desperate attempt to reverse the tide which threatened to sweep him towards inevitable destruction.

In Salt Lake City, Cassidy approached Judge O. W. Powers, one of the most widely known criminal lawyers in the West. In a private meeting in Powers' office the harried outlaw requested that the Judge approach Utah Governor Heber Wells with a request of amnesty in exchange for a promise to go straight.[1] Although the Judge's initial reaction was negative he was impressed with the earnestness of the man's pleas. Finally deciding that the idea of amnesty had merit, Powers arranged for a hearing with Governor Wells.

The Utah Governor also was taken with the outlaw's straightforwardness, but told Cassidy there was no legal precedent for such a move. He could not pardon Cassidy for crimes committed in another state, especially crimes for which the outlaw had not yet been tried.

The Governor then suggested an alternative. If Cassidy would request the Union Pacific to drop charges in exchange for a promise that depredations would cease, Wells would use his influence in helping the outlaw get a fresh start. It was further agreed that Cassidy would volunteer his services as a railway express guard, believing the railroad would see the advantage of having the notorious Butch Cassidy guarding the through safe.

Working through lawyer Douglas Preston and aided by Governor Wells' influence, Cassidy arranged to meet with Union Pacific representatives to negotiate a truce. To avoid any chance of doublecross he asked that Preston bring the officials to the Lost Soldier stage station at the base of Green Mountain in Wyoming.

The railroad contingent was delayed en route, and when the hour of the rendezvous had come and passed without Preston and the Union Pacific representatives showing up, Cassidy gave up in despair, leaving a blistering note of accusation: "Damn you, Preston, you double-crossed me. I waited all day but you didn't show up. Tell the U. P. to go to hell. And you can go with them."[2]

Quite naturally Butch Cassidy's next strike was on the Union Pacific. The August 29, 1900 train robbery at Tipton, Wyoming, is described in detail in the "Bandit Invincible" manuscript:

"Say fellows, I understand the Union Pacific is looking for more trouble," remarked Butch. "What do you say if we give them a little exercise? They tell me they have a bunch all lined up and ready for an emergency."

"All trains stop at the top of the hill west of Rawlins at a coaling station called Tipton. It is an out of the way place & we could make an easy get away to the South into Elk Basin & across into the Green River country in Utah. What do you think of it?"

"You've been over the road. If you think it can be pulled, it's fine with me," answered Curry.

"What say you fellows?" addressing Maxwell & Woodward.

"We're in for anything," they replied. "Anything for action."

"And besides," added Maxwell, "I'd like to see how fast those bench warmers can ride."

"Okay, we're off in the morning. We can pick up fresh horses along the sweet water. I want to see Dusty Jim if I can & try & head the Hawleys away from Lander. If them geezers ride into town they'll sure find it Plenty uncomfortable, for there laying for them all over."

The following morning the bandits broke camp at daybreak for their 3 hundred mile ride. All were jolly & anxious for the time they would again try theyr skill at dodging men hunters.

Butch did not see Dusty Jim on the way but he left a note with a friend of Dusty's who, he was sure would deliver the message.

Several changes of horses were made before they reached the sweet water. But they continued to lead their saddle horses, reserving them for the second relay, as they were more realiable than strange horses would be.

Arriving at the sweet water, Butch selected as fine a string of horses as he could find, in the herd of his would-be persecuter, and these they tailed to the horses they were riding, thus making a string of three horses each. That they would have a tough ride after the holdup, there was no doubt, so it was planed to use two relays, this would allow them to make a hundred miles easely in the first 12 hours of the get away.

After working their way South across the dessert to the railroad, they continued south to a low range of hills, about 15 or 18 miles distant. Here they left one string of horses in a small patch of the meadow, and proceeded southwest for another twenty miles, where they made camp on a small stream, well up in the hills. After stoping at this place over nite they carefully staked theyr last string of horses where they could easely reach water & returned to their first relay. There they found all as they had left it. and the horses were quite rested up, from the trip across the Red desert and in good condition for the return trip to the road. Remaining at this place for the night, they went over all theyr plans carefully and were fully prepared for the next nights work.

Leaving the hangout about 5 o'clock in the afternoon, they made their way slowly toward the railroad. there was no hurry they had plenty of time to make Tipton before train time, which was about two thirty in the morning, and besides, they wanted to keep their horses as fresh as possible, for the hard ride on the return trip.

They arrived at Tipton about one thirty and after Carefully scouting around, finally located a place where they could get water for their horses, by packing it in a bucket which they discovered near the coal chute. Then, they sent young Woodward to a point about a mile west of the station, where he was instructed to build a small sage brush fire which was to be a signal for the location of the horses. after staking the horses to some bunches of greasewood, Woodward got together some greasewood and sage brush and then settled down to await the time when the train would arrive.

The tactics to be used in this holdup were the same as used at Wilcox; which were to cut the express car from the main train, and run the engin and express car up the track for a mile or so, before attempting to forse the car door, which was sure to be locked.

The train arrived on time, and no sooner had it come to a stop, than Cassidy climbed into one side of the engin cab, & Curry the other. Curry, Pointing a gun at the side of the fire man, ordered him out of the cab and forsed him to uncouple the express car. after this was done, Maxwell clung to the rear of the car, While Curry returned to the engin. As soon as Curry was in the Cab, Butch ordered the engineer to Pull ahead, and seeing that it was suicide to resist, he immediately Put the engin in motion, and in about two minutes time, they were opposite the small fire which Woodward had built as a signal, and the train was brought to a stop. Uncoupling the engin from the car, Butch again ordered the engineer to Pull ahead a mile or so, and wait there until they had finished the job. this the engineer was glad enough to do, and soon they were alone with the car, & ready for the final job of forsing the express messenger from the car.

Dynamite, which they had brough with them from the canyon, was all prepared, and it was only a minute or so, till a charge of two sticks of dynamite was exploded against the door, but failed to bring out the agent. Butch shouted to the agent to come out, but there being no response he quickly prepared another stick of powder which he threw into one end of the car, where it exploded, but did not bring the agent out. Throwing a nother stick to the other end of the car, brought his man out. as he jumped to the ground, Butch searched him, and relieved him of his double action pistol, and turned him over to Maxwell for safe keeping while he and Curry entered the car to blow the safe. It took several shots before it finally yielded, but they soon had all the contents which were of any value to them, safely tucked away in their saddle bags, and were on their way.

Denver's *Rocky Mountain News,* under the headline, "Looks Like Work of Butch Cassidy Gang," corroborates the Phillips manuscript with quotes from Conductor Ed J. Kerrigan: "We had just passed Tipton and reached the 771-mile post from Omaha when I felt the train stopping. I knew something was wrong and went up ahead to see what it was. There was a small fire by the track, and I saw some men going down toward the baggage car. As soon as I reached the engine a man covered me with a Winchester. . . . When he saw I was the conductor, he . . . told me to uncouple the mail, express and baggage cars, so they could run them down the track. I started to do this, but the train was on a steep grade, and the passenger cars started to move down by themselves. They let me set the brakes on the coaches to hold them, and they ran the front part of the train down the track about half a mile. After they stopped they ordered Woodcock, the baggage and expressman, to unlock his car and come out. This he refused to do for a minute. Then, when I saw they were going to blow up the car I told him to come out, and he did so."[3]

For Earnest Woodcock this was the second experience with Cassidy's Wild Bunch. At Wilcox the previous year he also forced the gang to resort to dynamite to dislodge him from his duty post. Conductor Kerrigan said the bandits did not rob the passengers, although they fired shots past the coaches to scare them. A deaf old gentleman stuck his head out a window and was nearly shot before Kerrigan could make him understand a holdup was in progress.

The newspapers also gave descriptions of the robbers:

> There is little or no doubt but that the men who held up No. 3 last night are the same famous Wilcox bandits who successfully held up and robbed a train about a year ago and made good their escape by the murder of Sheriff Hazen. . . . The two gangs are almost identical.
> The leader in each case answers the same description, light hair, gray eyes, light complexion, five feet ten inches in height.[4]

Another report of the robbery said the bandit leader, "talks very fast," also adding to the conclusion that Butch Cassidy directed the robbery.[5] These contemporary accounts, in contrast to books written on the subject, confirm William T. Phillips' assertion that Butch Cassidy took part in both the Wilcox and Tipton holdups.

In a later report, full descriptions of the other robbers also were given: ". . . second man five feet seven inches, sandy complexion, talks very coarse, had on a canvas coat, corduroy pants and badly worn shoes. This is the fellow who first boarded the train at Tipton. Third man, five feet nine inches tall, dark complexion, wore dark flannel shirt, no coat. No description is given of the fourth man."[6]

Following his accurate portrayal of the Tipton holdup, Phillips
detailed the bandits' getaway:

> The following nite found the bandits well over a hundred miles
> from the scene of the robery. They made their way almost directly
> west to a Point South of Lehi City, where they decided to rest for a
> day or too before continuing west across the great Salt lake desert.
> and continued their way into Nevada in the Diamond Mountain
> region. As far as the posses were Concerned they were completely
> lost.
>
> The Hole in the Wall was closely Watched as usual also all the
> localities to the South but no attention was given to the west.
> They were almost entirely unknown in the Nevada State, except
> for hearsay.
>
> Butch had some verry close friends who had a small ranch in
> the foot hills ten miles from a place call Huntingon and after they
> had ben in camp for four days he decided to Ride out and see some
> old friends of his where he hoped to gain some information of
> what was going on in the out side world. he was familiar with
> that country and had no trouble in locating Hammits ranch 15
> miles from where they were captured [?]
>
> Hammit was surprised and glad to see him and told him all the
> rumers he had heard and showed him some recent papers he had
> brought from Huntington the day before. There was the usual
> rumer about the amount of money taken and the manner in which
> the job was done and the asurance that the possies was hot on their
> trail and their capture was expected soon. There was much talk
> weather much or any money was taken. The fact was they got
> $45,000 which was burried as it was too dangerous to try to
> dispose of it at that time.

Although the railroad widely publicized a mere $54 cash loss, in
contrast to Cassidy's figure of $45,000, Joe LeFors mentioned find-
ing money wrappers at one of the robbers' camps during his pursuit.[7] Earnest Woodcock has been quoted as saying the loss was in
the vicinity of $55,000.[8]

The manuscript continues, introducing the gang's plan to hit the
bank at Winnemucca, Nevada:

> Butch was quite happy that they had so complitly out witted
> the possies. Hammit supplied Butch with a grub stake and Butch

gave him $2,000 and headed for the bandit camp in the hills. It was at this camp where the Winnemucca hold up was planed.

In that part of the country they was not much known and every body was hunting for them in other parts of the world. Butch thought it an excellent time to surprise them by pulling another robbery in a country where they was least expected and the get away would be easy. They decided to make one more raid before fall and decided Winnemucca was the best prospect.

They moved over in the Sanoma Range twelve miles from Galconda and made camp. food and horses colected.

Vic Button was a boy of ten when the robbers camped near his father's ranch in the area described. "I remember them well. It was roundup time and these three men made their camp near a haystack about four miles down the river from the ranch.

"Each day I would ride down and visit with them. The reason I would go was because they had this white horse. I'd never seen such a horse.

"Butch would ride the white horse, and I would ride against him with the horse I had brought, but could never win. Butch told me, 'You like that horse? Someday he will be yours.'"

Button remembered Cassidy as a likeable man with a broad grin. "In fact, all three bandits were good natured. I didn't know they were casing the bank in Winnemucca, and I was very helpful. They would ask me all kinds of questions about Soldier's Pass, a shortcut to Clover Valley."[9]

The "Bandit Invincible" gives the outlaw's narrative of the September 19, 1900 holdup of the Winnemucca bank:

After a rest for a few days the bandits began their arangements in earnest. Circleing around to the north of Winnemucca they arange a relay of horses at the usual distance of 15 miles from town and got enough food together for a couple of days in case they were held up some where. They rested there horses for one day so if they had to run for their lives the horses would be in good shape. They set out the next fore noon all dress very ordanary and no suspicion was aroused along the way.

After entering the town they rode right to the bank. then Butch Curry Maxwell after leaving their horses a short distance away with Woodward to guard them entered the bank and Butch pushing a slip of paper. at that Instant they ordered everyone to put up his hands and Butch Went behind the counter picked up their guns and all the change and currency from the vault and also Safe while Curry and Maxwell stood guard. Butch ordered all behind the counter to lye face down on the floor then sent Maxwell out to see if the horses were in readiness for a quick get away. Butch & Curry followed and were soon in their saddles & were soon on their way at full speed through the town.

The Hold up being so thorough and quiet they were well out of town and heading for the hills before any one was aware of the hold up. Wires of the hold up were Wired all over the Country but the boys were fifty miles away in the cotton wood range of hills by night fall. They pulled their saddles from their horses & had something to eat and divided the money between the 4 of them which was $32,000.00. after a short rest for men & horses they road all night. Morning found them across the Oregon line by little Owyhee river. Then decided to go their own seperate ways. Maxwell went West to Yreka, Calif., Curry, Woodward went south and Butch went east. Their arangement to get in touch With each other was simple. They would address a letter to Frank Beal who acted as an information Bureau and formed the connection link. They were well hunted after the Winnemucca robery. Sherif and possies hunted far and near.

Contemporary Reno *Evening Gazette* accounts of the robbery and resulting chase were in complete agreement with the Cassidy narrative.[10] Vic Button added a personal note: "After the holdup, the posse caught up with them in Clover Valley. Butch, the Kid and Carver were changing their packs to fresh horses when the posse rode up. That's when Cassidy shouted, 'Give the white horse to the kid at the CS ranch,' and they left the horse behind when they rode off. I can only say that for Butch to remember his promise to a kid when the posse was hot on his trail, he couldn't have been all bad."[11]

Chapter XVII

Exit at Exeter

AFTER PARTING with the other Winnemucca bandits, according to the Phillips manuscript, Cassidy made his way eastward into the Idaho Falls country, where he happened upon a stagecoach with a broken wheel. "To his surprise," one of the passengers was Bishop Ethelbert Talbot:

> Well, well, remarked the Biship, You of all people are the last one I ever expected to see   I never thought you would turn out to be a bandit   Something must of happened to you to make you do so. You had such a wonderful character. tell me about yourself.
>
> Well Bishop in one way it is a long story and in another it is verry short but I will tell you first hand and he told his story of how he had been driven to his life   so far I am not a common thief as I hate one. The man who swore out the Warrents for my arrest both times I was framed by him and he is lower than a snakes belly and I am just getting eaven for the money I take belongs to him and men just like him and any body who stood in their way would get just what I got.

The man Cassidy again blames for his life of crime is the rancher "Ainsley" of the Beaver Rim country of the upper Sweetwater Valley. The rancher who twice swore out warrants against Cassidy, leading to his imprisonment, however, was Otto Franc of the Big Horn Basin, acting in Richard Ashworth's behalf. In 1903 Franc was found beside a range fence shot to death. Whether it was accidental, suicide, or murder was never completely resolved. When Phillips wrote his manuscript in 1934 he could have been aware of Franc's demise, and possibly created a fictional "Ainsley" to avoid any implication of his bandit invincible in the death of Otto Franc.

The discussion with the bishop continues:

> I don't hate any one but for it is a terrible sin but there are a lot of people I do not like and he & his kind are the ones. I don't

mind being chase. I got so I like it. Just think of the thousands of people who are looking for me all the time. It is good sport to out wit them. No, Bishop, I would rather go right into the banks and get it at the point of a gun than to get it the Way they do   many people have been left homeless by their doings. I have often given some of the Victoms back their part if the Bank expected their pound of flesh. I know how you feel Bishop, That a man should obey the law, but in my mind there is but one law. That is the law of the All mighty God and God did not order that familys should be turned out of their homes and go hungry so their bank roll should grow fatter. An animal will leave a carcus after he gets his belly full, but you never see a banker do that sort of thing no matter what misery and eaven to death. A banker or a loan shark they all look alike to me.

Then you believe all bankers are alike?

I know only three. There may be more but I have never heard of them yet.

Would you think it right to kill a man for his money?

No I wouldn't take a mans life for a million dollars. in other words if he was lying on a million $ and I had to take his life to get it I would go with out no matter what or who he was.

There have been several men killed in these hold up affairs. how do you reconcile your self to that?

Well if these people are fool enough to chase me to get the reward that is on my head and to get the other fellows money back I figured that is their business and it is his life or mine. I have never taken a mans life yet and never hope to be compelled to do so.

Well I can't say I am wholly in sympathy of your way of thinking and things I know that many people have suffered by the greedyness of bankers and money linders, but can't feel that they are all alike.

I don't expect you to agree with me Bishop, but I think your almighty God furnished sufficient food on this old earth of ours to feed every human alike and according to my faith he has extended no special privilages to any man or body of men where by they should be allowed to keep it from the ones he intinded it for.

You seem to be inclined to socialism.

No, only to the extent of a Guarantee of shelter, food, clothing for those who are unfortunate enough in losing all they have thrugh no fault of their own. I never feared no man and I would

not take a life but they have delibertly lied and delibertly pushed
me in this situation.

I [illegible] live life like the good honest straight forward way
and have tried to be that way but some certaine people are such
busy bodys that haft to make some one the goat for their doings
and it had to be me   They won't let me go straight   I served my
time when they framed me the 1st time. and the man who swore
out the second warrent was a liar and a thief. and he and his
friends wanted to pin some more rot on me [illegible] so they had
the Judge release me before my full time was up. so they could get
me more securally the second time. so now let come what will
they won't catch me if I can help it.

Well Butch I see my man has the old wagon about [illegible]
ready to go so I will bid you goodby and trust you will see things
differently before it is too late. And I earnestly hope we will meet
again. Goodby Butch and good luck.

After bidding goodbye to the bishop Cassidy continued his journey into Wyoming, eventually making his way to his hideout on
Green Mountain—a cabin in a mixed stand of aspen and lodgepole
pines overlooking the terraces of beaver ponds stairstepping down
the Willow Creek Valley above Jesse Johnson's ranch.[1]

In February Butch rode into Lander to see his sweetheart, stopping by at the O'Neal ranch on the Little Popo Agie, and at the
home of his widower friend "Joe," where he learned that his
sweetheart and family had moved to California in the early fall:

He then hastened to another friend in Lander being sure that this
friend would know the address of his sweetheart.

This friend, the wife of a high government official, felt greatly
obliged to him for saving the life of her only son at a great risk of his
own life, so he felt safe in calling on her. He soon obtained the
correct address of his sweetheart. Then he returned to the home of
the bachelor friend.

Cassidy again places his lover in the Lander area. The one girl in
the vicinity who fits his description was Mary Boyd, by then the
wife of Ol Rhodes.[2] Friends and relatives of Mary indicated she and
Cassidy did continue their relationship, meeting in secret, even after
she had married. The family did not move to California. However,
Mary took an extended trip to Missouri to visit her father's relatives

at about the time discussed in the manuscript. Mary's aunt, married to Sheriff Orson Grimmett, may have been the "wife of a high government official" mentioned.

There also are striking similarities between this account and Ardythe Kennelly's novel, *Good Morning, Young Lady*. Cassidy visited "Dorney Leaf" in Salt Lake City during early 1901. The heroine's family was in the process of selling their home and moving to California. "Dorney" was well acquainted with Judge Powers, the official through whom Cassidy appealed to Governor Wells for amnesty.[3]

At this point Cassidy discussed his long visit with Sheriff Orson Grimmett and his deputy Jim Baldwin, detailed earlier in Chapter XIII. On his return trip he ran into a blizzard:

> He arrived at Lone bear's camp near the mouth of muskrat creek and after getting some jerked Venison from the indian he continued up the muskrat.[4] The Wind was blowing and it was snowing but Butch kept going till he could reach the tall sage where there would be more shelter before making camp that night. As he came to a sharp curve around the ledge of cut bank in the creek bottom, he discovered a lone rider fifty yards ahead of him.
>
> As he came nearer the fellow began to talk but butch could not [illegible] him and understand a word he said and he was shaking like a leaf. Finally, the man made him under stand he was lost and allmost frozen as it was bitering cold. Butch told the man to follow him and he would try to help him out. They hurried along to the tall sage. They soon reached the one of Butches former camp. When they swang from their horses the stranger man slumped and feel to the ground Butch pulled him behind a bank out of the wind and made a sage fire. The stranger was a boy of eighteen or nineteen. After getting his old coffe can from its hiding place and with snow had a pot of hot coffe some Venison and Bread. The boy was two weake to hold the can of coffe. Butch held the can so the boy could sip the warm coffe and it was not long till the boy began to get warm and gain his strength back. The bluff was about eight feet high and Butch kept a good hot fire so it was not to uncomfortable.
>
> Butch asked the boy where he was headed for. The lad said he was over at Hailey last night stopped on my way to the sub

agency. my name is Ainsley   I am a nephew of John Ainsley over on the sweet water. Left Hailey this morning but the Blizzard had ben so bad I guess I must have gotten turned around for I have ben riding all day. It has never taken me this long to ride to Wind river before.

I guess you are lost all right. do you have any Idea where you are?

No.

You are away over on the [illegible] fork of the muskrat creek twenty five miles out of your Way, and if I dont miss my guess, you are a dam lucky guy that I happened along just when I did as there isnt a camp with in 20 miles of either way from here.

The next morning Cassidy and the boy backtracked to a sheep trail and located the sheep wagon. When they reached the camp the sheepman "refused them food for horse and man." Incensed, Cassidy proceeded to help himself to provisions and feed for the horses. In turn, the unwilling host, a man named McDougall,[5] pulled a rifle on Cassidy and the boy:

So that's your game is it? asked Butch. Well old timer you had better learn how to use a small gun That one might back up and hurt you.

Watching the fellow to see that he did not get the drop on him he walked up and demanded the fellow to hand over the gun. The fellow stepped back raised the gun but to his surprise seen Butch had the draw on him [illegible] hip and right straight for his belly. Butch ordered him in no mild tone of Voice to throw the gun out side the tent.

Have you any more guns?

No.

Well then build a fire. I am getting something to eat and dam quick. And don't make any more passes or something will happen to you dam quick.

When the boy returned from watering the horses Butch told him to untie a bundle of hay for the horses and also give them a good helping of oats. The horses tended to, the boy came in the tent. Butch told him to sit on the bed and rest and thaw out while he got some food ready. The tent was warm from the little camp stove as Butch prepared for their supper the fellow became more surley but Butch paid verry little atention to him. After frying some bacon to get the fat he fried several thick mutton chops, warmed over some cold biscuits and potatoes made coffe and opened a can of peaches for desert. The owner of the out fit lay on one of the beds while Butch and the boy ate their meals. Butch had put a pan full of snow on the stove for dish water and the boy washed the dishes while butch lay on the bed to rest. Butch asked the owner what his name was.

My names Mcdougal. I'll have the law on you for this, he returned.

Oh Thats the way you [illegible] feel about it. Your damed luckey to get off this easy. It would sirve you right if I took every dam thing you have. Where in the hell are you from   You havent been in this country long or you would know that no man here would turn another out in the cold with out any thing to eat you dam fool. Any one would be insulted if you offered pay for food. Maby I insulted you if so I apologize right now.

The owner continued silence and surleyness. Butch decided they would stay all night. He fed the horses more hay and loosened their sinches so they could realy eat their fill and left the saddles & Blankets on them for warmth as he knew the horses would not lye down.

The hearder proved to be a pleasing tipe of a fellow on his return to camp and was glad to talk with Butch. The hearder prepared his own supper thinking the owner had eaten. The owner then prepared his own supper and still was silint. When it came bed time Butch ordered the boy to get in bed with the hearder, and butch said he would sleep with Mcdougal. Soon all were asleep and their troubles for gotten for the time being.

In the morning, the hearder was the first one up and prepared breakfast for the 4 of them. Butch and the boy washed the dishes and put things in order fed their horses and were ready to leave.

Well Mcdougal, What do I owe you?

Nothing, sd Mcdougal.

I want to be sure of that so here is ten dollars and if that isn't enough [illegible] best say so and I will give you what you want. And if you ever run into my camp just go in and help your self.

Cassidy titled this chapter, "The Meanest Man in Wyoming," in reference to the unthinkable attitude displayed by the sheepman McDougall. After leaving the sheep camp the outlaw gave "young Ainsley" his slicker to break the biting wind, and pointed him in the right direction. In parting he told the boy:

when you get back to the ranch, You can tell your old uncle John that butch Cassidy is eaven with him now.

What, exclaimed the kid You are Butch Cassidy?

And it was your old uncle who started me to the bad but I am over looking it now. Goodby and good luck.

After leaving the youth on Muskrat Creek, Cassidy returned to his cabin on Green Mountain, where he remained until April 1. Then he started on a long trip to meet Kid Curry, who was "hiding out in the hills up near Miles City:"

> Cassidy's route to the Powder river range, lay through the Hole in the Wall, and on, to Sheridan, down Goose creek, over the Rosebud creek, and from there down to and across the Powder river. All went well until he was near the end of his journey when things began to happen. Arriving at the mouth of Lame deer creek, he stopped over night at the home of a friend named Precey.

The man referred to as "Precey" was Nathan Pressey, who resided at the mouth of Muddy Creek, a short distance from Lame Deer Creek. Cassidy said he was asked by Pressey to take a note to another settler up Rye Grass Creek, and after delivering the note he stopped at a nearby spring:

> he took a drink of the cool spring water, and it occured to him that a good face bath would make him feel much fresher, so he unbuckled his belt and hung it with his six shooter in it, on a nearby limb and proceeded to wash his face in the cool running water.
>
> He emmedeately heard a heavy thud behind him, and before he could straighten up, a gun was pressed against his side and a Voice said, I want you.
>
> Well I guess you got me, said Butch and looking up, he discovered a deputy sheriff who had backed around between he and his gun, there by cutting off any possible chance of putting up a fight, so, there was but [one] thing to do, and that was to submit, and take his chances of making a break, later. It seems that, somehow or other, Morgan had gotten wind of his being in the country, and had been following him all the way from Sheridan a distance of over a hundred miles. and had discovered in some way, that he had gone up Ryegrass creek.

Morgan took no chance with his prisoner. he ordered him directly to his horse. and after getting to his horse, he tied his feet under the horse, and also hand cuffed him. after removing the shells from his six shooter, he put it in his (Morgan's) saddle pocket, also belt and cartridges in the opposite pocket. When he finally had Butch secured to his satisfaction, they started on their long ride back to Sheridan. The first day's ride took them as far as Thompson's ranch, where they stopped for the night. Morgan kept the hand cuffs on Butch but released his feet, so he could Walk. he did not eaven remove the hand cuffs while they were eating but kept them on until bed time.

At bed time he released one of the cuffs, and attached it to his own Wrist, and they climbed into bed together. The following morning, Morgan slipped both the hand cuffs on Butches Wrists, but did not tie his feet under the horse, as he did the day before. After leaving the head of the Rosebud, there was not a single residence, for a strech of about 30 miles. and Morgan felt little uneasiness as to the safety of his prisoner, as he knew the chances of meeting any of Butches friends was Verry slim.

So after riding, perhaps, a distance of twenty miles or so, the weather growing quite cold, he concluded it would be safe to remove the hand cuffs and accordingly did so. After a further ride of about ten miles, they came to a place called Big Spring. here they stopped to water their horses.

Morgan's horse would not drink With the bit in his mouth, so he was forced to get off and remove the bit. as he did so, Butch rode up a little closer to his horse. as Morgan was bending over to remove the bit from his horses mouth, Butch quickly picked his gun from the saddle pocket. and slipping a couple of shells, which Morgan had overlooked, in his pocket, into the six shooter, he had the drop on Morgan, before he could reach his gun.

Stick 'em up Morgan, you're to slow this time. now toss your six shooter into the middle of the spring.

Morgan realizing that he was dealing with a desperate man, did as he was told and tossed the gun [illegible] to the spring.

Now, ordered Butch, lie down on your belly, and if you care to get back to Sheridan, don't make a move. for it's my inning now.

Morgan did as he was told, and then Butch swung of his horse, and taking a short piece of rope, which he had in his saddle pocket, he quickly secured Morgan's hands behind his back. This done, he made a quick search of his pockets. he was but a moment removing his belt from the pocket where Morgan had placed it and after buckling it about his waist, he was ready for the return trip. Removing the saddle and bridle from Morgan's horse, he gave him a sharp slap on the rump and started him back over the trail they had just come over, then he returned to Morgan and released his hands, warning him to remain as he was until he told him to get up. After mounting his horse, he told Morgan to get up on his feet. As he did so, Butch, pointing toward Sheridan, said,

Morgan, the shortest way to Sheridan is right across them hills.

Butch knew that there was a ranch about four or five miles distant and that Morgan would suffer no ill effects from the Walk, so he left him afoot. and drove his horse ahead of him for several miles before turning him loose. The last he saw of Morgan, he was walking in the direction of Prairie Dog Wilson's ranch, and packing his saddle on his back.

This had been a pretty close shave for Butch. in fact, it was the second time in his life, that he had been under arrest. and it was also the last.

Ryegrass Creek still exists by that name. The spring where Cassidy was captured —famous for its soft water—is known as Isaac Kye Spring. Big Spring, located on the present Glen Mock Ranch north of Decker, Montana, is now under the waters of Tongue River Reservoir. The Thompson ranch on the Rosebud—called the OD Ranch after its brand—was a Minneapolis outfit owned by Hubbard and Thompson. There also was a "Prairie Dog" Wilson who ranched on Lower Prairie Dog Creek near the present Bud Perkins ranch, in the place Cassidy described.[6] "Morgan" may have been Frank Morrow, Sheriff of Sheridan County during 1895–96, or a man named Matt Morgan, who was a law enforcement officer there for a short time.[7]

After reversing the situation on "deputy Morgan," Cassidy wasted no time in making his way directly to Kid Curry's hideout "at the foot hills ranch" near Miles City.[8] That Cassidy's misadventure may have occurred in 1898, and not 1901, as the context of the story would indicate, is revealed in their conversation, led by a question from Curry:

I suppose they told you all about Tom's trial over in Deadwood?

Yes old Bob [McCoy] did a good job of it didn't he?

Well, Bob is a slicker all right; he stayed right on the job till Tom was free.

I knew he would, said Butch.

Well, I'm glad old Tom got out all right. . . . Well old timer, I've got plenty of grub here to last two or three weeks, so I guess we might as well stick around here till Maxwell shows up.

That's what I figured on, said Butch. This is a good safe place to hold out and we can pass the time away some how or other.

There is a haunting similarity between Cassidy's episode and the capture of the Belle Fourche robbers near Lavina, Montana, in the fall of 1897. After a lengthy divergence, also indicating a chronology other than the spring of 1901, the manuscript sets the scene for the last organized robbery by the infamous Wild Bunch. In late June 1901 the outlaws proceeded from their hideout in Big Horn Canyon to Wagner, Montana[9], for the holdup of the Great Northern Coast Flyer:

After a few days, the bandits left the canyon for their last venture together. They took a coarse North to the Mussellshell river, from there they made their way to the Missouri river, and on northwest to the Milk river country. Picking up three men, who were well known to Curry, and went on to a point near Chinook, about twenty miles east of Havre, here camping and making plans for the holdup. They decided on the mail train and after twenty minutes stopping the train, were in their saddles and on their Way.

Outside of some unsigned currency there was about seventeen thousand dollars.

From the descriptions given by eyewitnesses to the holdup at Exeter Switch near Wagner, Montana, during midday, July 3, 1901, two of the three men Curry recruited were O. C. Hanks and Ben Kilpatrick. Camillo Hanks had just been released from the Montana State Penitentiary at Deer Lodge, on April 30, 1901, after serving eight years for the holdup of a Northern Pacific train near Reed's Point on August 27, 1893. Hanks had auburn hair, sandy complexion, and blue eyes. Because of his deafness he had developed a habit of tilting his head to the left. At the time of the Exeter, or Wagner, robbery in 1901 Hanks, alias Charley Jones, was thirty-eight, stood five feet ten inches tall and weighed 156 pounds.[10]

Ben Kilpatrick, the Tall Texan, had been implicated in both the Wilcox and Tipton robberies, and probably saw action in other Wild Bunch escapades.

According to Alan Swallow, editor of the anonymously authored book, *The Wild Bunch,* Logan's third recruit was Jim Thornhill. Jim took over Kid Curry's former ranch in the Little Rockies area after Curry killed Pike Landusky in 1894. His intimate knowledge of the country, and his close friendship with Curry, would have made him a logical choice.[11]

Harvey "Kid Curry" Logan boarded the westbound Great Northern Coast Flyer when it pulled into Malta on July 3 for a water stop. He climbed onto the blind baggage and, as the train pulled out of the station, he crawled over the coal tender and dropped down on the engine platform to cover the engineer, Tom Jones, and his fireman, Mike O'Neil, with his six-shooter. A few miles down the track, at the Exeter Switch, Logan ordered the train halted near a bridge where the other outlaws were hidden. At that point on the line the Milk River takes a bend close to the Great Northern tracks.

Two bandits covered the train. To keep curious passengers from coming forward, they occasionally fired random shots into the coaches. Three of these warning shots ricocheted badly, wounding the brakeman and two passengers.

While the Winchesters distracted the passengers, Logan and one other outlaw ordered the train disconnected back of the express car and pulled a short distance up the track, where the through safe was summarily blown open. The take included $40,000 in unsigned bank notes, shipped from the U.S. Treasury in Washington, D.C. for delivery at the National and the American National banks in Helena, Montana.

The outlaws politely bid the trainmen a good day, then dropped over the roadbed bank to cross the Milk River at a nearby ford to make their escape.[12]

Almost as soon as news of the robbery spread, reports of sightings of the outlaws came in from every direction. Harvey Logan was among the first to be identified. Posses were quickly formed and the area from the Milk River south to the Missouri Breaks was combed, to no avail. Then several days after the robbery, an eastern Montana rancher named Morton tried to cash some of the stolen notes in Miles City. Under questioning he revealed that the outlaws had convinced him to trade four of his best saddle horses for $100 and their four badly used horses, some forty-eight hours after the holdup.[13] The information was of little help. The robbers had vanished.

The end to the notorious Wild Bunch is given but short note in "The Bandit Invincible:"

Butch thinking this was a good time to quit the bunch, suggested they split the bunch, and make their way in pairs, and after shaking hands, seperated for the last time, and headed for Miles City.

Express car blown up in holdup at Wilcox, Wyo., June 2, 1899.

Courtesy Union Pacific Railroad Museum Collection.

Outlaw grave, Burnaugh Road Ranch, Muddy Creek, Wyoming.

Photograph by author.

185

Express car blown up in holdup at Tipton, Wyo., August 29, 1900.

Union Pacific posse loading their horses into specially designed stable car, following Wild Bunch holdup at Tipton, Wyoming.

Courtesy Union Pacific Railroad Museum Collection.

Isaac Kye Spring, Rye Grass Creek, Montana. At this spring Butch Cassidy, the "Bandit Invincible," was captured by "Deputy Morgan."

Author Photo.

Harry Longabaugh and Etta Place, New York, 1901.

Harvey "Kid Curry" Logan, after his arrest for the Belle Fourche Bank Robbery, 1897.

Cholila, Argentina. Butch Cassidy's ranch lay within this area.

SKYLAB photograph, 1973. Courtesy United States Geological Survey, EROS Data Center, Sioux Falls, South Dakota.

BANDIDOS
YANQUI'
EN
ARGENTINA

★ Butch Cassidy's Ranch

💰 Reported Robberies

192

Chapter XVIII

Bandidos Yanquí

Cholila. Ten Chubut
Argentine Republic S. Am.
August 10, 1902

Mrs. Davis
Ashley, Utah

My Dear friend.

I suppose you have thought long before this that I had forgotten you (Or was dead) but my Dear friend I am still alive. and when I think of my Old friends you are always the first to come to my mind   It will probably surprise you to hear from me away down in this country but U.S. was to small for me. The last two years I was there, I was restless, I wanted to see more of the world. I had seen all of the U.S. that I thought was good, and a few months after I sent A——— over to see you, and get the Photo of the rope jumping (of which I have got here and often look at and wish I could see the originals, and I think I could liven some of the characters up a little for Maudie looks very sad to me.) Another of my Uncles died and left $30,000, Thirty Thousand to our little family of 3 so I took my $10,000 and started to see a little more of the world. I visited the best Cities and best parts of the country of South A. till I got here, and this part of the country looked so good that I located, and I think for good. for I like the place better every day. I have 300 cattle, 1500 sheep, and 28 good Saddle horses, 2 men to do my work, also good 4 room house, wearhouse stable, chicken house and some chickens. The only thing lacking is a cook. for I am still living in Single Cussidness and I sometimes feel very lonely. For I am alone all day, and my neighbors dont amount to anything, besides the only language spoken in this country is Spanish, and I dont speak it well enough yet to converse on the latest scandles so dear to [?] the [?] hearts of all nations, and without which conversations are very stale. but the country is first class   the only industry at present is stock

193

raising (that is in this part) and it cant be beat for that purpose, for I never seen a finer grass country, and lots of it hundreds and hundreds of miles that is unsettled, and comparatively unknown, and where I am, it is a good agricultural country, all kind of small grain and vegetables grow without Irrigation. but I am at the foot of the Andes Mountains. and all the land east of here is prarie and Deserts, very good for stock, but for farming it would have to be Irrigated, but there is plenty of good land along the Mountain for all the people that will be here for the next hundred years, for I am a long way from Civilation   it is 16 hundred miles to Buenos Aires the Capitol of the Argentine, and over 400 miles to the nearest RailRoad or Sea Port, in the Argentine Republic, but only about 150 miles to the Pacific Coast to Chile but to get there we have to cross the Mountains. which was thought impossible till last summer when it was found that the Chilean Gov. had cut a road almost across so that next summer we will be able to go to Port Mont [*Puerto Montt*], Chile, in about 4 days, where it use to take 2 months around the old trail and it will be a great benefit to us for Chile is our Beef Market and we can get our cattle there in 1/10 the time and have them fat. And we can also [illegible] supplies in Chile for one third what they cost here. The climate here is a great deal milder than Ashley Valley. the Summers are beautiful, never as warm as there. And grass knee high every where. and lots of good cold mountain water. but the winters are very wet and disagreeable, for it rains most of the time, but sometimes we have lots of snow. but it dont last long. for it never gets cold enough to freeze much. I have never seen Ice one inch thick.[1]

With this August 10, 1902 letter to Elzy Lay's mother-in-law in Ashley, Utah, Butch Cassidy's presence in Argentina is first documented. Although the remainder of the letter is missing, it does reveal a clear picture of Cassidy's fresh start as a rancher in the frontier province of Chubut. His movements following the Wagner train robbery are detailed in "The Bandit Invincible:"

From Miles City he took the train to Minneapolis. After three days there he boarded the train for Duluth and about a month later he took passage by boat to Sault Ste. Marie. staying for a month. During the Winter he made a study of the route he intended to take to South America. Leaving the middle of March he made his way to the Canadian "Soo," from there to Montreal where he stayed six weeks. In May, he went to Liverpool.

Arriving in Liverpool, he found he had only about a week to spend in England, so he took the first boat out for Pernambuco. It was a long trip from Liverpool to Montevideo. The first stop was at the Canary Islands the second Cape Verde Islands and then Pernambuco. After leaving there it seemed they would never arrive at Montevideo as there were several stops the most prominent being Rio De Janerio.

Butch spent about two months around Montevideo while he waited for Maxwell. About the first of September they met each other as planned. After about three days they left for Buenos Aires. and from there to Rawson City and on to a small village called Gaiman.

Here they purchased saddles & pack mules and continued on their inspection tour for a suteable location for stock raising. Finding a place about a hundred miles northwest from Lake Chacabucco and near Rio Negro. Here they purchased about thirteen thousand acres of land and eight hundred cattle.

The manuscript's assertion that Cassidy went to Liverpool is corroborated in a Wyoming Writers Project manuscript by A. F. C. Greene, which states that Cassidy "went to Liverpool on a cattle boat; thence he made his way to the Argentine and joined his companions."[2] All of the places in Cassidy's itinerary check out. Rio Negro is a district in Argentina, named after the "Black River." Cholila, in Chubut Province, is not far from the Rio Negro boundary.

The Pinkerton National Detective Agency operatives' records, preserved in the Pinkerton Archives, constitute the largest single source of information relating to the activities of Cassidy and Harry Longabaugh during the years 1901 and 1902. In a letter to his brother Robert, William Pinkerton wrote that during the time the Phillips manuscript places Cassidy in the cabin on Green Mountain above Jesse Johnson's ranch during the winter before the Wagner, or Exeter, train holdup, "Longabaugh" and his party "have been in New York City. It shows how daring these people are; while we're looking for them in the mountains and the wilderness they are in the midst of society."[3]

The trio's activities in New York are detailed in a Pinkerton memorandum dated New York, July 29, 1902, and signed by Robert Pinkerton:

> This is to advise all offices that the above named holdup [Harry Longabaugh] was in New York City February 1, 1901, at which time he lived with a woman he called his wife, at the boarding house of Mrs. Taylor, 234 East 12th St. There he used the name of Harry E. Place. . . . Longbaugh had with him George Parker. He was at this boarding house under the name of Ryan. . . .
>
> We have ordered copies of a photograph which Longbaugh had taken of himself and the woman with him at this time by De Young this city.
>
> The woman with him is said to be his wife and to be from Texas. . . .
>
> We also learned that Longbaugh under the name of Place was treated in the Pierce Medical Institute, Buffalo, New York, and by a Dr. Weinstein, 174 Second Ave., New York City. We do not know the nature of the ailment he was being treated for.[4]

Informant reports[5] had indicated Longabaugh suffered from catarrh—membrane inflammation of the nose and throat—but a Philadelphia memo said he was treated in Buffalo for "a pistol shot wound he said he got in the extreme West."[6]

In New York City the trio took in the sights, and Etta Place received a Tiffany lapel watch as a gift from "Ryan." The photographs Harry Longabaugh and Etta Place posed for were taken at De Young's photographic studio at 857 Broadway. Longabaugh was outfitted in a dress suit and Etta wore a velvet gown highlighted with her new Tiffany watch. The photographer thought the elegant pair were "perhaps Western society." Ryan was not present.

The New York Pinkerton memorandum also noted their departure: "On Feb. 20, 1901, Place and his wife sailed for Buenos Aires, Argentine Republic, South America." Sailing for Buenos Aires that day was the R. P. Houston Company liner, *Herminius,* a British ship.[7] Again, Ryan was not present.

The couple's subsequent activities are detailed by operative Frank P. Dimaio, who went to Buenos Aires in March 1903: "At the London and River Platte Bank I met the manager who advised that Harry A. Place had opened an account with the bank on March 23,

1901, depositing $12,000 in gold notes. He gave his address as the Hotel Europa, Buenos Aires."[8]

Dimaio also interviewed a "Clerk Porter of the Prince Line and other lines who recognized photo of Place and wife but not Cassidy. He sailed them March 1902 on 'Soldier Prince', Buenos Ayres to UA."[9] The Soldier Prince docked at Bush Terminal in Brooklyn on April 3, 1902.[10]

Pinkerton detectives also discovered that both "Mr. and Mrs. Harry A. Place," upon returning to New York, checked into a hospital in the city during May 1902.[11] No record of the reason for their stay was located, but operative Dimaio learned from the London and River Platte Bank that "on May 16, 1902, Place cashed a check for $3546, dated April 2, 1902, endorsed by one Angelo Bottaro, Treleu, Argentine Republic."[12] The check, cashed in New York, and signed by Bottaro the day before the couple's arrival in New York, had to have been mailed to them from Argentina.

Dimaio's continued research in Buenos Aires took him to the Registry of the Colonial Land Department where he "learned that on April 2nd, 1902, Place and Ryan [notified] Argentine Republic Government they had settled on 4 square leagues of Government land within the Province of Chubut, district 16th of II October, near Cholilo and had 1300 sheep, 500 head of cattle, 35 horses, and asked for the first right to buy some [land] and were settled on land improving it. This petition was signed by Place and Ryan, per Santiago," with the added note, "Not Sold Yet, Place and Ryan are squatters."[13]

This filing, made by Cassidy in his partner's absence, gives good indication that the two outlaws were well on their way to success as ranchers in the Argentine interior. It also corroborates Cassidy's letter to Mrs. Davis some four months later.

The persistent Dimaio also was able to determine Longabaugh's return sailing: "At Houston Line learned they left New York July 10, 1902, on steamer Honorious. Arrived Buenos Ayres August 9, 1902, as Harry A. Place, Purser, Mrs. Harry A. Place, Stewardess, which was OK as no passengers were carried, hence put them in the crew's list."[14] When Cassidy wrote his August 10 letter to Mrs. Davis, he was, indeed, alone as Longabaugh and his consort had not yet returned from their New York trip.

Dimaio learned from the bank that "Place drew out his balance of $1105.50 August 14, 1902, and it was worth 44ᶜ to the dollar in gold. The manager had no record of Place since, but it was believed he was still at Cholilo. When shown the photographs of these people, the manager readily recognized them."[15]

"August 15, 1902, HA and wife sailed on *Chubut* from Buenos Ayres, got off at Madryn on Gulf of Nuevo, then probably by horseback to their ranch at Cholilo."[16]

Dimaio's investigation completed, he returned to the United States, arriving in New York the last of June 1903.[17]

Perhaps the most authoritative source as to the outlaws' activities in Argentina is a series of three articles written by Justo Piernes, and published in the Buenos Aires newspaper, *Clarin,* in 1970. The series is based on Argentine provincial police reports.[18] According to Piernes, Cassidy, Longabaugh, and his "wife" Etta arrived at the City of Trelew, in Chubut, in 1902, putting up at the Globe Hotel, today torn down. From there the trio left "on foot" for Patagonia. At Cholila, a beautiful region of lakes and mountains near the city of Esquel, they established their ranch. They began to acquire a herd of mares and sheep, the latter purchased from a company called Lands of the South, in Leleque, a few kilometers from Cholila.

The new arrivals began to make themselves known in the mountain region, and were conspicuous in their behavior. The married couple as well as Butch Cassidy were honorable ranchers. While in Argentina the outlaws used their names, George Parker and Harry Longabaugh. Etta was known as Señora Longabaugh.

Butch was described as the gentleman of the trio, Longabaugh as a supernatural gunman, and Etta as slender, with chestnut hair and green eyes. She wore breech pants and at one time, riding bareback, she demonstrated shooting with her Winchester as her horse was at full gallop. She mounted a horse as though she were a horse breaker.

They joined in the fiestas in the neighboring town of Esquel, and at one inaugural ball Etta danced with the territory's governor, a Dr. Lezana. She was described by neighbors as free, forward, and very playful, while Cassidy was the least communicative of the three. As he indicated in his 1902 letter to Mrs. Davis, Cassidy was having difficulties with the language.

According to the Phillips manuscript, all went well for three years, until:

> a stock buyer by the name of Apfield came through the country. had at one time been a sheriff in Wyoming and as he had known Cassidy quite well, he at once recognized him. Apfield thinking he might be able to collect part of the large reward, began negotiations for the arrest of both Cassidy and Maxwell.
>
> Realizing there was little chance of peace for them in any part of the world, they decided to resume their life of banditry.

In a fascinating account of how the outlaws finally left the ranch, the 1970 *Clarín* series said they were paid an unannounced visit by Argentine provincial authorities:

> "Why do you want to arrest us?" asked one of the outlaws, when a frontier police commisar named Tasso rode up to the ranch. They offered the officer a drink of whiskey and when one of the outlaws spoke, Tasso recalled it was in Castillian "which was not too good."
>
> "We only pick upon the powerful, never the poor people. Furthermore, officer, we're going to tell you we have no idea of going with you." The outlaw then took out a Colt revolver and shot a couple of bullets in the air. The bandits also threw rocks in the air and shot them. At last, one said to the officer, "Pardon us for shooting like this. It's in order that we are not bored." The policeman decided to withdraw without his quarry.

This visit occurred in 1906, the same year other reports have the outlaws disappearing from Patagonia.

The Piernes articles, however, put the outlaws' first return to banditry a full year before they were forced to leave their sanctuary. "In all of this region they had never done anything out of the ordinary or that could be considered wrong until 1905. That is to say, Cassidy and his band were authentically retired from activity" until, on February 11, 1905, they made an assault on the Bank of Loudres and Tarapaca at Rio Gallegos, some one thousand kilometers from their ranch.

In leaving Cholila, the three ranchers told neighbors they were going to Chile. Upon reaching Rio Gallegos, in the southern tip of Argentina, they rented a small house on the edge of town. Twice a week they galloped into town for provisions and left in the same manner. They called so much attention to themselves that the people always commented, "Here come the crazy Yankees." When they pulled off the robbery, obtaining 20,000 pesos and a small box containing an undetermined amount of gold ingots, their rapid escape was hardly noticed by the citizenry.

In the Rio Gallegos holdup the trio was assisted by a man identified as "Harvey Logan, Kid Curry, 41 years of age. 1.71 meters [5 feet, 7 inches] in height; body slender; color, white but tan; eyes dark, nose prominent; teeth noticeably white; he has a scar back of wrist, two on his back and on left shoulder; middle finger on his hands is extraordinarily long."

Only one source would have had so complete a description of Harvey Logan: the Pinkerton National Detective Agency. Logan, following the Wagner holdup, had been captured in Tennessee and sentenced to twenty years at hard labor in the Columbus (Ohio) federal penitentiary. Before he could be transferred to the prison he escaped the Knox County jail on June 27, 1903.[19]

Attempts to capture Logan were futile. Then in June 1904 three bandits held up a Denver and Rio Grande passenger train near Parachute, in western Colorado. In the chase that followed one of the outlaws was wounded, and rather than face certain capture, the man sent a bullet through his own brain.[20]

There was much controversy over the identity of the dead robber. Lowell Spence of Pinkertons claimed the man to be Harvey Logan; other law officers equally well acquainted with Logan swore to the contrary. Following a lead based on an envelope addressed to "Tap Duncan," found in the dead man's coat, Denver and Rio Grande detective R. Brunazzi traced the letter to its origin in Texas, and upon interviewing the dead man's relatives, verified that the outlaw was, indeed, Tap Duncan of Knickerbocker, Texas.[21]

Following this revelation the Pinkertons again revived their search for Logan and in 1907 publicly verified that Harvey Logan, alias Kid Curry, had turned up in Argentina.[22]

Piernes placed the four back at Cholila in March 1905, but indicates they stayed only about ten months before they learned the police had received an order to detain them. Butch Cassidy found "the long hand of the Pinkerton Detective Agency" had reached him and "he planned his second bank robbery."

"One day they left the ranch, the married couple and Logan. Another day, in the morning, Butch Cassidy did the same."

They never returned to the ranch and the next word on the outlaws was the report of a bank robbery at Via Mercedes in San Luis, on March 2, 1906.

In contrast to the *Clarin* articles, the "Bandit Invincible" manuscript says Cassidy's first criminal act was to hold up the bank in an Argentine town called Neuquen, located more than two hundred miles north of Cholila:

> They held up the bank in Newquein, went to San Martin and then took the train for Mendoza. Here, they made plans to hold up the express train running between Mendoza & Valparaiso.
>
> Geting two men by the name of Fowler and Haines to join them, the bunch retired to a place near Mendoza to complete their plans. After the robbery, they [illegible] spent a year between Mendoza & the Bolivian Border. During the time they robbed three banks two express trains and four pack trains.

San Martin is approximately six hundred miles from Cholila, in Mendoza Province in the Andes foothills. The identities of Fowler and Haines have not been established.

The last known of Cassidy, Longabaugh, and Etta Place, according to the *Clarin* account, was a letter from Harry Longabaugh to a friend in Chubut, announcing that "tomorrow we will leave for San Francisco. . . . We have done well in business and we've received our money. . . . I do not wish to see Cholila ever more."

Longabaugh's letter compares favorably with the Cassidy narrative:

> With the hope that he might some day find a way that he could give up his life of banditry Butch concluded to work his way northward into Bolivia.
>
> Shortly before leaving Argentine country, he notified several of his friend of his intention of leaving and that if any other crimes were comited in Argentina would be comited by some one else besides he and his bunch as they were leaving for all times.

His friend [illegible] encouraged him to abandon his life of banditry intirely. some of them offering flattering inducements of positions in Chille or Perue with companies with which they were asociated but none of these offers were considered, as he felt that sooner or later some one would stumble up on him or put the authorities on his trail in hopes of gaining the [illegible] large rewards which were offered for his capture. The idea of some day becoming a respectable citizen had never been intirely abanded but he felt that it could never be accomplished simply by changing locations.

Cassidy was of a Verry determined disposition and when an Idea or desire became rooted in his mind he never abanded it and nothing but death could force him from the hope, that some day some how he could leave the life, with the women he so dearly loved in the far off united states. He could find no definate plan, but the Idea rangled in [him] to accept the first opportunity that presented it self. It was with this Idea that he decided to work his way to the northwest into Bolivia.

Justo Piernes' series concluded with additional information on the activities of Harvey Logan, who was accompanied by two other North American bandits identified by Argentine authorities as Robert Evans and Williams Wilson: "In 1906, part of the gang left. There remained of the band, Logan, Evans and Wilson. They launched a trip filled with attacks in Patagonia. The documents we begin to see at this particular time seemed to show that they lacked the leadership of Butch Cassidy. . . ."

On December 29, 1909, Logan, Evans, and Wilson made an attack on the Mercantile Company in Rio Pescado within the Province of Chubut. During the robbery Mercantile agent Lloyd Apjuan was shot and killed.

The Argentine newspaper also detailed another raid in the zone of Rio Pico where the three tried to rob a house, and an engineer there was shot and killed. "It is evident in the last operation there existed much clumsiness." Apparently also, the bandits failed to obtain any money.

Piernes reported it was believed that Logan was killed by "his own companions some months afterwards in a place close to Corcovado," a gulf on the Chilean coast directly west of Cholila.

At the present time it is impossible to select from the bewildering maze of stories the true fate of Harvey Logan, alias Kid Curry.

The *Clarín* told of the demise of the unidentified "Evans and Wilson" in a bloody shootout with Argentine authorities in the Rio Pico region, on December 9, 1911. From Don Pedro Penia, at age 103 the surviving member of a police patrol involved, Justo Piernes learned what happened:

"The battle flared when the two outlaws were cornered. Evans unloaded his Winchester and six-shooter at the patrol. He was the first to fall. An officer named Montenegro, at Penia's side, was shot through the heart by the remaining bandit, Wilson.

"Wilson dashed back of a tree, reloading his carbine. I had discharged three cartridges from my arms," Penia said. "As the bullets went by, I felt I had been caught in the arm. Then I fell, but Wilson also fell, tumbled end over end, and did not get to his horse. He had eight bullets in his body. A lieutenant in the patrol rushed over to the dying Wilson and gave him on the ground the shot of grace."

What an eerie parallel to the reported demise of Butch Cassidy and the Sundance Kid.

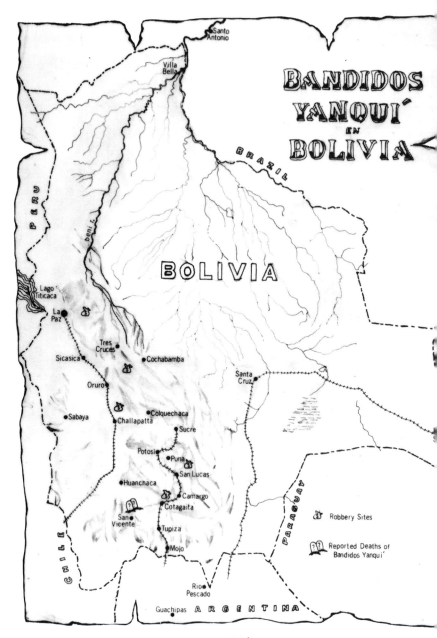

BANDIDOS
YANQUI'
EN
BOLIVIA

BRAZIL

PERU

beni r.

BOLIVIA

Lago Titicaca

La Paz

Tres Cruces

Sicasica

Cochabamba

Oruro

Santa Cruz

Sabaya

Colquechaca

Challapatta

Sucre

Potosi

Puna

San Lucas

Huanchaca

Camargo

Cotagaita

San Vicente

Tupiza

Mojo

CHILE

PARAGUAY

Rio Pescado

Guachipas   ARGENTINA

Santo Antonio

Villa Bella

🐝 Robbery Sites

🪦 Reported Deaths of
Bandidos Yanqui'

204

Chapter XIX
San Vicente

IN RELATING the move of his outlaw band to Bolivia, Cassidy described their near-capture in the mountains west of the village "Gaciayo [or Gaciapo] inconder." Before he left the village, natives informed Cassidy "that plans had been made to attempt the capture of he and his pals in one of the passes in a low range of mountains on their way from Gaciayo to Lipez [Lipez Province, in southern Bolivia]."

In a plan to dodge the posse, Cassidy set up a fake camp the first night out, and "fixed up three verry natural looking dummies which he left lying close to a verry slow smoldering fire. He had also piled several small bunches of brush here and there to resemble the usual pack outfit in the dark." Then, under cover of darkness, the gang made their way westward, reaching the summit of the range by daybreak.

After resting a few days in the Bolivian village of Huanchaca, the bandits made a reconnaisance trip through the new country before resuming criminal activities in southern Bolivia:

Leaving Huanchaca, horses, mules & pack out fit went by train to La Paz where they stoped for two weeks posing as prospectors. They [received] much information about several mining camps as well as train movements, bullion shipments.

Then they made a trip up to Lake Titicaca and on down to the Pacific coast. The West coast of the Andes mountains did not apeal to them so they went back to La Paz where there atention was turned to the South & East. Leaving La Paz they returned to Huanchaca, packed their mules and set out for Potosi and Sucre.

Their first hold up in Bolivia was a suply pack train between Oruro and Cochabamba. the hold up easy, rewards small [compared] with other hold ups in Argentina. Then the Bandits made their way South to a point near the Village of Colquehaca where they stoped for a week. then went West to the railroad, where they stoped near Challapatta, and made their first holdup in Bolivia.

From there, they made their way to Sabaya. To allay suspicion they left their out fits, seperated and secured seperate occopations for the time being.

In late 1906 or early 1907 the two outlaws secured employment at the Concordia Tin Mines, near the village of Tres Cruces, ninety miles southeast of La Paz. As noted by Arthur Chapman, "Cassidy and Longabaugh made it a practice to secure employment, far from the scene of their latest holdup, while they looked over the field and studied the possibilities for another robbery. In this way, Cassidy and Longabaugh familiarized themselves with a considerable part of South America."[1]

Chapman received much of his information from Percy Seibert, an American engineer associated with the Bolivian Supply, and assigned to the Concordia Tin Mines at the turn of the century. Seibert also was the source of author James D. Horan's information on the two outlaws' association with the mining company. Seibert had first come to Bolivia in 1905 as an engineer detailed under W. L. Sisson to survey proposed routes for construction of the Bolivian Railway.[2] Seibert, or Sy, as he was called, was among several dismissed by the controversial Sisson during the ensuing year, after unintentionally becoming entangled in disputes between Sisson and others, including the Bolivian government, the American legation, and influential United States citizens living in La Paz.[3] Some time after May 1906, Seibert became associated with the Concordia operation.

Cassidy applied to Concordia manager Clement Rolla Glass for employment. At that time Glass needed a man to carry the payroll remittances and to purchase the necessary livestock for camp sustenance and transportation of materials. He put Cassidy to work and found him an excellent, trustworthy employee.

In a previously unpublished letter written in 1964, Percy Seibert provides a glimpse of the outlaws' association with those at Concordia and added insights into the personalities of Cassidy and Longabaugh:

> Butch Cassidy was an agreeable and pleasant person, a grandson of an elder of the Mormon Church. He took well with the ladies and as soon as he arrived in a village he made friends with the little urchins and usually had some candy to give them.

When he visited me he enjoyed hearing the gramophone records, as I had a large selection of choice music. He allowed no other bandits to interfere with my camp and told them when they needed an animal shod or they needed a meal I would take care of them, but that they should move on and keep their backs toward my camp and not give it the reputation of being a bandit's hang-out. When he last visited me, he asked me a couple of times if I was sure he did not owe our comissary store anything more than the six or eight dollars I told him of and which he immediately paid. . . .

They said after a holdup or two, they had to continue as the Pinkertons, U.S. Cavalry and Bankers Association and Railroad detectives were constantly on their trail. I never had the slightest trouble getting along with them. Cassidy purchased cattle and mules for us and always was scrupulously honest as far as we were concerned. He went to a mining camp owned by a pair of wealthy Scotchmen, to get the lay-of-the-land and to learn when their payroll remittances would arrive so as to pick it up. They gave him a job as a night watchman and told him they really needed no one, but wanted to give him a chance to make a little money so he could continue prospecting for mines, as on applying for work he told them he was a prospector and had run out of money and supplies. They told him the meal hours, told him the sideboard had a supply of whiskey, appolinas water, gin, and beer and whenever he felt like a drink to help himself. He told me after, that he had not the heart to hold up people who treated him so kindly.[4]

The "Bandit Invincible" manuscript makes no mention of Cassidy's stay at the Concordia Mines, but describes the various strikes made by the gang in Bolivia:

After a stay of six weeks in Sabaya the bandits again hit the trail for Puna and San Lucas. during six months, several holdups were made between Camargo and Puna. The only rail road train hold up was near Catagaita.

That Train happened to be transporting a Troop of Calvery and [the gang] almost meet their Water lue. Cassidy, Maxwell, Haines & Betty Price consisted part of the Bandits at this time. The cavuly opened fire on them but after a firce battle all were on their way to a safe hide out. from there they went to San Lucas and from there to Sucre, abanded their horses and all entered the city seperately so as not to atract atention. got lading and then got together

Arthur Chapman, relying on Percy Seibert's information, indicated the outlaws held up a Bolivian Railway pay train at "the station of Eucalyptus," in the vicinity of Cochabamba. As with the Cassidy account, "There was a regiment of Bolivian cavalry close at hand, but the Colonel commanding would not allow his troops to pursue the bandits." Chapman gave McVey, rather than Haines, as the name of the trio's accomplice.

At this point, Cassidy tells of Etta's departure: "Betty Price returned to Buenos Aires as the hard ships would be two much for her. Maxwell gave betty all his money as they figured it would be their last meeting on this earth."[5] Etta Place also is conspicuously absent in Cassidy's next documented whereabouts, on November 12, 1907, when he wrote "To the Boys at Concordia" from Santa Cruz, some four hundred miles to the east, on the Bolivian plains:

> We arrived here about three weeks ago after a very pleasant journey and found just the place I have been looking for for 20 years and Ingersoll likes it better than I do. He says he wont try to live any where else. This is a Town of 18,000 and 14,000 are females and some of them are birds. This is the only place for old fellows like myself [Cassidy was forty-one], one never gets to old if he has blue eyes and a red face and looks capable of making a blue eyed Baby Boy.
>
> Oh god if I could call back 20 years and have red hair with this complection of mine I would be happy. I have got into the 400 set as deep as I can go. The lady feeds me on fine wines and she is the prettiest little thing I ever seen but I am afraid Papa is going to tear my playhouse down for he is getting nasty. But there is plenty more. This place isnt what we expected at all. There isnt any cattle here all the beef that is killed here comes from Mojo a distance of 80 legues and are worth from 80 to 100 Bs. But cattle do very well here and grass is good but water is scarce. There isnt any water in this town when there is a dry spell for a week. The people here in town have to buy water at 1.80 per barrel, but they can get good water at 40 feet but are to lazy to sink wells.
>
> Land is cheap here and every thing grows good that is planted. But there is damd little planted, every thing is very high. it costs

us Bs100 per head to feed our mules, 250 each for ourselves. We Rented a house, hired a good cook and are living like gentlemen.

Land is worth 10 cts. per hectare 10 leagues from here and there is some good Estancias for sale, one 12 leagues from here of 4 leagues with plenty of water and good grass and some sugar cane for 5,000 and others just as cheap and if I dont fall down I will be living here before long.

It is pretty warm and some fever but the fever is caused by the food they eat. At least I am willing to chance it.

They are doing some work now building a R. R. from Port Suares [Puerto Suarez, Bolivia] here and they claim it will be pushed right through so now is the time to get started for land will go up before long.

It is 350 miles here to Cochabamba and a hell of a road just up one mountain and down another all the way not a level spot on it is big enough to whip a dog on and most of the way thick brush on both sides. But there is people all along and lots of little towns in fact it is thickly settled. There is plenty of game on the road but it is safe for it is impossible to get it for brush. [illegible] Killed 1 turkey, 1 sand hill crain and 1 Buzzard. We could hear the turkeys every day and seen some several time but I only got one shot. it wont do for Reece [A. Basil Reece, Glass's assistant] to come over the road for he would Kill himself getting through the brush after birds. We would of left here long ago but we had a little trouble with the old mule Ingersoll [a companion traveler with Cassidy] hobbled her and tied her to a tree and wore a nice green pole out on her but I didn't think he had done a good job so I worked a little while with rocks. Between us we broke her jaw and we have been feeding her on mush ever since but she can eat a little now and we will leave in a few days for a little trip south to see that country. I am looking for the place Hutch [James Hutcheon, owner of a transportation company in Tupiza] wants, 8 leagues long, ½ league wide with big river running through it from end to end.

We expect to be back in Concordia in about 1 month.

Good luck to all you fellows.

J. P. Maxwell[6]

Cassidy's last letter, addressed to C. R. Glass, evidently in La Paz at the time, was written February 16, 1908, from the Concordia Mine at Tres Cruces:

Scarberry [George Scarbury, manager of a mine near the Concordia] leaves here for Sicasica on the 18. He will be there the 20. I dont know how long he will be there but I will let you know when he leaves. every thing is OK here as far as I know.

Yours Truly,
Gilly[7]

The "J. P. Maxwell" alias was Cassidy's most frequently used name during his association with the "Boys at Concordia." "Gilly" was an unknown Cassidy alias until discovery of this letter, although the bandit's mother's maiden name was Gillies, remarkably similar. The handwriting is the same as that in other Cassidy correspondence.

This second letter is the last documented evidence of Butch Cassidy's presence in South America.

In quoting Percy Seibert, Arthur Chapman set the demise of Cassidy and Longabaugh following the holdup of a payroll remittance pack train headed for the Aramayo mines in the Department of Potosi, and near the town of Quechisla. A few weeks after this holdup two heavily armed Americanos, on jaded mules, rode into the patio of the police station at the Indian village of San Vicente, Bolivia.[8] They ordered a meal at the police station, which served as an inn, as "there was no place else in the village where wayfarers could find food and shelter."

The constable in charge recognized one of the mules as that belonging to his friend, a muleteer who was helping transport the payroll at the time of the holdup. The suspicious constable alerted the captain of a Bolivian cavalry outside the village, and the bloody shootout was initiated when the captain attempted to arrest the two bandidos Yanqui'.

In contrast to Chapman's narrative, the "Bandit Invincible" account places Cassidy and his cohorts some distance outside La Paz, instead of at San Vicente. The location was not far from Tres Cruces, where Cassidy wrote his last letter in February 1908:

Rewards of thousands were offered dead or alive for the Bandits. They seperated in Sucre after the excitement had died down some and meet again in La Paz. They went from there to Beni river, to look that part of the river country over for a get away.

It was 3 o'clock the following afternoon after the train left La Paz that the bandits hear the tinkling of the lead Bell on the lead mule as the cavvalcade advanced up the steap trail. The bandits except Billings who had been set up the Gorge to look after the horses, were in readiness for the holdup. As the leader of the pack train made his appearance around the point of the rock on the sharp curve on the trail.

"Hands up," commanded Cassidy. "All of you and quick."

Up went the hands of the half dozen riders near the head of the train and while Maxwell and Hains held the drop on them, Cassidy quickly disarmed them and the lotting of the train began. before the bandits had nicely began to examine the various packs which were suposed to contain the treasur, a commotion was heard at the rear of the train beyond the curve and before they realized what was hapening a detachmint of Bolivian cavalry made its apearence around the curve and opened fire on them. The Bandits were suprised and hurried to shelter behind some large boilders which lay at the mouth of the Gorge, before it begin to rain bullets and spattered against the rocks from all directions.

Billings was wounded in the first atact but the bandits killed eleven soldiers. and 7 wounded. Billings was finaly kill and at that point Cassidy and Maxwell blew the heads practly of Two Soldiers. Where Cassidy and Maxwell were hiding they could get good aim and was much protected from the firing of the soldiers.

After fifteen or more soldiers were killed and several wounded. the firing seased for a while as the soldiers knew it was instant death to come out in open fire. Such deadly fire had never been seen before. Later on in the evening, Hains was wounded and with what care Maxwell & Cassidy could give him helped for a while, but, finaly he was Weakened from loss of Blood and slumped in an expand position and was shot by the soldiers.

That left Maxwell and Cassidy to fight their way out. Later on Maxwell recived a shot through the body and a scalp wound. Butch managed to get to Maxwells side and began to give him what aid he could. but Maxwell had been hard hit and Butch saw at once the best he could do was to make him as comfortable as possible as they lay there behind the rocks. Maxwell gave Butch a letter from Betty and requested him to notify {her} of his death in case he got away. He also informed Butch that Betty was his legal wife and had been for many years.

Butch got down two more soldiers who were working around

the uper edge of the canyon to get a better shot at he and Maxwell. It finaly grew dark and Maxwell a long sigh and said, "Good
by butch my old pal   dont forget Betty. take my belt with you if
you can get away and send it to little Betty and she will know I
died fighting and thinking of her." And with these last words he
quietly passed on.

Butch had seen many people die but never did any thing affect
him as did the passing of his old Friend, Maxwell.

Forgetting him self for the moment. he had forgotten he was
surrounded by soldiers. hearing a sudden voise not far. he lisened
carefully for the direction from where it came took dead aim and
got his man. He heard the thud of the body as it hit the ground.
Waiting silently and [illegible] watching careffuly for some time
after every thing had became silent in the darkness he removed
Maxwells money belt and buckled it about his own body and then
bagan to think of a plan by which he hoped might gain the
summet of the Canyon wall. And once on top he might evade the
troop. which he knew were some where up there among the rocks.
He fired a couple of shots in the direction where they had hid and
tied their horses.

For an hour he cralled on his hands & knees so he could not be
seen or heard so easily and every now & then he would stop and
listen careffuly for any possible sound.

After going three or 4 hundred yards he lay quietly for some
time to rest & listen again. Hearing no sound he got to his feet.
The horses could not get out of the Gorge on either side but butch
was afraid they might have broken their tie ropes and worked
their way out of the head of the Gorge two miles from where they
were tied and he, two, was worried that the soldiers might have
found them and made away with them.

He was relived by hearing one of the horses move some distance
ahead and stoped to listen and reasoned if the troops had discovered the horses they would undoubtedly have followed on down
the Gorge and atacted them in the rear instead of remaining with
the horses. he listend again and hearing no noise except the horses
he made his way to the first one. Being dark could not tell at first
which one was his. locating his own horse he removed all the food
from the saddle packs and filling his own, and roaling the remainder in his coat he tied it with the bags and water bottles on
the back of his saddle. Then, he & horse made their way slowly to
the head of the Gorge.

Gaining the summit of the Canyon wall, he continued on toward the Plateau of Cacaca. from the plateau he set his course East as near as he could due to darkness and continued on till day break next morning.

Allowing his horse to rest a while, he continued on east ward where he knew he would reach one of the streams following north to the Beni river. That evening he was at the head waters of a stream that flows into La Paz river which was twenty miles where the La Paz emptied into the Beni.

Feeling no pursuits he made camp for the night then would continue on down the Beni river to some point in Brazil. Rest and breakfast. he went down the La Paz to Beni. Day [illegible] day, on & on, he reached the Mederia river near Villa Bella from Villa Bella to Santo Antonia and on down the Maderia river to Parare and stoped for a Week. The trip down the Maderia was made by boat and the scenery was beautifull. both banks covered with [illegible] timber and tropical Vegetation.

Had it not been for the resecint loss of his pall Maxwell. he could have injoyed the trip Verry much. He finaly concluded since he was all alone now and no one to Identify him he would settle down to a normal life.

He went to Parare to Para, spent two weeks Waiting for a boat down the coast to Pernambuca. At Pernambuca he had to wait a month for a boat to Europe. Before leaving for Europe, he wrote a letter to the one girl in the world which he Explained every thing for their future and would write her as soon as he arrived there.

At Pernambuca he sent by express Maxwells belt to Betty Price in Buenos Aires. he knew that Betty would understand and he did not write her. Betty would never know who sent the belt and no women would ever know except to one he loved that he alone survived the tirrible battle.

The troopers had seen but three bandits and there were three horses left behind. In his haste to take the belt from Maxwells body he Butch had lost a small folder which he had carried for several years with some clippings & a letter and a little gold chain & cross.

Finding the folder with the three dead men the world would feel that Cassidy and his band had been killed. he would let it be that way.

From Pernambuca he [went] to Liverpool and to England then Paris. At Paris he entered a private hospital where he submited to several minor operations. three weeks left the hospital he could see Verry little trace of his old self in the mirror, so clever had the transformation been worked out. He got a room in a comfortable hotel wrote a letter to his sweet heart in Calif. telling of his intintions and where to meet him in the united states Retired for the night defying any one to identify him.

Reports from the troopers with Cassidy and his Bandits in the pass in Bolivia The various governments of North & South America accepted their story as authentic and the name of Butch Cassidy became only as a memory.

Chapter XX

Phillips Manufacturing Company

AMERICA in 1908 was a foreign country to one who had been away from her shores for six years. The intervening years had seen the advent of Orville and Wilbur Wright's airplane, the radio-telephone, an infinite array of devices and gadgetry, and that ridiculous contrivance, the automobile—no more than a fascinating toy in 1902—was now huffing its way down the boulevards of the nation.

Frontiers were being pushed back in every direction as man explored the air, the sea, and every remote area on earth. The Panama Canal was fast becoming a reality—the crowning feat of technological advance—and within a year Robert Peary would plant the Stars and Stripes on the North Pole.

As national attention turned to the campaign ballyhoo of presidential hopefuls William Howard Taft and William Jennings Bryan, even the horrifying San Francisco fire of 1906 became but a dim memory. There was no time for backward glances.

These were glorious times with excitement at every turn. Men were embarking on prosperous careers in thrilling new endeavors unheard of in 1902. Boundless opportunity beckoned.

Butch Cassidy had long coveted such opportunity. Now there was nothing to prevent him. The slate was clean.

Springtime of 1908 found him strolling down the maple-canopied avenues of Adrian, Michigan, a little farming community just southeast of the hardwood-covered Irish Hills. To the bowlegged man with sparkling grey eyes the community was especially attractive. He had been here possibly but once before at a different time, under different circumstances. He liked what he had seen, and he came back.

William Phillips was his name, he told those he met; William Thadeus Phillips, to be exact. Late of Des Moines, Iowa, where he'd been in the machine shop business, he just came to Adrian to get away from it all, to see a little country. As he ambled by the Adrian Baptist Church, so he later claimed, he heard the melodic strains of a piano within. Curious, he entered the church and there he met Gertrude Livesay. That meeting was to change the course of his life. William T. Phillips fell in love.

A plain woman, Gertrude Livesay in 1908 was even a little sickly. She had a chronic asthmatic condition, and at age thirty-two it wasn't getting any better. She also wasn't getting any younger.

Gertrude had been born not far from Adrian, at Fairfield on July 25, 1875. Her parents, Richard M. and Mary Jane Locke Livesay, were Baptist farmers with holdings in the Morenci area just above the Ohio line. Gertrude was raised in Fairfield and for a time had worked in a millinery store in nearby Morenci. In 1905 she boarded in Adrian and may have attended Adrian College there. At the time William T. Phillips entered her lift she was again living in Morenci and was in nearby Adrian on a visit.[1]

The courtship was short and, over family objections, Gertrude became Mrs. William T. Phillips on May 14, 1908. A Methodist minister performed the ceremony and two of Gertrude's closest friends were witnesses. Her mother, who resided in Adrian, and her sister Blanche probably attended the services. Her father had died five years before.

On the marriage license Phillips put his age at thirty-four (he would have been forty-three); his residence as Des Moines, Iowa. He said he was born in Michigan and was a "mechanical engineer."[2]

After an extended honeymoon—Gertrude's relatives thought the couple went camping in the Colorado mountains—the couple settled in Globe, Arizona, where Phillips found work on various ranches and in housing construction. He may also have acquired some skills as a draftsman.

Phillips later confided that he also spent some time as a sharpshooter for six dollars a day in the Mexican Revolution.[3] While the couple was in the Southwest, Francisco Madero with the aid of Pancho Villa began his revolt against the Mexican government, touching off twenty-three years of bloodshed for the struggling republic. Phillips may have joined the "Falange de Los Extranjeros," a company of mercenaries formed in El Paso under the command of Captain Linderfelt to fight on the side of the revolutionaries.[4]

During this same period Phillips evidently was recognized as Butch Cassidy in Mexico. Henry Bowman of Cedar City, Utah, later told author Charles Kelly he had seen Cassidy in the company of Pancho Villa early in the revolution. Bowman, a member of a Mormon colony in Mexico, said Cassidy saved him from execution at the hand of the volatile Villa.[5]

George West Musgrave, infamous member of the original "Black Jack" gang, and his bride, the former Janette Magor of Baggs, Wyoming, also met Cassidy in Mexico. Janette, who had known Cassidy since she had witnessed the celebration of the Wild Bunch in 1897, as a young girl in her mother's Baggs boarding house, clearly remembered that Cassidy had a woman with him whom he loved very much.[6]

The third person who claimed Butch Cassidy was in Mexico during the early part of the Mexican Revolution was his sister, Mrs. Lula Parker Betenson of Circleville, Utah. Mrs. Betenson recently revealed this information in her book, *Butch Cassidy, My Brother*, adding it was her understanding that Harry Longabaugh and Etta Place also were in the country![7]

By late summer 1910 Phillips and his wife, her asthma arrested, left Arizona and headed north. In making their way eventually to the state of Washington, the two stopped over in Wyoming where Phillips took his wife on a leisurely float trip on the Big Horn River, through the Big Horn Basin, photographing sights along the way.[8]

In the final paragraph of "The Bandit Invincible," written twenty-four years later, Phillips made the following statement, reflecting his 1910 visit to Wyoming:

> All of the members of the original Wild bunch of the Hole in the wall gang, as they were usually spoken of except two had been wiped out. The one who had been most sought and now become a man of mystery and the man who he first meet upon the day he entered the Hole in the wall, Tom O'day. O'day is yet living and at the same place where he Welcomed Cassidy on his first Visit to the Hole in the wall.

O'Day was indeed alive and living at Lost Cabin, Wyoming, at the time the Phillipses passed through the area in 1910. Following his release from the Deadwood jail in 1898, O'Day had returned to northern Wyoming, and on November 23, 1903, he was arrested on a charge of horse theft. He was sentenced at the February 1904 term of distrct court and, at age forty-two, entered the Wyoming State Penitentiary. After serving four and one-half years of his six-year sentence, he was released on June 1, 1908, to return to the Lost Cabin country.[9]

As late as 1912 O'Day was still living in the same dugout hovel near Lost Cabin. He later left the area and married an Indian girl in South Dakota. Tom was killed at Forte Pierre, South Dakota, in 1930, when a runaway team of horses overturned a wagon in which he was riding—four years before Phillips wrote his manuscript.[10]

Phillips' closing paragraph in "The Bandit Invincible" was given added significance elsewhere in Wyoming in the summer of 1910. At the Dan Hilman ranch at the base of the Big Horns, Fred Hilman, then a young man of twenty-five, came in from haying to find a man standing under a tree in the ranch yard. The two exchanged pleasantries and, as the visitor looked around, Fred felt he had seen the man before, but couldn't quite place him.

The stranger asked how the hay crop was doing and then turned to look directly at Fred with grey eyes twinkling, "Have you had any rattlesnakes tossed up on the hay rack with you lately?" Fred Hilman then knew he was talking to Butch Cassidy.

When the former hired hand learned Dan Hilman was on an extended trip, he bade Fred good luck and left. Fred Hilman never saw him again. For Fred's wife the passing years would never obscure the date of that visit. It definitely was 1910, the year she and Fred were married.[11]

William and Gertrude Phillips spent the fall in Billings, Montana—140 miles north of the Hilman ranch—and arrived in Spokane, Washington, two days before Christmas, 1910. They took a room in the Globe Hotel, and Phillips hocked a six-shooter for enough money to buy a few groceries. That Christmas Eve they ate peanut butter loaf cooked over a gas burner in their room.[12]

The day following Christmas, Phillips went to the Washington Water Power Company to apply for a job he had seen advertised. The position required training in drafting and he would have to apply trigonometry in his work. When asked if he knew trigonometry, Phillips quickly assured his interviewer that he did. He was desperate.

William Phillips spent the next week in the Spokane library pouring over textbooks on trigonometry before beginning work as a draftsman for the Washington Water Power Company. His first projects included drafting bridge plans, and he successfully performed all assignments, including those requiring trigonometry.[13]

Phillips learned rapidly and expanded his efforts to encompass other ventures. The 1911 Spokane City Directory, the first to record Phillips' residence there, listed him as "second vice president, American Stereotypewriter Company." The nature of the enterprise hasn't been determined. In subsequent years Phillips was listed as an "engineer," first for the Washington Water Power Company, and then on his own.

In 1912, with an unidentified partner, Phillips went to Alaska in a gold-seeking venture. The operation aborted the same season and the two prospectors divided their joint property—including a Hudson's Bay blanket—down the middle, and Phillips returned to Spokane.[14]

During the period Phillips prospected in Alaska he also was recognized as Butch Cassidy. Wyatt Earp, who ran a gambling joint in Anchorage, later said he made Cassidy's acquaintance in Alaska, and commented of the man, "Outlaws are made, not born."[15]

In her book, Lula Parker Betenson corroborated, saying ". . . after leaving Mexico, he went to Alaska, where he trapped and prospected. . . . But Alaska was too cold for him, and he stayed there only a year or two."[16]

By 1915 Phillips had started his own business, the Phillips Manufacturing Company, the main enterprise being the development of "adding and listing machines" invented by Phillips. With a small downtown office, Phillips operated the enterprise in his home, a stark dwelling in Peaceful Valley beneath the Highbridge railroad trestle, a structure he may have helped design during his years as a draftsman for the power company. Phillips also invented a variety of other devices, including parts for farm equipment, an automatic garage-door opener, and a gas mileage indicator for inside the automobile. He also toyed with a steam-car creation. None were patented.

The Burroughs Company expressed interest in his mechanical adding machine, and in 1916 Phillips traveled to Detroit to discuss selling his rights. When the company failed to meet his asking price, Phillips returned to Spokane. Burroughs later produced an adding machine of their own—remarkably similar to that of Phillips—and the inventor was without a market. The invention was never sold.[17]

By 1918, seven years after arriving in Spokane, Phillips was able to open a small machine shop on North Monroe. As work expanded the machine shop was moved first to East Sprague, where Phillips also rented an apartment on the second floor, and finally to North Division, a major thoroughfare.

Athol Evans began employment in Phillips' shop during 1921: "When I went to work, he had two steadies, Frank Frueschuetz and Bill Hartman, and one or two extras. I started as an extra and then worked as a steady. Bill Phillips was not a master machinist, but mechanically minded and a good inventor. Frank did most of the hand work. Phillips always told us he learned the trade in New York."[18]

Later analysis of the man's handwriting—performed by graphoanalyst Jeannine Zimmerman—also pointed to his mechanical aptitude and creative abilities.[19]

In the mid-1920s most of the shop's work involved subcontracting for the Riblet Tramway Company, a firm which built ski lifts and tramways in North and South America. Phillips soon couldn't work fast enough to supply the firm's metalworks needs. As the Riblet Company prospered, Phillips own operation flourished, and by 1925 his business had reached its zenith.

For several years William and Gertrude Phillips attempted to have children. Then in 1919, after several miscarriages, they adopted a six-month-old son, William Richard. To distinguish him from his father the boy was nicknamed "Billy Dick."

In 1925 Phillips moved his family into a spacious home on West Providence, in an affluent neighborhood. The home had large picture windows, the latest in furnishings, a grand piano, the finest china, and costly silverware. The den included a large collection of books, many of them western. Billy Dick and neighbor children often played at the Phillips' basement pool table, a neighborhood status symbol.

Phillips had a penchant for fine automobiles, much as he had loved fine horses in earlier years, and for several of his successful years he bought Mr. Riblet's year-old Oldsmobile trade-ins, preferring the make to others.

During the early years in Spokane, Bill and Gertrude Phillips enjoyed each other's company. With little money to spend on entertainment, they would join friends on picnics, on swimming parties, or in camping trips in the nearby mountains.

Phillips was outgoing and loved mingling with others. Social acceptance was primary in motivating the striving businessman. He was a genial man, and his charisma attracted all he met. As his enterprise prospered he was accepted into the Elks Lodge in 1925, and into Spokane Lodge thirty-four of the Masons the following year.

Gertrude, in contrast, was shy and withdrawn; her reserve often taken for snobbery. As her husband's circle of friends widened, she became more introverted and turned her attentions toward their adopted son.

The strait-laced Gertrude especially objected to Phillips' drinking. Like the outlaw Butch Cassidy, William Phillips enjoyed drinking, but had a reputation of seldom drinking to excess and always retaining control of his faculties. He would get together with drinking buddies for a drink or two after work in mid-afternoon, and at night he joined in parties in the homes of his various friends. At first Gertrude gamely tried to smoke, drink hard, and lead a fast life, but she simply was no match for her husband.[20]

As she grew more embittered by her husband's activities, Gertrude grew less tolerant of his friends. One family friend recalled that, at a party in her home during Prohibition when many made home brew and wine, Gertrude slipped into the kitchen and began pouring the precious home-made raspberry wine down the sink. When the guests caught her, the indignant hostess grabbed Gertrude by the throat and nearly strangled her before other guests could intervene.[21]

When Prohibition came to Spokane on January 1, 1916, Phillips and his friends moved their afternoon sessions to the back of a moving and storage company, and their evening socializing to the basement hideaway of William C. Lundstrom, a former Spokane bartender.

Lundstrom and Charles F. "Fred" Harrison were Phillips' closest friends. Both men had spent some time in Wyoming at the turn of the century. Lundstrom had worked at various jobs before hiring on as bartender in Fred Harrison's White Owl Saloon in Sheridan, Wyoming, during 1905. The two later worked in the Owl Saloon in Billings, Montana, before eventually settling in Spokane in 1910. Before opening his saloon in Sheridan, Harrison had been associated with a Mr. Zant in a cigar business in Lander, Wyoming. Both Lundstrom and Harrison had known William Phillips as Butch Cassidy in Wyoming.[22]

Athol Evans said his boss seldom talked to his employees about his past. Evans did witness Phillips demonstrate expert marksmanship, and he knew the man was an excellent horseman. What the shop employees learned about Phillips came to them through Frank Frueschuetz. Phillips often discussed his outlaw past with Frueschuetz and Frank passed the information on to Evans as the two became good friends. Frueschuetz told Evans that William Phillips was Butch Cassidy, leader of the notorious Hole-in-the-Wall Gang.

Only once, Evans recalled, was Phillips recognized as Cassidy by a stranger. Phillips told Frueschuetz he was in the Clausen & Schutte saloon shortly after he came to Spokane, and the bartender, Barney Clausen, remarked, "You're Butch Cassidy, aren't you?"

"How did you know?"

Clausen showed Phillips a reward poster with a photograph.

"Why don't you turn me in?" Phillips asked.

"I wouldn't turn you in and besides, after this much time, the reward wouldn't be offered," was the reply.[23] The statute of limitations had run out; Butch Cassidy was a free man.

Along with his fast cars and whiskey, Phillips liked the women and it frequently was the talk of the machine shop employees. Phillips was a well-built, attractive man, and as his marital difficulties became more severe, romantic affairs often were rumored. Anna Galusha, a floor detective for the Crescent, a large Spokane department store, was considered by the men who knew Phillips to be his mistress for several years. On one occasion Athol Evans unexpectedly ran into Phillips and the tall, beautiful widow on a Seattle ferry during a holiday weekend. To insure Evans' silence Phillips gave his employee an immediate two-week paid vacation.[24]

Gertrude Phillips posing with rifle, Globe, Arizona vicinity, 1909.

Courtesy William R. Phillips.

Gertrude Phillips with lady friend, Globe, Arizona vicinity, 1909.

225

"Big Horn River scene, 1910." Photograph taken by William and Gertrude Phillips during their 1910 visit to Wyoming.

Courtesy William R. Phillips.

"Hole in the Wall cabin." Photograph taken by William and Gertrude Phillips during their 1910 visit to Wyoming.

Courtesy William R. Phillips.

227

William and Gertrude Phillips with unidentified draftsman in first office of Phillips Manufacturing Company, 325 Lindelle Block, Spokane, Washington. The calendar dates the photograph as taken in March 1916.

Courtesy William R. Phillips.

William T. Phillips in his machine shop. The Phillips Adding Machine is on the bench at right. On Phillips' left hand is the Mexican Fire Opal ring later given to Mary Boyd Rhodes.

Courtesy William R. Phillips.

Phillips Manufacturing Company, Adding and Listing Machines, N1612
Monroe, Spokane, 1919.

Courtesy Athol Evans.

Interior of Phillips' machine shop, *c*1921. From left: Frank Frueschuetz, unidentified employee, Athol Evans.

Phillips' residence and machine shop, E1326 Sprague, Spokane.

231

Gertrude and Billy Phillips, *c*1923–1924.

Courtesy William R. Phillips.

William Phillips' home, W 1001 Providence, Spokane.

Photograph by author.

William T. Phillips. The back of the original photograph was dated 1916.

234

William T. Phillips, possibly in 1918. The Mexican Fire Opal ring is
readily visible on his left hand.

William T. Phillips, driving Oldsmobile sedan originally owned by A. N. Riblet, for whom the Phillips Manufacturing Company did subcontracting during the 1920s.

William T. Phillips, *circa* Winter, 1936.

Courtesy William R. Phillips.

238

Billy Phillips, Spokane, Washington, September 1976.

Photograph by author.

Last known photograph of William T.
Phillips, c 1937.

Courtesy William R. Phillips.

Chapter XXI
Finis

Back to old Wyoming where I roamed in the days of your,
Searching for the faces of my pals, of long ago.
Gone, are they, forever, from the mountain and the dales;
Ne'er, again I'll see them, midst the hills I love so well.
WILLIAM T. PHILLIPS

Boyd Charter was seventeen the summer of 1925 when a man driving a Model T Ford pulling a two-wheel trailer loaded with camping gear rolled into the Charter's Spring Gulch Ranch in Jackson Hole, Wyoming. Bert Charter, Boyd's father, welcomed the stranger heartily, like a long-lost friend. As they exchanged pleasantries Boyd believes he heard the man say his name was Phillips. Bert helped the visitor set up his tent in a grove of trees below the ranch house. There the man remained camped for an extended stay over the summer.

The Charters' pleasant, but tight-lipped guest often invited Boyd to hunt sage chickens with him on the ranch. Phillips cooked the birds on a crude, home-made camp stove similar to the Coleman stoves used today. It was the first such contraption Boyd had ever seen and he used every excuse possible to be around when Phillips cooked his evening meals.

After the stranger had departed Boyd chanced to overhear a private conversation between his father and Will Simpson, prosecuting attorney at Butch Cassidy's 1894 trial. Bert told Simpson, then a lawyer in Jackson, that Butch Cassidy had just spent a long visit at the ranch. To others, neither Bert nor Will Simpson ever admitted any knowledge of Butch Cassidy's return.[1]

Author John Rolfe Burroughs was told by John Taylor, retired Rock Springs mechanic, that "one day in 1922 Butch Cassidy drove into the shop in a Model T to get some work done on the car. He was pulling a two-wheel trailer loaded with camping gear. He asked me a lot of questions about old-timers around Rock Springs. He didn't tell me who he was, but I recognized him."[2]

Bert Charter and John Taylor were not the only men to see Cassidy at that time. Tom Welch, a southwestern Wyoming pioneer who had known the outlaw Cassidy well, recalled it was 1924 when Cassidy stopped to visit him in Green River, Wyoming, just a few miles from Rock Springs. Welch remembered that Cassidy used an alias, and was driving a Model T with a two-wheel trailer loaded with camping gear.[3]

In Baggs, Wyoming, mayor Tom Vernon said he also was visited by Cassidy in the mid-twenties. Vernon had played the fiddle at dances during the 1897 Wild Bunch celebration in the little community.[4]

In 1970 Lula Parker Betenson first revealed that Cassidy also had visited the family home in 1925. In his visits with the Utah Parker family, the former bandit leader never did mention his wife and adopted son, nor did he discuss his extended trip with his family in Spokane upon his return. The two families were totally unaware of each other's existence.

Phillips' good times, with his shiny cars, parties, and fast company, came to an end with the Great Depression. During the late 1920s, the Riblet Tramway Company had increasing cutbacks in contracts and began to lose money. Phillips' manufacturing company, in turn, ceased getting work and William T. Phillips began losing money heavily.

In January 1929 his financial condition forced him to sell a third interest in his business for $3,500 to Gardner L. Farnham, a retired lawyer who had practised in Spokane at the time Phillips was first getting established. The agreement provided a stipulation that if Farnham were dissatisfied with the transaction, within one year he could recall his investment. On October 28, 1929, he demanded repayment. Phillips could not come up with the money.[5]

In May 1930 Frank Frueschuetz and Athol Evans bought Farnham's one-third share—by then shared with Spokane attorney George A. Preston. Then, on June 6, 1930, Phillips turned over the remaining two-thirds to the two former employees, who in turn assumed all debts he had accrued. Phillips owed the men back wages amounting to $1,000 each.[6]

That summer Phillips again returned to Wyoming. This time, however, his vacation was with a different purpose: He returned to locate buried caches of money hidden during his outlaw days.

In Lander, where he was recognized by former deputy sheriff Harry Logue,[7] Phillips hired Herman LaJeunesse and Charley Boyd, Mary's brother, to drive him to the home of another brother, Will Boyd. When he discovered Will was in Jackson Hole contracting bit parts for the film, *The Big Trail,* he arranged for Will's cousin, Dan Boyd, to pack him into the back country of the Wind River Mountains. He stayed but a few days.[8]

If Phillips found any outlaw caches, it was never reflected in his living style once he returned to Spokane. In 1931 he was forced to sell the big home on Providence and buy a more modest place on Kiernan. It was an especially bitter pill for Gertrude, to whom the large home had meant security as well as prestige.[9]

During the years from 1933 on, Phillips and Bill Lundstrom made money working at odd jobs and by peddling Phillips' various inventions. Phillips also prospected for gold along the Columbia River near the town of Daisy, Washington, since moved to avoid inundation by Lake Roosevelt behind Grand Coulee Dam. In Daisy, Phillips struck lasting friendships with mechanic Harold Miles and postman J. K. Mutterer. Miles, later a sheriff in Colville, Washington, was especially impressed with Phillips' show of marksmanship during shooting practices with his six-shooters, for diversion while on his prospecting excursions. The Mutterers often hosted Phillips during his trips. Both Miles and the Mutterers were taken into Phillips' confidence and told of his existence as Butch Cassidy. They also later were allowed to read his "Bandit Invincible" manuscript.[10]

Phillips again arranged a trip to Wyoming in 1934. Mrs. Ellen Harris, who with her late husband had socialized with Phillips in Spokane, financed the venture, and with her son Ben "Fitzharris," accompanied Phillips on the trip.

In 1973 reporter James Dullenty located Ben Fitzharris and interviewed him in his North Hollywood home. Ben recalled that he and his mother left Los Angeles to rendezvous with Phillips at the Hotel

Utah in Salt Lake City: "To me it was a summer vacation. . . . Phillips said he'd like to get back there because he thought he could find a certain gold deposit that an old Indian back in his early days told him about. This old Indian was named Whiskey Jack."

Fitzharris said they met in May and took Phillips' car to Wyoming:

> Instead of going east directly along the Union Pacific there, we cut off through Fort Bridger. He knew a short-cut, through a little old mining town called Atlantic City and then we landed in Lander.
>
> And we stopped at what I think was the first auto court they had there, the only one, and we didn't go into the town. So we took rooms there.[11] Mother was all in and she got in her room and lay down.
>
> I walked down the street with him and that's where he first met this banker, the son of the original banker that knew Bill. . . . When we went across the street to the grocery store, I guess you'd call it a general store, why, my God, this guy threw up his hands and threw his arms around Bill and asked, "George, how are you? My God, it's been ages." Well, they were all taken with him. They threw their arms around him and called him "George" and "Cassidy, Cassidy."
>
> And the old marshal of Lander at that time remembered him. That's why we went across to one of those old hotels there—if you go to Lander, you'll know it, it's right across from the bank, those high ceilings you know, about thirty feet high. And we had quite a night there, with those old-timers sitting around and tossing them back. But they all knew George Cassidy.[12]

Phillips stocked up in Baldwin's grocery store, "then we went out to Washakie. Bill saw the Indian agent and he got a permit for us to go up there. Then we went down to Bill and Minnie [Boyd], who were in their tepee at the time, you know, Minnie didn't like the government-built log cabins. . . . And then that first day there was a great to-do. Old Bill Boyd got me to one side—old Bill didn't talk much—and he said, 'You know don't you that Mr. Phillips is Butch Cassidy?' I said, 'Yes, I know.' So even old Bill told me 'that's Butch Cassidy.' Because he remembered him from those days and I think in those days Bill [Phillips] used to hide out with those Indians."

Ellen Harris had told her son that Phillips was Butch Cassidy before the trip. Phillips had taken her into his confidence during their association in Spokane. "But nobody knew it for a fact, you know, it was like a dream. It was to me anyway until I met these old people around Lander and Fort Washakie."

Will and Minnie, with the help of Bert Chamberlin and his son Jesse, helped the visitors pack into the Wind River Mountains to Mary's Lake, where they set up camp. The party remained there from late May to about October 1.

Will Boyd was so excited to have his old friend visit him, he sent his nephew Roy Jones after his sister, Mary Boyd Rhodes, Cassidy's old sweetheart. Mary, by then a widow, was living in Riverton, Wyoming, with her teen-age granddaughter, Ione Campbell. Roy used a buckboard to take Mary and Ione up to Mary's Lake. When they arrived, the camp suddenly became the site of an emotional reunion.

"For God's sake! **Mary!** What are you doing here?" Phillips exclaimed in astonishment. Recognition between the two was immediate. [13]

Ben Fitzharris recalled the occasion, "And another thing. Minnie's sister, Mary, I believe that's the name. She was laughing so much about it, that she was a childhood sweetheart of George Cassidy's in those days back in the '90s. We used to sit around the campfire and they'd sing old songs that were popular as long as I can remember. 'My Sweetheart's the man in the moon, I'm going to marry him soon.' "

Phillips told his life story repeatedly at Mary's Lake, and Fitzharris learned it by heart. "He was falsely accused, taking cattle that didn't belong to him. He had a little ranch at that time called the Quien Sabe, somewhere in the vicinity of Riverton, and that's where they accused him of rounding up somebody else's cattle. It was why he was sent to the Wyoming Penitentiary and the Governor pardoned him and when he got out he said that 'if you think I'm an outlaw, I'll show you what an outlaw is' and he really started in then and gathered these other men with him."

Fitzharris remembered Phillips' stunning Mexican Fire Opal ring—the same ring which later played an important part in verifying William Phillips' true identity.

Both Fitzharris and members of the pack trip were dazzled by Phillips' exhibitions of marksmanship with his small pepper-box Derringer and two Colt revolvers. "We'd get about 20 feet from a tree and he'd put a little piece of paper up and squeeze the trigger. Boy, he could really bear down—pull down and bam! He really was a marksman. I'd try it and I'd land back on my bottom."

"He was a man who could pick up anything; he had a clever mind. In fact the furniture—we cut down those lodgepoles up there and he'd build the tables and chairs and when we broke camp and went down Bill insisted on taking some of those chairs down to Fort Washakie, they were so well-built. All he had was a hammer, and nails and a saw and axe, and he built all that furniture right there. He could turn his hand to anything. He was that kind of a man."

Fitzharris said his impression of Phillips was that of "an honorable man and a very powerful character, not only physically, but mentally powerful. And those blue eyes, that would just, oh brother, bore right through you. When his steel blue eyes got a little angry, oh, I'm telling you. . . ."

Phillips and Fitzharris occasionally prospected but "all we ever found was fools' gold. All those streams up there have copper pyrite, tons of it. We were going over those mountains and walked ourselves silly. We wound up fishing."

Snow began flying about October 1, forcing the trio to pack their things and return to Lander. Fitzharris told of seeing Phillips off: "He was pretty glum. Course he was despondent over not having found anything and having to face what he did when he went home. He knew he didn't have any money and that was it. But, we helped him out the best we could."

Ellen Harris and her son paid the Boyds for the horses and food and prepared to return to Hollywood by train while Phillips drove off in his automobile. Before returning to Spokane, Phillips first stopped for an extended visit with his old sweetheart, Mary Boyd Rhodes. While there he was treated royally. Mary's granddaughter Ione even served the celebrated house guest breakfast in bed.[14]

After Phillips left the mountains several people who had noticed his peculiar style of "prospecting" retraced some of the area where he had been seen. In the canyon between Mary's Lake and Moccasin Lake, they found a series of freshly dug holes, each at the base of a tree, and always on the north side. These observations correspond with the local legend that Cassidy and Elzy Lay had buried some of their Montpelier loot at the base of an old tree in the Wind River Mountains. Phillips had often complained to Will Boyd that "the country has shifted. It's not the way it used to be."[15] Although there are stories to the contrary, William Phillips evidently did not find the treasure for which he was searching, for his financial plight continued to worsen once he returned to Spokane.

In Spokane, Phillips wrote his "Bandit Invincible" manuscript. Repeated efforts to market the story were met with rejection slips from the publishing world, and he gave up on the effort.

Unable to realize any returns from the story of his life, desperation turned his ingenuity toward illegitimate pursuits once again. This time he decided to kidnap someone for ransom!

Phillips' decision was not wholly original. By 1935 America had been rocked by a series of kidnappings. In 1932 the infant son of Charles Lindberg was kidnapped and murdered. 1933 saw the Mary McElroy nabbing; the abduction of Denver philanthropist, Charles Boettcher; followed by the kidnappings of St. Paul brewery magnate, William A. Hamm Jr., and Oklahoma City oilman, Charles Urschell.

While the capture of Bruno Richard Hauptman for the Lindberg kidnapping made headlines in 1934, the Ma Barker–Alvin Karpis gang shocked the nation with the nabbing of Minneapolis banker, Edward G. Bremer.

By 1935, when Butch Cassidy, alias William T. Phillips, turned to thoughts of kidnapping as his last resort, the trial of Hauptman and the Bremer kidnapping trial of corrupt Chicago politician, John H. "Boss" McLaughlin, were dominating the front pages of the nation's newspapers.[16]

Phillips had a definite victim in mind: William Hutchinson Cowles. Cowles was not only the most prominent man in Spokane, he was one of the wealthiest men in the western United States. He owned the community's two newspapers and much property in the Spokane area. While the rest of the nation slumped into the hellish nightmare of soup lines, eviction proceedings, hobo jungles, and door-to-door begging, Cowles rolled on successfully, not unlike the cattle barons of old.[17]

The Cowles mansion stood on the hill above Peaceful Valley, where Phillips had first lived in Spokane. During the years Phillips lived there, until he was able to buy a better home, he could look up to that mansion and hope to attain that level of success in the community. Now broken, William Phillips knew his dreams of social prominence in Spokane were forever behind him. He was sixty-nine, broke, and dying of cancer.

Ronald L. Smith, Bill Lundstrom's son-in-law, spent much of his time in Lundstrom's back yard repairing automobiles during the lean years of the mid-thirties. When Phillips began building a "gold cradle" for use up north along the Columbia River, Smith thought little of it.

After constructing the device Phillips disappeared. About a week later Smith remembered a tool he needed and had left in Lundstrom's basement room. Several times he tried the door before it opened. Sitting in a chair facing him as he walked into the dark room was William T. Phillips. The man was extremely unhappy at having been discovered and Smith quickly exited.

The young man immediately told his father-in-law of the incident. Lundstrom was distressed to learn Smith had seen Phillips in the basement. He took his son-in-law aside and explained, "That nut, he has an elaborate plan to kidnap William Cowles, owner of the Cowles Publishing Company, and hold him for ransom. He wants me to get involved and help him, but I'm not going to do it. I didn't get involved with him before, and I'm not going to now. I haven't talked him out of it yet, but you leave it to me."

Lundstrom told how Phillips had staked a hideout in a wooded area near the Little Spokane River, west of Spokane. Here he had planned to hold Cowles for ransom. Phillips had made arrangements with someone out of town who was willing to testify he was with them during the time of the kidnapping. But he needed one man to help him with the kidnapping, and that was the hitch.

Several days later, Phillips reappeared and Smith facetiously asked him, "How was the prospecting?" Phillips' glare was answer enough; the matter was never mentioned again.[18]

Billy Phillips also told of his father's desperate state of mind in 1935. The elder Phillips had been drinking at the time. He took Gertrude and Billy to Newman Lake east of Spokane, late at night.

"He had a gun in his hand and he backed us out the door to the end of the dock. He threatened to shoot us, my mother and me. We were scared to death. Boy was he sore. He resented me and felt mother had turned her affection away from him when I came along. Just as he had us backed up to the water's edge, somebody came along in a car with headlights on and they flashed onto the beach. When he turned to look back to see who it was, I guess mother grabbed the gun out of his hand. I don't know who drove up on that beach right then, but if they hadn't come I wouldn't be sitting here."[19]

Phillips' depressed state also is dramatically revealed in the letter he secretly mailed to Mary Boyd Rhodes during the Christmas season:

My Dear Mary:
    Perhaps you think I have forgotten you. but I haven't. I am not so sure but you owe me a letter but maby not I just can't remember. I have been confined to the house now since I came back from Idaho about two months back or more. I don't know if I will ever be able to do much any more as I am getting quite weak. I have gradualy been going down since I came back from Wyoming. Just cant seem to gather any strength. maby I am just geting old and cant realize it! every thing I touch seems to flop. Did you answer my letter I wrote you from Idaho? I remember very clearly that I wrote you while I was down there. but cant remember geting a reply. I wrote a short letter to Harry Baldwin a couple of days ago. I thought if any thing was wrong with you he would rite and tell me. I didnt ask him about you for certain reasons. but I thought he would understand.
    Well Mary dear Christmas is about here and Ill be glad when its over perhaps I wont be bothered about another one, who knows? can't never tell and it sure don't matter to me. I always liked to give, give, give, but now as I am broke my only pleasure I ever enjoyed was when I could help some poor cus along but those days are gone unless the Townsend plan [Dr. Francis Townsend's social reform plan which turned public thought toward our present Social Security program] goes over. if it does we old cocks will have a good time for a little while anyhow. I am going to try and get out and work for it if posible and you tell all the boys over to work for it for they will all be old some day and

the way things are going they will soon need it or the big corporations are surely picking up every thing and fast too.

If you see Will and Minney also Verna as well as the rest of the boys tell them you heard from me and that I send them my very best wishes. And now wishing you all a very happy holliday season and trusting life is treating you a little better than it is me

I am as always your old sweetheart   *Geo*

W. T. Phillips
adress as before

One of my old friends from Montana came to see me the other day and is going to take me down town today to mail this as I never trust any one to mail my letters. I dont want them to know any thing of my afairs you understand.[20]

Phillips' health rapidly declined. For a time he stayed with a Lewiston, Idaho–Clarkston, Washington family while taking "irrigations," or flushing of the bowels. He also was treated by a Pendleton (Oregon) physician, and was in contact with a cancer sanitarium in Savannah, Missouri.[21]

During the summer of 1936 Phillips made one final futile effort to locate outlaw caches in the Wind River Mountains of Wyoming. He visited a few friends in Lander and stayed for a short time in the Dubois area before returning empty-handed to Spokane.[22]

To meet mounting expenses Gertrude started work in January 1936 as a clerk and librarian at Opportunity Elementary School in Spokane Valley.[23] In early 1937 Phillips' condition was such that he became too much of a burden for his working wife. She had him removed from the home and placed in a nursing home. It was from this home that Phillips wrote his last letter to Mary Boyd Rhodes. Mary had just written him at his wife's address at 828 Glass:

Dear Mary:

Your letter came all right but I only got to see part of it. Why did you change the adress? 828 Glass is my home adress and my wife got the letter so now you can imagine what happened and me confined to my bed as I have been for the past 14 months. It is a terrible trial for me to write but all my friends seem to think that I could write even if I had both arms cut off. I must tell you now that I am going to write to no one again until I am up on my feet or at least able to sit up. so dont expect it. I am sending you under seperate cover my ring which I wore for over 35 years, as a keepsake I hope you will like it you will never see another like it. Well I must close and get ready for my treatment. am in a private sanitarium you can write me here the adress is 123 North Cook St Spokane Wn

best wishes to all my old friends but dont ask me to write or you will only get your feelings hurt.[24]

During the first week of July, 1937, Phillips' friends reported to Bill Lundstrom, "Bill Phillips said to tell Bill Lundstrom to come and get me out of this God damn place or I'll jump out the window." Blanche Lundstrom described the sight greeting them when they arrived at the nursing home: "They put him up in the attic. It was terrible up there. It was hot, and he was stuck way up in a dinky little room, with one little window, and no air. You couldn't go in the room where he was, his bed and he always smelled and his clothes were soiled."

On July 10 the Lundstroms hired an ambulance and transported Phillips from the home to Broadacres, the county poor farm at Spangle, a few miles south of Spokane: "He was kept clean and neat and in good condition at Broadacres. He had a white uniform on and his bedding was clean and white."[25]

The county poor farm at Broadacres was William Phillips' last home. Ten days later, on July 20, 1937, he passed away. Time, at last, had run out for Butch Cassidy, the Bandit Invincible.

Chapter XXII

Epilogue

FOLLOWING cremation by the Hazen and Jaegger Mortuary, a Rose Croix memorial service was conducted for William Phillips by the local Masonic Lodge. Some time later Gertrude Phillips scattered the ashes over the Little Spokane River, near Dartford, in keeping with Phillips' wishes.

Gertrude Phillips and her son continued to reside in the little house on Glass. Mrs. Phillips found various employment until she ceased working altogether in the early 1950s. During her last years in Spokane, Gertrude kept close to her home. She never again was asked to publicly explain her husband's background. In her last years she developed cancer and, at age eighty-three, she died at a Spokane hospital, on April 16, 1959. As with her husband, her remains were cremated.[1]

William R. Phillips still lives in Spokane, where he finds occasional handyman and custodial work. A portion of the proceeds from this book will supplement his earnings. With all the publicity his father has received in recent years, it is Billy's wish that Butch Cassidy be remembered, not so much for his lawless years, but for his self-rehabilitation and his technological contributions to our present way of life. Certainly his efforts in development of "adding and listing" machines deserves proper recognition.

Of Phillips' closest friends in the Spokane area, Blanche Lundstrom Glasgow survives at age ninety-three. Anna Galusha passed away in 1943, after a lingering illness.

Cassidy's sweetheart Mary Boyd Rhodes survived her former lover by only one year, passing away in Riverton, Wyoming, in 1938.

"Dorney Leaf," Cassidy's Salt Lake City girlfriend later married and died of childbirth fever in Utah.[2]

Lula Parker Betenson is the last remaining member of her generation of the Utah Parker family. In 1975, at age ninety-one, she published her book, *Butch Cassidy, My Brother*. Dan Parker died in

Cedar City, Utah, in 1941; his daughter-in-law Ellnor passed away in Seattle, Washington, in September 1975.

Mike Cassidy, Robert LeRoy Parker's outlaw mentor at the Jim Marshall ranch, left Utah to avoid prosecution for rustling. He was last reported living in Mexico.[3]

On September 7, 1893, Tom McCarty, with his brother Bill and nephew Fred, held up the Farmers and Merchants Bank in Delta, Colorado. While attempting their getaway, Bill and Fred were shot down in the street by Ray W. Simpson, a hardware merchant. Tom escaped, but abandoned the outlaw life. Drifting to Montana, he eventually settled near Rosebud, Montana, in self-imposed exile as a sheepherder.[4]

After a shooting scrape near Vernal, Utah, in which two men were killed, Matt Warner, with William Wall, was sentenced to five years in the penitentiary, not to be released until January 11, 1900. Both then decided to seek a quieter livelihood. Warner, by then well versed in the law, eventually worked both sides to his benefit during Prohibition, serving as a justice of the peace while bootlegging on the side. He died on December 21, 1938.[5]

Al Hainer's role as "Judas" was given further credence in that, during Cassidy's absence, he was again acquitted of horse thievery while his co-defendant, Jakie Snyder, was sentenced to five years at the July 1896 term of court.[6] There is no evidence that Cassidy ever took revenge against Hainer. The 1896 Lander directory listed Al Hainer as working at the local livery and staying at the Cottage Home Hotel. Author Pearl Baker believes the man eventually settled in Utah under an assumed name.

After Bub Meeks was committed to the Idaho State Correctional Institution he immediately began plotting to escape. His first opportunity came on Christmas Eve, 1901. While on work detail at the prison hog pens Meeks cut the traces on one of the work horses and escaped in a blizzard. The heavy snowfall made tracking the desperate man an easy task and he was soon recaptured. His sentence was doubled.

On February 2, 1903, after a period of erratic behavior, Meeks made a desperate dash out of the prison's front gate. A bullet from the rifle of Deputy Warden R. H. Fulton stopped his flight, shattering his left leg below the knee. The wound was so severe the leg had to be amputated.

After returning from Boise's St. Alphonse Hospital he twice attempted suicide, "by jumping from a 35 foot wall and later stabbing himself with a pair of shears." On April 22, 1903, he was transferred to the insane asylum at State Hospital South in Blackfoot, Idaho, by order of probate court.

On August 9, 1903, Meeks made his escape from the Blackfoot facility by overpowering his attending physician and stealing the doctor's French coach mare from the hospital stable. Although he was located at his brother's ranch at Fort Bridger, Meeks was left free, it evidently being felt a one-legged outlaw was no outlaw at all.

Bub's erratic behavior increased and finally became violent. Relatives fearing for their lives had him committed to the Wyoming State Hospital at Evanston. He died in Evanston on November 22, 1912.[7]

Walt Punteney ranched on Bridger Creek, above Lost Cabin, until 1912. He later owned the Camp Stool Ranch near Crow Heart Butte, and in 1923 moved to Pinedale, Wyoming, where he bought a saloon. He died in Pinedale in 1949.[8]

Bob McCoy, whom Phillips revealed had been the courier of the funds Cassidy put up for Tom O'Day's defense, came to a violent end. Long suspected of being a consort of outlaws, McCoy was murdered in 1905 while riding along the Big Horn River near his homestead at the mouth of the Wind River Canyon. McCoy's killer was never apprehended.[9]

Emery Burnaugh was run over by a train while shipping cattle in 1907. He was buried on the knoll above Cassidy's hideout at Burnaugh's Muddy Creek road ranch. Alice Burnaugh sold the ranch to move to Riverton, near her friend Mary Boyd Rhodes.[10]

Bert Charter remained in Jackson Hole until his death in 1939. His ranch on Spring Gulch is now the property of Wyoming Senator Cliff Hansen.[11]

After serving only five years of his life sentence for his part in the 1897 Folsom train robbery, Elzy Lay, alias William McGinnis, was pardoned by New Mexico Governor Miguel Otero for exemplary behavior while in prison. Following his release on January 10, 1906—some say December 1905—Lay returned to Alma, New Mexico, for about a year before drifting north to settle at Baggs, Wyoming, where he met Mary Calvert, daughter of a local rancher. Lay's first wife, Maud Davis, had divorced him while he was in prison, and Elzy eloped with Mary to Thermopolis, where they were married on March 27, 1909.

Lay stayed in the Baggs vicinity for a short time, managing his father-in-law's ranch, and participating in petroleum explorations with local banker Louis Maupin and a visiting petroleum geologist from New York. Lay next moved to Shoshoni, Wyoming, where he entered the saloon business with a man named Liedick. The results of his oil exploration did pay off, but not for Lay. Ironically, beneath the old Powder Springs hideout of the Wild Bunch was one of the most lucrative petroleum reservoirs in the West.

Sometime after settling in Shoshoni, Elzy Lay disappeared, not to be located until several years later when his family got word from him in California. Much of his absence is still a mystery. For a while he was a professional gambler in Tijuana, Mexico, and later he worked as a water master for the Imperial Valley Irrigation Company in California. After a prolonged illness, aggravated by a life of intemperate living, he died on November 10, 1934.

Both Tom Vernon and Josephine Bassett Morris, Brown's Park girlfriend of Cassidy, whom Butch visited in the 1920s in Rock Springs, claimed Cassidy was in the company of Elzy Lay when they saw him. It would have been during Lay's mysterious disappearance that he was reported with Cassidy. Elzy never elaborated on his escapades, nor did he admit to others that Butch Cassidy had not died in South America. He apparently carried many secrets with him to his grave, this "paladin amongst cow punchers."[12]

Following his release from the Wyoming State Penitentiary on February 13, 1907, Harvey Logan's cousin Bob Lee returned to Dodson, Missouri to work as a bartender.[13]

Will Carver was killed in Sonora, Texas, by Sheriff Elijah S. Bryant. His dying words, "Die game, boys," were an omen for many of the Wild Bunch.[14]

Harry Tracy, the outlaw whose murder of rancher Valentine Hoy forever closed Brown's Park as an outlaw sanctuary, was later imprisoned in the Oregon State Penitentiary. In 1902, with an accomplice, David Merrill, Tracy broken out of the prison, killing guards with firearms smuggled in to them. Tracy led officers of Oregon and Washington on one of the largest manhunts in the annals of crime before, surrounded in a grain field near Spokane, he took his own life on August 6, 1902.[15]

After the Great Northern holdup at Exeter, near Wagner, Montana, O. C. "Deaf Charley" Hanks narrowly escaped capture in Nashville, Tennessee, on October 26, 1901. Detectives tracked him to San Antonio, Texas, following his trail of unsigned Helena bank notes from the robbery. Before officials could apprehend the man Hanks was killed on April 15, 1902 by two officers while resisting arrest for shooting up a San Antonio dive. His mother claimed the body.[16]

Ten days after Hanks escaped capture in Nashville, Ben Kilpatrick was arrested in St. Louis where he had used some of the damning unsigned notes at a jewelry store. Also captured was his common-law wife, Laura Bullion. Ben and Laura were charged, tried, and found guilty of forgery. Laura was sentenced to five years; Ben was given fifteen years at the maximum security federal penitentiary at Atlanta.

Upon Ben's release in July 1911 he was extradited to Texas to stand trial for the 1901 murder of Kilpatricks' neighbor, Oliver Thornton. The case was later dismissed for lack of evidence, and, for a time, it appeared the Tall Texan had abandoned his outlaw life.

Just before midnight on March 12, 1912, two masked men darted out of the shadows and climbed onto the blind baggage of the westbound flyer of the Southern Pacific as it stopped at Dryden, Texas, to take on water. As the train continued its journey across the desolate stretch of track near Lozier, Texas, where Tom Ketchum's gang had robbed a Southern Pacific train back in 1896, the two men slipped over the coal tender and covered the engineer and fireman.

The bandits forced engineer E. Grosh to lead them to the express car and had him order the door opened. When messenger David Trousdale complied, the taller of the two bandits climbed into the car and proceeded to rummage through the parcels. The shorter bandit foolishly left his companion to his work and marched the engineer and fireman back to the engine.

As the outlaw bent over a package, temporarily turning his back on Trousdale, the messenger grasped an ice mallet with both hands and brought it down on the unsuspecting bandit's head, crushing his skull.

Trousdale then grabbed the robber's rifle and crouched behind some baggage. After some time the other bandit came back to the express car to see what had detained his companion. As the outlaw stood at the open door of the express car, his head silhouetted in the dim starlight, Trousdale squeezed the trigger of the Winchester in his hand and the robbery was over.

The two outlaws' bodies were taken to Sanderson, Texas, and Pinkerton agents identified the taller of the men as Ben Kilpatrick. The Tall Texan had robbed his last train.

The identity of Kilpatrick's accomplice was the object of much speculation for some time. Some said he was Howard Benson, a former cellmate of Kilpatrick, while others thought the dead man was Ed Welch. The body also was identified as that of Ole Beck. Jeff Burton, in his *Dynamite and Six-Shooter,* stated the man actually was Nick Grider, and cited his source as Grider's cousin, Jim Harkey. [17]

Following the release of the movie *Butch Cassidy and the Sundance Kid,* an itinerant toured the West giving talks to all who would listen. Variously giving his name as Robert Longabaugh, and Harold Longabaugh, the man said he was the illegitimate son of the Sundance Kid. He claimed his mother was a sister to Etta Place, whose maiden name was Thayne. He said that Etta died in Marion, Oregon, in 1940, under the name Hazel Tryon. "Longabaugh" also claimed his father died as Harry Long on August 28, 1957, in Wyoming.

The proclaimed son of Longabaugh was killed in a Missoula (Montana) hotel fire in December 1972. Research has proven his testimony erroneous, and his claimed relationship to Harry Longabaugh is seriously doubted.

The identity of Harry Longabaugh's mysterious lover, Etta Place, is one of the most intriguing riddles in western history. Leads develop only to dissolve in ambiguity. The problems besetting the Pinkerton operatives of 1900 have been compounded by the seventy-five years which have elapsed, yet there remains the optimistic hope that the next lead might hold the necessary clues to solving the mystery.

Equalled only by the Butch Cassidy–William T. Phillips controversy, the problem of documenting the final fates of Harvey Logan and Harry Longabaugh continues to fascinate historians of the western frontier. Perhaps even the answers to these puzzles will be located someday.

The "Bandit Invincible" manuscript also will long be a document of intrigue for western historians. Of particular interest are descriptions of four robberies not generally attributed to Cassidy's Wild Bunch. The first of these as-yet-unverified holdups was placed in the context of the gang's stay in San Antonio following the Wilcox train robbery. Etta Place, or "Betty Price," was sent to Oklahoma where she scouted "the busy little town of A——[Alva?] located on one of the main railroads." After the robbery of the town's bank, which Cassidy said netted the gang $26,000, the outlaws were intercepted by a posse from a cowtown fifty miles to the west. Driving their pursuers back in an exchange of gunfire during which Etta "received a crease across the shoulder," the bandits made their escape to eventually return to Wyoming.

Cassidy also described a sequence of robberies between his escape from "deputy Morgan" in Montana, and the gang's final holdup, that of a Great Northern train at Exeter Switch. From Miles City the outlaws traveled by rail to Pueblo, Colorado, and made a reconnaisance trip into Kansas, where they robbed a bank in a town "about sixty miles west of Dodge City."[18]

After a short stay in Pueblo the bandits next made their way west to Durango where "they decided on a holdup of the Rio Grande mail trains." With the help of recruits including "Gentleman Black Jack," they robbed a train "about 20 miles north of Durango." Cassidy said the train carried two express guards and in an exchange of gunfire, one of the outlaws was killed and "Black Jack McKinney" was shot through the shoulder."

The only Durango area train robbery was that of the Rio Grande southern flyer Number 6, on July 6, 1898, at Stoney Creek, a station twenty-four miles south of Rico, Colorado.[19] None of the holdup details fit those of the Cassidy manuscript. Black Jack Ketchum was shot in the arm in a train holdup attempt, but at Folsom, on the Colorado and Southern, near Raton, New Mexico, on August 16, 1901. He was thought to have attempted the robbery alone.[20]

The last of the robberies described by Cassidy was a bank robbery in "a small town near Hemingford" Nebraska, where the take "amounted to about $12,000."[21]

Confounding continued research in locating these robberies is the warning prefacing the "Bandit Invincible" manuscript: "As all the characters depicted in this book have taken an actual part, I find it essential to substitute some of the real names of both persons and places which I shall mention. Also, some places of the holdups have been changed."

The "Bandit Invincible" manuscript will continue to be a challenge for years to come, in search of Butch Cassidy.

Notes

CHAPTER I.   The Legend of Butch Cassidy

1. Mart T. Christensen, memorandum, "The above related by Wm G. Johnson, Register of the U. S. Land Office, one time resident of Lander, Wyo., July 1936," Wyoming State Archives. Christensen served the State of Wyoming both as State Treasurer and later as Secretary of State. He had more than a passing interest in Butch Cassidy and his gang. As a youth he worked in Thomas Magor's general store in Baggs, Wyoming. His fiancée, Mary Calvert, jilted him in 1909 to elope with former Wild Bunch outlaw, Elzy Lay, who had settled in Baggs following his release from the New Mexico prison in 1906.
2. Walker to Christensen, August 8, 1936.
3. Walker to Kelly, August 1, 1936.
4. Christensen to Kelly, December 1, 1936.
5. Christensen to Kelly, June 19, 1937.
6. Certificate of death: William Phillips, June 22, 1937. Washington State Department of Social and Health Services.
7. Gertrude Phillips to Kelly, October 4, 1938.
8. Charles Kelly, *Outlaw Trail*, 319.
9. Spokane *Spokesman-Review*, July 7, 1940.
10. Spokane *Spokesman-Review*, July 23, 1940.

CHAPTER II.   William T. Phillips

1. *Billings Gazette*, November 8, 1970.
2. *Ibid.*
3. Ray Picard, interview with author, Lost Cabin, Wyo., November 21, 1972.
4. Graham K. French, attaché, American Legation, La Paz, Bolivia, to author, March 18, 1974.
5. Pinkerton report, "informant #85" (signed H-), San Francisco, Calif., April 5, 1909.
6. Frank P. Dimaio, Pinkerton memorandum, September 17, 1941.
7. William Pinkerton, memorandum, undated.
8. Arthur Chapman, "Butch Cassidy", *Elks Magazine*, April 1930.
9. Lula Betenson, *Butch Cassidy, My Brother*, 184.
10. Lula Betenson, interview with author, Kanab, Utah, August 10, 1973.

11. Betenson, *Butch Cassidy, My Brother,* 195.

12. Certificate of death: William Phillips, June 22, 1937, Washington State Department of Social and Health Services.

13. The author was assisted in this research by James K. Dullenty.

14. *Ibid.*

15. Butch Cassidy to Mrs. Davis, August 10, 1902.

16. Justo Piernes, "Butch Cassidy in Patagonia," Buenos Aires *Clarin,* May 2, 1970.

17. The Percy Seibert scrapbook is in the possession of Mrs. Robert W. Cline, Williamsport, Maryland.

18. Ellñor Parker, interviews with James K. Dullenty, June 30, July 12, 1975; to Dullenty, July 20, August 11, 1975; Max Parker, son of Dan Parker, interview with author, September 12, 1975.

19. Spokane *Daily Chronicle,* August 18, 1973.

20. Harry Jackson, sculptor, interview with author, Billings, Mont., March 6, 1976.

21. Roy Jones, interview with author, Fort Washakie, Wyo., August 28, 1973; Herman LaJeunesse, interview with author, Fort Washakie, Wyo., March 8, 1973.

22. Ellen Harris to Will and Minnie Boyd, October 8, 1940.

23. William R. Phillips, interview with author, Spokane, Wash., September 9, 1976.

24. Blanche (Lundstrom) Glasgow, interview with author, Spokane, Wash., August 16, 1974.

25. Esther Chamberlin, interview with author, Arapahoe, Wyo., August 7, 1973.

26. Ione Manning, interview with author, Riverton, Wyo., September 11, 1973.

27. Mary Boyd Rhodes to W. Fields, August 20, 1937.

28. William Lundstrom to Mrs. O. Rhodes, August 28, 1937.

29. Jeannine Zimmerman, master certified graphoanalyst, to author, November 19, 1973.

CHAPTER III.   The Bandit Invincible

1. Ben Fitzharris to author, July 1973 (undated).

2. Blanche (Lundstrom) Glasgow, interview with the author, Spokane, Wash., August 16, 1974. Of the 188 pages of hand-transcribed manuscript, Blanche copied a total of 63 pages. Her daughters Cleo and Veryl copied 48 and 45 pages, respectively; and her sister, Mrs. Madge Fields copied 29 pages. The sequence shifted 8 times among the transcribers. Careful scrutiny of the copied material reveals a pattern of inconsistencies which can be attributed to variations among the transcribers in the degree to which the original spellings and punctuation was followed. Blanche rarely made paragraphs, and her material most closely follows

writing patterns consistent with other examples of the man's writing. Cleo created more paragraphs, and correctly spelled words which her mother misspelled. Veryl used the & sign in place of "and," but otherwise wrote in a manner similar to that of her mother. The greatest contrast is found in the 29 pages copied by Madge Fields, wherein spelling and punctuation are quite correct—not at all consistent with the other sections, nor with other samples of his writing. The over-writing by James K. Dullenty for the most part has been corrected, but there are certain obliterations which the author could not decipher. As best as possible—with the exception of spacing changes to effect separation of unrelated expressions—the author has recorded the manuscript as originally transcribed.

3. Sheriff's Record Book, Fremont County, Wyoming.

4. Information in the 1896 Lander City Director was provided to the author by Jay Trosper.

5. The photograph, owned by John Henry, of Lander, was located by Minnie Woodring of the *Wyoming State Journal,* Lander.

6. Esther Chamberlin, interview with author, Arapahoe, Wyo., July 25, 1974.

7. Vincent Brown, son of Lone Bear, interview with author, Riverton, Wyoming, July 26, 1974.

CHAPTER IV.   Robert LeRoy Parker

1. Utah State Census, 1880.

2. Lula Betenson, interview with author, Kanab, Utah, August 10, 1973; Betenson, *Butch Cassidy, My Brother;* Parker family genealogy records, The Church of Jesus Christ of Latter-day Saints; Nema Anderson, "Butch Cassidy and his home," no date.

3. Nema Anderson to James Dullenty, March 26, 1974.

4. Betenson, *Butch Cassidy, My Brother,* 38.

5. *Ibid.,* 37.

6. Nema Anderson, "Butch Cassidy and his home."

7. Betenson, *Butch Cassidy, My Brother,* 51.

8. *Rocky Mountain News,* August 30, 1900.

9. James D. Horan, *Desperate Men,* 377.

10. *Wyoming State Tribune,* May 7, 1942.

11. Kelly, *Outlaw Trail,* 12–13.

CHAPTER V.   Telluride

1. Eugene Cunningham, *Triggernometry.*

2. *Rocky Mountain News,* June 27, 1889.

3. Matt Warner, *Last of the Bandit Riders,* 80–81.

4. Pearl Baker, *Wild Bunch at Robbers Roost*, 159–160.

5. Boyd Charter, interview with author, Billings, Mont., December 1, 1973.

6. Wilson Rockwell, *Memoirs of a Lawman*, 183–184. Rockwell blasted the myth of Butch Cassidy's participation in the November 3, 1887 holdup of a Denver & Rio Grande train in this well-documented biography of early day lawman, C. W. "Doc" Shores. Shores successfully brought to ground and secured conviction of Jack and Bob Smith, Cawker City, Kansas, and Ed Rhodes and Bob Boyle, alias Bob Wallace, Paola, Kansas, for perpetrating the affair.

7. John Rolfe Burroughs, *Where the Old West Stayed Young*, 114–135.

8. Several published accounts have discussed the origin of Cassidy's nickname "Butch." Rock Springs (Wyoming) pioneer Joe Gras was told Cassidy was given the epithet while working in Otto Schnauber's meat market prior to Gras's employment there in 1893. Outlaw Matt Warner said he gave Cassidy the nickname after an incident involving Warner's needle gun, also named Butch. When Cassidy first fired the gun, the recoil knocked him flat on his back in a bog. Historically, William Phillips' account is valid in that the men on roundups who were responsible for securing meat for the camp were called "butches."

9. C. A. Guernsey, *Wyoming Cowboy Days*, 43–44.

10. Ethelbert Talbot, *My People of the Plains*, 96.

11. *Fremont Clipper*, April 15, 1892.

12. Warner, *Last of the Bandit Riders*, 146; Bertillion Book, Wyoming State Penitentiary; Frankie Moriarty, interview with author, Dubois, Wyo., June 15, 1974; Harriet Woolery, interview with author, Kinnear, Wyo., June 27, 1974; Essie McCullough, interview with author, Kinnear, Wyo., June 27, 1974. Cassidy and Hainer were together when the John Burlingham family moved to the Dubois area in 1889, according to Frankie Moriarty, Burlingham's daughter. Accounts of Cassidy's activities in the area also came from interviews with Dubois pioneers and their descendants, including Frank Welty, whose father sold Cassidy cigars at the J. K. Moore general store in Fort Washakie; "Dutch" Nipper; Bill Burlingham; Mae Shippen; and George Peck, son-in-law of Eugene Amoretti, Jr.

In 1936, Leon Warnock was hunting on the mountain above the Wind River ranch, some twenty miles above Dubois. He lost his footing in the snow and slipped down the slope, grabbing what he thought was a stick on his way down the incline. At the end of the skid, he discovered his stick was the barrel of a six-shooter. After cleaning the Colt .44 later at camp, he discovered an inscription carved inside the pistol's wooden handle, "Butch Casidy." The gun was old and Warnock's discovery was certainly the authentic item. That gun, serial #99736, is now on display in Welty's General Store in Dubois.

Cassidy may have spelled his name differently in early years, although by the time he appeared in court in Lander in July 1893 he was spelling it "Cassidy." Pearl Baker, *Wild Bunch at Robbers Roost*, 210, reprints a photograph of an inscription in a sandstone rock with the spelling, "Casidy," and the *Fremont Clipper*, April 14, 1893, had notice by the post office that among their unclaimed letters was one for George Casidy.

In 1895, Francis Nicol, father of Harriet Woolery and Essie McCullough, moved into the Horse Creek cabin vacated by Cassidy and Hainer.

13. *Historical Encyclopedia of Wyoming,* 1030; George Peck, son-in-law of Eugene Amoretti, Jr., interview with author, Dubois, Wyo., June 8, 1974.

14. A.F.C. Greene, "Butch Cassidy in Fremont County," unpublished manuscript, Wyoming State Archives.

15. Mae Shippen, interview with author, Dubois, Wyo., January 11, 1973.

16. *Wyoming State Journal,* April 6, 1950.

17. Ludwig Stanly Landmichl, "Hank Bedeker [sic] Tells of Old Times," unpublished manuscript, Wyoming State Archives.

18. Bud Burnaugh, interview with author, Riverton, Wyo., November 1, 1972; Elmer Stagner, interview with author, BarGee, Wyo., August 12, 1972.

19. Ione Manning, interview with author, Riverton, Wyoming, September 11, 1973. Information was also obtained from Dora Lamorreaux's stepson, Bill Robertson, and his son, Allan, both of Lander, Wyo.

CHAPTER VI.   Alias Tom Ricketts

1. Unless otherwise noted, all information in Chapter VI was obtained from the trial transcript, Case No. 30, *U. S. vs. William Brown and Dan Parker,* Archives Branch, Federal Records Center, Denver, Colo.

2. Bertillion Book, Wyoming State Penitentiary.

3. Max Parker, interview with author, Billings, Mont., September 5, 1975.

CHAPTER VII.   The Hole-in-the-Wall

1. Paul Frison, *Grass Was Gold.*

2. Alfred Mokler, *History of Natrona County,* 264–269.

3. Paul Frison, *First White Woman in the Big Horn Basin.*

4. Thelma Gatchell Condit, "The Hole-In-The-Wall," series of articles in *Annals of Wyoming,* October 1955 to April 1962.

5. Evelyne Currie Marcinck to James Dullenty, October 28, 1974.

6. Joe LeFors, *Wyoming Peace Officer,* 103–104.

7. Condit, "The Hole-In-The-Wall."

8. Nell Bullock, daughter of Walt Punteney, interview with author, Riverton, Wyo., August 25, 1974.

9. Ethyl Taylor, interview with author, Blue Creek Ranch, Wyo., July 5, 1974.

CHAPTER VIII.   Prison Walls

1. Helena Huntington Smith, *War on Powder River.*

2. Tacetta B. Walker, *Stories of Early Days in Wyoming.*

3. Raymond Picard, interview with author, Lost Cabin, Wyo., November 21, 1972.

4. Case Nos. 144, 166, *State of Wyoming vs. George Cassidy, and Albert Hainer,* Third District Court, Lander, Wyoming. Unless otherwise cited, all information on Cassidy's arrest and trials was obtained from the court record.

5. *Fremont Clipper,* April 15, 1892.

6. *Wyoming State Tribune,* June 16, 1939. In his column "In Old Wyoming," John Thompson printed letters by Bob Calverly, obtained from the officer's son, James Calverly. These documents refute the widely publicized notion that Calverly arrested Cassidy in 1894.

7. Smith, *War on Powder River.*

8. *Ibid.*

9. *Wyoming State Journal,* April 6, 1950.

10. Bertillion Book, Wyoming State Penitentiary.

11. Hank Boedeker, Jr., interview with author, Dubois, Wyo., March 14, 1973.

12. Bertillion Book, Wyoming State Penitentiary.

13. *Ibid.*

14. *Ibid.*

15. Case No. 167, *State of Wyoming vs. Thomas Osborne Shepheard,* Third District Court, Lander, Wyo.

16. Bertillion Book, Wyoming State Penitentiary.

CHAPTER IX.   The Wild Bunch

1. Smith, *War on Powder River,* 113.

2. *Fremont Clipper,* January 1893.

3. Record of Pardons, Wyoming Territory, T. Moonlight Governor, Wyoming State Archives.

4. Sheriff's Record Book, Crook County, Wyo.

5. Percy A. Seibert to "Elizabeth," letter in the possession of Mrs. Robert W. Cline, Williamsport, Md.

6. Pinkerton report by JTC, Philadelphia, March 4, 1902, Pinkerton Archive; Census of Pennsylvania, 1880, National Archives; Census of Pennsylvania, 1900, National Archives; Edward M. Kirby, "Butch, Sundance, Etta Place Frolicked in 'Fun City,'" *Newsletter of the National Association and Center for Outlaw and Lawman History,* Winter, 1975–76.

7. Boyd Charter, interview with author, December 1, 1973; Great Falls *Daily Tribune,* November 30, 1892; Dolores Munden, Records Supervisor, Montana State Penitentiary, to author, March 25, 1976.

8. Harry Gourley, interview with author, Lost Cabin, Wyo., November 8, 1972; Bill Hamilton, interview with author, Lander, Wyo., July 27, 1972; Louis Meeks, interview with author, Thermopolis, Wyo., February 3, 1974.

9. Jeff Burton, *Dynamite and Six-Shooter*, 4; Kelly, *Outlaw Trail*, 260–62; William French, *Some Recollections of a Western Ranchman*, 271–72.

10. Burton, *Dynamite and Six-Shooter*, 4.

11. *Fremont Clipper*, August 5, 1895.

12. Buffalo *Bulletin*, August 22, 1895; *Fremont Clipper*, September 13, 1895.

13. Thomas Crawford, *The West of the Texas Kid*, 72–79. Crawford places his robbery—similar to that described in the Phillips manuscript—in 1893 or 1894 in a town "about fifty miles south of Salt Lake City." Three men were involved, one possibly Crawford himself. One was shot through the right side during the pursuit which followed. Jakie Snyder, Cassidy's friend of the Lander area—who also stood trial with Al Hainer during Cassidy's internment—fits Crawford's description of the wounded outlaw, including the gunshot scars. The robbery's take, according to Crawford, was $12,000.

14. The situation of the widow in Salt Lake City, with some variation, is reported in contemporary Salt Lake City newspapers, in which Salt Lake deputy sheriff Harris interrogated a woman who came under suspicion after purchasing a lot and building a $2,000 house. She was the widow of a miner and had two small children. Since the woman had been destitute for several years previous, she was questioned as to the source of her windfall. It was revealed that Butch Cassidy had given her the money. The news item gave the impression that Cassidy was the woman's common-law husband and the father of the two children. Brown Waller, *Last of the Great Western Train Robbers*, 134–37.

15. Phil Boyd, interview with author, Lodge Grass, Mont., September 28, 1975.

CHAPTER X.   Montpelier

1. Condit, "The Hole-in-the-Wall."

2. Mary B'Hat Harris, daughter of Mary Boyd, interview with author, Riverton, Wyo., July 26, 1974.

3. *Ibid.*

4. Marriage license is in the possession of Mary Boyd Rhodes' granddaughter, Ione Manning, Casper, Wyo.

5. Ruth Beebe, *Reminiscing Along the Sweetwater*, 100, 104–105; Florence Kirk, interview with author, Jeffrey City, Wyo., June 11, 1974; Jim McIntosh, interview with author, Jeffrey City, Wyo., June 9, 1974. Some time after Cassidy's visits, Jesse Johnson moved a few miles west along Green Mountain to Middle Cottonwood and founded the 46 Ranch, where he lived out his years.

6. R. H. Burns, A. S. Gillespie, and W. G. Richardson, *Wyoming's Pioneer Ranches*, 430.

7. Kelly, *Outlaw Trail*, 176–79.

8. *Ibid.*, 261–65.

9. The boat *City of Petoskey* was built at Manitowoc, Wisconsin, in 1888, and

made nightly cruises between South Haven and Chicago, along the route described by Phillips. Research performed by James K. Dullenty. Sand Beach most probably was Harbor Beach, Michigan.

10. Ardythe Kennelly Ullman to author, April 5, 1976. In relating the information on Cassidy's Salt Lake City lover, "Dorney Leaf," Mrs. Ullman exacted the promise that the true identity of the young girl, Annie F., not be revealed.

CHAPTER XI.   Castle Gate

1. Baker, *Wild Bunch at Robbers Roost,* 201–210.

2. Fred W. Hilman, interview with author, Big Horn, Wyo., July 6, 1972. Other pioneers in the Dayton (Wyoming) area testified as to the contrary nature of Mr. Mock. Mock rode a horse with just one spur, reasoning that where one leg went the other wouldn't be too far away. That one spur is said to have drawn blood all too often when Mock used a horse. Despite the obvious alibi, Cassidy knew Mr. Mock well.

3. Fred Hilman was 88 when interviewed in 1972. The Hilmans still had the .44 carbine given Fred by Cassidy, in their Home Museum collection of antiquities dating to the Crusades, and artifacts from throughout the West, valued at more than $100,000. All was lost in a fire on July 13, 1974. Hilman is the founder of the Wyoming Archaeological Society.

CHAPTER XII.   Belle Fourche

1. Just before Bub Meeks' arrest, his brother William had participated in the robbery of Charles Guild's Fort Bridger general store and post office, with Henry Lee, John Henry, and Charlie "White River" Stevens. William was caught and spent time in the Wyoming Penitentiary. Rock Springs *Miner,* June 17, 1897; Bertillion Book, Wyoming State Penitentiary.

2. Willard Hayden, "Butch Cassidy and the Great Montpelier Bank Robbery," *Idaho Yesterdays,* Spring 1971, 2–9.

3. Millicent James, interview with James K. Dullenty, Kaycee, Wyo., April 1974.

4. Buffalo *Bulletin,* April 22, 1897.

5. *Wyoming State Tribune,* February 13, 1942.

6. Elmer Stagner, interview with author, BarGee, Wyo., August 12, 1972.

7. Mokler, *History of Natrona County, Wyoming,* 286–88.

8. Bertillion Book, Wyoming State Penitentiary.

9. Buffalo *Bulletin,* August 5, 1897.

10. Paul Frison, in *Grass Was Gold,* printed an 1896 settler census in which Harvey Ray was listed as ranching near Ten Sleep, Wyoming.

11. R. I. Martin, "A Lively Day in Belle Fourche," *True West,* March–April 1962.

12. Butte County, South Dakota, Justice Court Records, June 29, 1897 to March 10, 1898, supplied by Gladys Rothermel, Clerk of Courts, Butte County, South Dakota.

13. Helena Huntington Smith, "The Truth About the Hole-in-the-Wall Fight," Michael Kennedy, *Cowboys and Cattlemen,* 253–262.

14. Carley Jebens, eye-witness to the Wild Bunch celebration, interview with author, Baggs, Wyo., May 29, 1974.

15. *Fremont Clipper,* October 1897.

16. Butte County, South Dakota, Justice Court Records, June 29, 1897 to March 10, 1898, supplied by Gladys Rothermel, Clerk of Courts, Butte County, South Dakota.

17. *Fremont Clipper,* November 5, 1897.

18. Waller, *Last of the Great Western Train Robbers,* 81–85.

19. Butte County, South Dakota, Justice Court Records, June 29, 1897 to March 10, 1898, supplied by Gladys Rothermel, Clerk of Courts, Butte County, South Dakota.

20. Billings *Gazette,* April 1, 1898.

21. Buffalo *Bulletin,* April 7, 1898.

CHAPTER XIII.   Handwriting on the Wall

1. Denver *News,* February 27, 1898.

2. *Fremont Clipper,* February 15, 1898.

3. *Wyoming State Tribune,* June 16, 1939.

4. Burroughs, *Where the Old West Stayed Young,* 157–169.

5. Denver *News,* March 11, 1898.

6. *Fremont Clipper,* March 25, 1898.

7. *Ibid.*

8. Walker, *Stories of Early Days in Wyoming,* 116–117.

9. Greene, "Butch Cassidy in Fremont County."

10. *Wyoming State Tribune,* June 16, 1939.

11. *Ibid.*

12. *Ibid.*

13. French, *Some Recollections of a Western Ranchman.*

CHAPTER XIV.   Wilcox

1. Buffalo *Bulletin,* June 8, 1899.

2. A line in the original manuscript transcription, obliterated in tracings by

reporter James K. Dullenty, may have contained the name of one additional bandit, possibly George Currie.

3. *Natrona County Tribune*, June 8, 1899.

4. *Ibid.*

5. *Ibid.*

6. LeFors, *Wyoming Peace Officer*, 109–115.

7. It is of note that Harvey Ray is never again mentioned in historical accounts of the Wild Bunch. Whether the grave at the Burnaugh Ranch is that of Ray remains conjecture.

8. Roy Jones and Herman LaJeunesse, interview with author, Fort Washakie, Wyo., October 22, 1973; Will Frackleton, *Sagebrush Dentist*.

CHAPTER XV.   Diamonds or Shackles

1. Charles Siringo, *A Cowboy Detective*, 305–325.

2. Warner, *Last of the Bandit Riders*, 131–33.

3. Waller, *Last of the Great Western Train Robbers*, 134–37.

4. *Ibid.*, 136.

5. *Ibid.*, 137–39.

6. Denver *Evening Post*, March 1, 1900; Kelly, *Outlaw Trail*, 261; Evelyne Currie Marcinck, George Currie's niece, wrote "identification was almost impossible due to the condition of the body. But to put my poor grandmother's mind at rest, my grandfather said it was George." The Currie family plot in the Greenwood Cemetery at Chadron has a tombstone for G. S. Currie, Age 29, Born March, 1871, but Mrs. Marcinck wrote that there is some question as to who is buried in the plot, Evelyne Currie Marcinck to James Dullenty, October 28, 1974; contemporary news accounts also voiced this question; Denver *Times*, May 2, 1900.

7. Cheyenne *Leader*, May 25–29, 1900.

8. Bertillion Book, Wyoming State Penitentiary.

9. Burton, *Dynamite and Six-Shooter*, 32–36.

10. Denver *Evening Post*, August 17, 1899; Theories that G. W. Franks was Harvey Logan are disproven by positive identification of Logan in Wyoming at the time of the Turkey Canyon shootout. Most New Mexico historians believe Franks was Bill Carver, but there also is the possibility that he was George West Musgrave, member of the original "Black Jack" gang of New Mexico. Musgrave was a close companion of Elzy Lay during the years immediately following Lay's prison release in early 1906.

11. French, *Some Recollections of a Western Ranchman*, 258–83.

12. Like Butch Cassidy the outlaw, William Phillips the businessman had a full repertoire of bicycle riding stunts. Even as a man in his upper sixties, Phillips was able to perform acrobatics with a bicycle. Ronald L. Smith, interview with author, Spokane, Wash., September 10, 1976.

13. The Sundance Kid's beautiful consort was first mentioned in the "Bandit Invincible" manuscript in relation to events prior to the Belle Fourche robbery in 1897. Phillips indicated that Longabaugh "had spent the past few weeks in Montana with his sweetheart Betty Price. . . ." Longabaugh did spend the 1896–97 winter with Etta Place, but at the outlaws' hideout in the Robbers Roost area of Utah. Also present were Elzy Lay and his bride, the former Maud Davis of Ashley, Utah. Baker, *Wild Bunch at Robbers Roost,* 171–74.

CHAPTER XVI.   Tipton and Winnemucca

1. Greene, "Butch Cassidy in Fremont County."
2. Kelly, *Outlaw Trail,* 266–72.
3. *Rocky Mountain News,* August 31, 1900.
4. *Ibid.*
5. *Ibid.*
6. *Ibid.*
7. LeFors, *Wyoming Peace Officer,* 123.
8. Baker, *Wild Bunch at Robbers Roost,* 191; There was a Huntington, Nevada. It and the surrounding valley, with a population of 54, had a post office from March 17, 1873 to July 15, 1904, and again from December 7, 1923, to January 31, 1931. It was no longer in existence when the Phillips manuscript was written. The man Hammit has not been identified, but in the area is a Hammet Canyon, at the headwaters of Huntington Creek, on the east side of the Diamond Range. Dugouts beside a spring in the area are in the approximate location described in the manuscript.
9. I. V. Button to Pearl Baker, December 28, 1970.
10. Reno *Evening Gazette,* September 19–20, 1900.
11. I. V. Button to Pearl Baker, December 28, 1970. Button also wrote that Cassidy sent him a copy of the famous Fort Worth (Texas) photograph of five members of the Wild Bunch. He identified Cassidy and Carver in the picture. The mention of Woodward and Maxwell in the manuscript, to the exclusion of Carver, is yet unexplained. The photo was loaned to the Humboldt County Sheriff's Office and an enlargement was placed in the First National Bank in Winnemucca.

CHAPTER XVII.   Exit at Exeter

1. Jim McIntosh, interview with author, Jeffrey City, Wyo., June 9, 1974.
2. For a time, Ol Rhodes worked as a ranch hand for Walt Punteney.
3. Ardythe Kennelly (Ullman), *Good Morning, Young Lady;* Ardythe Kennelly Ullman to author, April 5, 1976.
4. Esther Chamberlin, interview with author, Arapahoe, Wyo., August 7,

1973; Ray Picard, interview with author, Lost Cabin, Wyo., October 20, 1973; Vince Brown, interview with author, Riverton, Wyo., July 26, 1974. Descendants of the O'Neals' mentioned in the manuscript also still reside in Fremont County.

5. There was a sheepman named McDougall whose range encompassed the area described at the time of Cassidy's outlaw career. *Fremont Clipper,* various dates 1887–1902.

6. Charles Pence, interview with author, Sheridan, Wyo., August 24, 1974; Pete Kegerris, interview with author, Sheridan, Wyoming, August 24, 1974.

7. Police Department Records, Sheridan, Wyo.

8. The foothills ranch may have been Big Mike Wehinger's Pine Hills road ranch. Mrs. Betty Parker, the author's mother-in-law, and Mrs. Violet Jones of Buffalo, Wyo., both raised in the area described, have indicated Wehinger's ranch best fits that mentioned in the manuscript.

9. Although the robbery is most often called the Wagner train holdup, the actual site was at the Exeter Switch, some two miles east of the small town of Wagner, Montana.

10. Waller, *Last of the Great Western Train Robbers,* 40.

11. Alan Swallow, *The Wild Bunch,* 89.

12. Great Falls *Tribune,* July 4–12, 1901. Early reports identified Harry "Lone Bow" as one of the robbers. With the arrest of Ben Kilpatrick, who was identified by eye-witnesses as "Lone Bow," the mistaken identity became apparent.

13. *Ibid.*

CHAPTER XVIII.   Bandidos Yanquí

1. Butch Cassidy's letter to Mrs. Davis was donated to the Utah State Historical Society by her great grandson Harvey Murdock, and is reprinted here as a courtesy of the Utah State Historical Society. Cassidy's mention of A—— may have been a reference to his sweetheart Annie F., the "Dorney Leaf" of Ardythe Kennelly's *Good Morning, Young Lady.*

2. Greene, "Butch Cassidy in Fremont County."

3. William Pinkerton to Robert Pinkerton, July 30, 1902, Pinkerton Archives.

4. Robert Pinkerton, memorandum, New York, July 29, 1902, Pinkerton Archives.

5. Charles Ayres, Pinkerton informant report, Dixon, Wyoming, October 1900, Pinkerton Archives.

6. J.T.C., Pinkerton memorandum, Philadelphia, April 3, 1902, Pinkerton Archives.

7. William Pinkerton to Robert Pinkerton, July 30, 1902, Pinkerton Archives.

8. Frank P. Dimaio, memorandum, Philadelphia, September 17, 1941, Pinkerton Archives.

9. Dimaio, undated memorandum to Pinkertons, following return to United States, June 1903. Between the two Dimaio memoranda, the writer altered his spelling of the Argentina capitol from "Buenos Ayres" to Buenos Aires."

10. Kirby, "Butch, Sundance, Etta Place Frolicked in 'Fun City,'" *National Association and Center for Outlaw and Lawman History Newsletter,* Winter 1975–76.

11. Pinkerton memorandum, New York, undated, Pinkerton Archives.

12. Frank P. Dimaio, memorandum, Philadelphia, September 17, 1941, Pinkerton Archives.

13. Dimaio, undated memorandum to Pinkertons, following return to United States, June 1903, Pinkerton Archives.

14. Dimaio, memorandum, Philadelphia, September 17, 1941, Pinkerton Archives.

15. *Ibid.*

16. Dimaio, undated memorandum to Pinkertons, following return to United States, June 1903, Pinkerton Archives.

17. Robert Pinkerton to Dr. Francis Beasley, Buenos Aires Chief of Police, July 1, 1903, Pinkerton Archives.

18. Piernes, Justo, "Butch Cassidy in Patagonia," Buenos Aires *Clarin,* May 2, 1970. The *Clarin* Series is based on a investigation conducted by Don Enrique Emshut, chief of Chubut Province law enforcement, who compiled a political history of the province. Emshut was aided in his project by federal judge Dr. Allehandro Godori, who researched archives. The material in the *Clarin* articles is supported in detail by records in the Pinkerton Archives. The author is indebted to Patsy Hamilton, Sheridan College Spanish instructor, for translating the articles.

19. *Rocky Mountain News,* June 28, 1903.

20. *Rocky Mountain News,* June 10, 1904.

21. Denver *Republican,* August 20, 1904. In support of Brunazzi's findings, William Pinkerton wrote his brother, "I am inclined to believe it is Duncan, yet the people in Knoxville who know Logan well assert positively it is Logan. [The description] does not show that there is a gun shot wound on his wrist, which we all know Logan had. Naturally the people at Knoxville, who are crooked in this matter, including the Sheriff, would try to make it appear that Logan is dead, to save their own skirts. Personally, I am inclined to believe the Knoxville identification is wrong." William Pinkerton to Robert Pinkerton, July 9, 1904, Pinkerton Archives.

22. Zortman *Little Rockies Miner,* July 8, 1907. The complete text of William Pinkerton's address, "Train Robberies, Train Robbers and Holdup Men," to the 1907 convention of the International Association of Chiefs of Police, at Jamestown, Virginia, as quoted in the *Little Rockies Miner,* is in the Pinkerton Archives. That same year, 1907, Robert Pinkerton wrote, "It is our belief that Logan joined Cassidy and Longabaugh in the Argentine." Robert Pinkerton, confidential Pinkerton memorandum, New York, January 15, 1907.

CHAPTER XIX.   San Vicente

1. Chapman, "Butch Cassidy," *Elks Magazine,* April 1930.

2. American Legation, Bolivia, correspondence 1904–1906, Microfilm T51,

Roll 22, Denver Archive and Record Center. Seibert could have accompanied W. L. Sisson to Bolivia in November 1904.

3. Percy A. Seibert to W. L. Sisson, Oruro, Bolivia, May 31, 1906, Microfilm T51, Roll 22, Denver Archive and Record Center.

4. Percy A. Seibert to "Elizabeth," January 15, 1964, letter in possession of Mrs. Robert W. Cline, Williamsport, Maryland.

5. The author was unable to locate Pinkerton records to support author James D. Horan's contention that Etta Place became ill with appendicitis and was taken back to the United States where, in a Denver hospital, she had her appendix removed. The *Clarin* articles by Justo Piernes do, however, make reference to a letter by Longabaugh in 1906 to friends in Cholilo, indicating intentions to sail for San Francisco.

6. Butch Cassidy to "The Boys at Concordia," Santa Cruz, Bolivia. November 12, 1907, letter in Percy Seibert scrapbook in possession of Mrs. Robert W. Cline, Williamsport, Maryland. A later Pinkerton report, from informant Milton Roberts of Chubut, also stated, "Ryan [Cassidy] had been in Bolivia under the name of Gibbon and I believe he actually is in Santa Cruz about 400 miles to the South of this place." Milton Roberts to Pinkertons, Chubut, January 29, 1910, Pinkerton Archives.

7. Butch Cassidy to C. R. Glass, Tres Cruces, Bolivia, February 16, 1908, letter in Percy Seibert scrabook in possession of Mrs. Robert W. Cline, Williamsport, Maryland.

8. There are two San Vicente villages in Bolivia. The first, with less than 2,000 inhabitants, lies in the mining district of the department of Potosi, and the second is located in a more agricultural area to the north, in the department of Cochabamba. To which village Percy Seibert, and therefore Arthur Chapman, referred is not clear, although the latter does not occur on the 1904 map.

CHAPTER XX.   Phillips Manufacturing Company

1. William R. Phillips, interview with author, Spokane Wash., September 9, 1976; Gerald Russell, nephew of Gertrude Phillips, telephone interview with James Dullenty, Fayette, Ohio, May 29, 1974; *Farmer's Directory, Lenawee County, Michigan,* 1916; *Directory,* Adrian, Michigan, 1905.

2. County Clerk's Records, Lenawee County, Michigan.

3. Athol V. Evans, interview with author, Spokane, Wash., August 17, 1974.

4. I. J. Bush, *Gringo Doctor.*

5. Kelly, *Outlaw Trail,* 317.

6. Janette Magor, interview with author, Denver, Colo., October 13, 1974.

7. Betenson, *Butch Cassidy, My Brother,* 186.

8. William R. Phillips, interview with author, Spokane, Wash., September 9, 1976.

9. Mokler, *History of Natrona County,* 327–28; Bertillion Book, Wyoming State Penitentiary.

10. Ray Picard, interview with author, Lost Cabin, Wyo., March 31, 1974; Harry Gourley, interview with author, Lost Cabin, Wyo., November 8, 1972; Jerry Eagan to author, May 1, 1974.

11. Fred W. Hilman, interview with author, Big Horn, Wyo., July 6, 1972.

12. William R. Phillips, interview with author, Spokane, Wash., September 9, 1976.

13. *Ibid.*

14. Mrs. George F. Cranston, interview with James Dullenty, Daisy, Wash., July 11, 1973.

15. Gayle R. Rhodes, "Butch Cassidy Didn't Die in an Ambush in South America," *The West,* January 1974.

16. *Los Angeles Times,* April 3, 1970; Betenson, *Butch Cassidy, My Brother,* 192–93.

17. Athol V. Evans, interview with author, Spokane, Wash., August 17, 1974. Phillips' office was at 325 Lindelle Block, his home at West 3023 Third. First mention of the Phillips Manufacturing Company in Spokane City Directories is in 1915. Phillips is listed as general manager. From 1918 to 1920, the firm is listed as the manufacturer of "Phillips adding and listing machines," and the address changes from 325 Lindelle Block (1915), to North 1612 Monroe (1918), to East 1326 Sprague (1920), to North 2303 Division, where it remained until Phillips turned the business over to Athol Evans and Frank Frueschuetz.

18. Athol V. Evans, interview with author, Spokane, Wash., September 10, 1976.

19. Jeannine Zimmerman, interview with author, Denver, Colo., September 24, 1976.

20. William R. Phillips, interview with author, Spokane, Wash., September 9, 1976.

21. Blanche (Lundstrom) Glasgow, interview with author, Spokane Wash., August 16, 1974.

22. *Ibid.*

23. Athol V. Evans, interview with author, Spokane, Wash., September 10, 1976.

24. *Ibid.*

25. *Ibid.*

26. William R. Phillips, interview with author, Spokane, Wash., September 9, 1976.

CHAPTER XXI. Finis

1. Boyd Charter, interview with author, Billings, Mont., December 1, 1973.

2. Burroughs, *Where the Old West Stayed Young,* 135.

3. George Reynolds, interview with author, Riverton, Wyo., May 7, 1974.

4. Ivan Daugherty, interview with author, Baggs, Wyo., May 29, 1974.

5. Athol V. Evans, interview with author, Spokane, Wash., September 10, 1976. The agreement between Phillips and retired Spokane lawyer G. L. Farnham was dated January 2, 1929, with an addendum dated October 26, 1929.

6. *Ibid.*

7. *Wyoming State Journal,* June 30, 1972.

8. Herman LaJeunesse, interview with author, Fort Washakie, Wyo., March 8, 1973.

9. William R. Phillips, interview with author, Spokane, Wash., September 9, 1976.

10. Harold Miles, interview with author, Colville, Wash., September 8, 1976.

11. The Teepee Lodge Auto Court, mentioned by Fitzharris, stood on a rise across the Little Popo Agie to the east of Lander. It was only recently torn down to be replaced with a Holiday Lodge. *Wyoming State Journal* issues of the 1890s are replete with mention of "Whiskey Jack."

12. The Fremont Hotel, to which Fitzharris referred, burned in 1971. Phillips visited with several Lander pioneers, including Eugene Amoretti, Jr., the banker who had hosted Cassidy at his Horse Creek ranch; Harry Baldwin, Lander businessman; and Hank Boedeker, former deputy sheriff who was in the party which delivered Cassidy to the Laramie prison in 1894. Riverton businessman Reg Logan was present when Phillips and Boedeker first met.

Jay Trosper and his mother reminisced with Phillips for several hours, after Boedeker took him to their house. Cassidy had been a habitué of Jay's father's saloon, today the Stockgrower's Bar. Jay also remembered seeing Ben Fitzharris.

Peaky St. John, Lander gambler who had spent many leisure hours with Cassidy, visited Phillips at the Teepee Lodge. Tom St. John accompanied his father and recalled Peaky and Phillips visited about incidents occurring in Lander during the 1890s. He also remembered seeing Ellen Harris. Tom was later told by his father that Phillips was Butch Cassidy.

Ada Calvert Piper, who's sister Mary became Elzy Lay's second wife, wrote in 1963 of Phillips' visit: "Butch Cassidy was not killed in South America. He was here in 1930 [sic] and I visited with him and he told several of us how he escaped with his life. I heard he died sometime later in Washington. He took his cache near Brooks Lake and his Model T and left in the dark of night with his little old spaniard woman [the dark-complected Ellen Harris]." Ada Piper to Blythe H. Teeple, February 6, 1963, copy supplied by Kerry Ross Boren.

13. Ione Manning, interview with author, Riverton, Wyo., September 11, 1973.

14. *Ibid.*

15. Roy Jones, interview with author, Fort Washakie, Wyo., August 28, 1973.

16. Information on kidnappings of the 1930s was gleaned from Lew Louderback, *The Bad Ones.*

17. Information on William H. Cowles was compiled from "Associated Press Biographical Service, No. 2795," issued May 1, 1940, and *Spokane Daily Chronicle,* January 15, 1946, and supplied by James Dullenty.

18. Ronald L. Smith, interview with author, Spokane, Wash., September 10, 1976.

19. William R. Phillips, interview with author, Spokane, Wash., September 9, 1976.

20. William T. Phillips to Mary Boyd Rhodes, December 17, 1935. Letter is in the possession of Ione Manning, Casper, Wyo.

21. Blanche (Lundstrom) Glasgow, interview with author, Spokane, Wash., August 16, 1974.

22. When Phillips returned to Wyoming briefly in 1936, he was again met by several persons who recognized him as Cassidy. Ken Milburn, who had just arrived in Lander that year, was introduced to Phillips by his employer, butcher and former Lander mayor, Billy Jones, who later told Milburn that Phillips was Cassidy. Ken Milburn, interview with author, Hudson, Wyo., January 1, 1974.

Lander businessman Ted Baldwin was working in his father's general store that same summer when he met Phillips. Ted, too, was told Phillips was Cassidy. Ted Baldwin, interview with author, Lander, Wyo., March 9, 1974.

In Dubois, Phillips spent time visiting the Welty General Store, Welty, who had sold Cassidy cigars at the J. K. Moore general store at Fort Washakie in 1889, recognized the former outlaw. Frank Welty, interview with author, August 9, 1974; Hugh Otte, interview with author, Lander, Wyo., July 6, 1973.

23. William R. Phillips, interview with author, Spokane, Wash., September 9, 1976.

24. William T. Phillips to Mary Boyd Rhodes, April 8, 1937. Letter is in the possession of Ione Manning, Casper, Wyo.

25. Blanche (Lundstrom) Glasgow, interview witt author, Spokane, Wash., August 16, 1974.

CHAPTER XXII.   Epilogue

1. William R. Phillips, interview with author, Spokane, Wash., September 9, 1976.

2. Ardythe Kennelly Ullman to author, April 5, 1976.

3. Kelly. *Outlaw Trail,* 12.

4. Burroughs. *Where the Old West Stayed Young,* 122.

5. Kelly. *Outlaw Trail,* 311-12.

6. Clerk of Court Records, Fremont County, Wyo., Lander, Wyo.

7. Information on Henry Wilbur "Bub" Meeks was obtained from the following sources: R. D. Newberg, Idaho State Correctional Institution, to author, April 22, 1976; Wyoming Vital Records Services, Cheyenne, Wyo.; Pinkerton memo, August 12, 1903, Pinkerton Archives, New York; *Denver Post,* October 19, 1903; Willard C. Hayden. "Butch Cassidy and the Great Montpelier Bank Robbery," *Idaho Yesterdays,* Spring, 1971; Harry Gourley, interview with author, Lost Cabin,

Wyo., November 8, 1972; Louis Meeks, interview with author, Thermopolis, Wyo., February 3, 1974.

8. Esther Chamberlin, interview with author, Arapahoe, Wyo., August 7, 1973; Nell Bullock, interview with author, Riverton, Wyo., August 25, 1974.

9. Walker. *Stories of Early Days in Wyoming,* 177–80.

10. Bud Burnaugh, interview with author, Riverton, Wyo., November 1, 1972.

11. Boyd Charter, interview with author, Billings, Mont., December 1, 1973.

12. Information on Elzy Lay was obtained from the following sources: Helen Bengtson, interview with author, Lander, Wyo., March 12, 1973; Baker, *Wild Bunch at Robbers Roost,* 178–80.

13. Waller. *Last of the Great Western Train Robbers,* 140.

14. Burton. *Dynamite and Six-Shooter,* 142.

15. James D. Horan. *Desperate Men,* 333.

16. Waller. *Last of the Great Western Train Robbers,* 199.

17. Burton. *Dynamite and Six-Shooter,* 166–67; Waller. *Last of the Great Western Train Robbers,* 184–97.

18. Garden City, Kansas, in the location described, has no bank robbery recorded during Cassidy's career.

19. Denver *Times,* July 6, 1898.

20. Burton. *Dynamite and Six-Shooter,* 98–103.

21. None of the banks in Nebraska towns—Harrison, Crawford, and Chadron—near Hemingford had recorded bank robberies at the time.

Bibliography

Books and Articles

Adams, Ramon. *Six-Guns and Saddle Leather, a Bibliography of Books and Pamphlets on Western Outlaws and Gunmen.* Norman, University of Oklahoma Press, 1969.

Alderson, Nannie, as told to Helena Huntington Smith. *A Bride Goes West.* New York, Farrar and Rinehart, 1942.

Anderson, Nema. "Butch Cassidy and His Home." Circleville, Utah, no date.

Baker, Pearl. *Wild Bunch at Robbers Roost.* New York Abelard-Schuman, 1971.

Beebe, Ruth. *Reminiscing Along the Sweetwater.* Boulder, Johnson Publishing, 1973.

Betenson, Lula, as told to Dora Flack. *Butch Cassidy, My Brother.* Provo, Brigham Young University Press, 1975.

Burns, R. H., A. S. Gillespie, and W. G. Richardson. *Wyoming's Pioneer Ranches.* Laramie, Top-of-the-World Press, 1955.

Burroughs, John Rolfe. *Where the Old West Stayed Young.* New York, Bonanza, 1962.

Burton, Jeff. *Dynamite and Six-Shooter.* Santa Fe, Palomino Press, 1970.

Bush, I. J. *Gringo Doctor.* Caldwell, Idaho, Caxton, 1939.

Chapman, Arthur. "Butch Cassidy," *Elks Magazine,* April 1930.

Condit, Thelma Gatchell. "The Hole-in-the-Wall," *Annals of Wyoming,* October 1955–April 1962.

Crawford, Thomas. *The West of the Texas Kid.* Norman, University of Oklahoma Press, 1962.

Cunningham, Eugene. *Triggernometry.* New York, Pioneers, 1934.

Farmer's Directory, Lenawee County, Michigan. Philadelphia, Wilmer Atkinson Co., 1916.

Findlay, Jack. "The Bowman Bank Robbery," *Password,* Fall 1969.

Frackleton, Will. *Sagebrush Dentist.* Pasadena, Trail's End Publishing, 1947.

French, William. *Some Recollections of a Western Ranchman.* New York, Argosy-Antiquarian Ltd, 1965.

Frison, Paul. *First White Woman in the Big Horn Basin*. Worland, Wyoming, Worland Press, 1962.

———. *Grass Was Gold*. Worland, Wyoming, Worland Press, 1966.

Guernsey, C. A. *Wyoming Cowboy Days*. New York, Putnam, 1936.

Hayden, Willard C. "Butch Cassidy and the Great Montpelier Bank Robbery," *Idaho Yesterdays*, Spring 1971.

Historical Encyclopedia of Wyoming. Cheyenne, 1972.

Horan, James D. *Desperate Men*. New York, Doubleday, 1949.

———. *The Gunfighters, the Authentic Wild West*. New York, Crown, 1976.

———. *The Pinkertons, the Detective Dynasty that Made History*. New York, Crown, 1967.

———. *The Wild Bunch*. New York, Signet, 1958.

———, and Paul Sann. *Pictorial History of the Wild West*. New York, Crown, 1954.

Kelly, Charles. *Outlaw Trail, a History of butch Cassidy and His Wild bunch*. New York, Bonanza, 1959.

Kennelly, Ardythe. *Good Morning, Young Lady*. Boston, Houghton Mifflin, 1953..

Kirby, Edward M. "Butch, Sundance, Etta Place Frolicked in 'Fun City,'" *Newsletter of the National Association and Center for Outlaw and Lawman History*. Winter 1975–76.

LeFors, Joe. *Wyoming Peace Officer*. Laramie, Powder River Publishers, 1953.

Louderback, Lew. *The Bad Ones*. Greenwich, Connecticut, Fawcett, 1968.

Martin, R. I. "A Lively Day in Belle Fourche," *True West*. March–April 1962.

Mokler, Alfred. *History of Natrona County, Wyoming, 1888–1922*. Chicago, R. R. Donnelley & Sons, 1923.

Piernes, Justo. "Butch Cassidy in Patagonia," *Clarin*. Buenos Aires, Argentina, May 2, 1970.

Rhodes, Gayle R. "Butch Cassidy Didn't Die in an Ambush in South America," *The West*. January 1974.

Rockwell, Wilson. *Memoirs of a Lawman, Autobiography of Cyrus Wells Shores*. Denver, Sage, 1962.

Siringo, Charles A. *A Cowboy Detective*. Chicago, W. B. Conkey, 1912.

Smith, Helena Huntington. "The Truth About the Hole-in-the-Wall Fight," *Cowboys and Cattlemen*. Michael S. Kennedy, editor. New York, Hastings House, 1964.

———. *War on Powder River*. New York, McGraw-Hill, 1966.

Swallow, Alan, editor. *The Wild Bunch*. Denver, Sage, 1966.
Talbot, Ethelbert. *My People of the Plains*. New York, Harper, 1906.
Walker, Tacetta B. *Stories of Early Days in Wyoming: Big Horn Basin*. Casper, Wyoming, Prairie Publishing, 1936.
Waller, Brown. *Last of the Great Western Train Robbers*. South Brunswick, New York, A. S. Barnes, 1968.
Warner, Matt, as told to Murray E. King. *Last of the Bandit Riders*. New York, Bonanza, 1938.

Newspapers

Billings (Montana) *Gazette*.
Buffalo (Wyoming) *Bulletin*.
Cheyenne (Wyoming) *Leader*.
Denver (Colorado) *Evening Post*.
Denver (Colorado) *News*.
Denver (Colorado) *Republican*.
Denver (Colorado) *Times*.
Great Falls (Montana) *Daily Tribune*.
Fremont Clipper (Wyoming).
Little Rockies Miner (Montana).
Los Angeles (California) *Times*.
Natrona County (Wyoming) *Tribune*.
Reno (Nevada) *Gazette*.
Rocky Mountain News (Colorado).
Spokane (Washington) *Daily Chronicle*.
Spokane (Washington) *Spokesman-Review*.
Wyoming State Journal.
Wyoming State Tribune.

Manuscripts

Greene, A. F. C. "Butch Cassidy in Fremont County," unpublished manuscript. Wyoming State Archives.
Landmichl, Ludwig Stanly. "Hank Bedeker Tells of Old Times," unpublished manuscript. Wyoming State Archives.
Phillips, William T. "The Bandit Invincible, the Story of Butch Cassidy," unpublished manuscript in possession of the author.

Court Records

Justice Court Records, Butte County, South Dakota: *State of South Dakota vs. Thomas O'Day and Walter Punteney.* Butte County Courthouse, Belle Fourche, South Dakota.

Records of the U.S. District Court, Wyoming. Case No. 30, *U.S. vs. William Brown and Dan Parker.* Archives Branch, Federal Records Center, Denver, Colorado.

Records of the U.S. District Court, Wyoming. Case No. 197, *U.S. vs. Robert E. Lee.* Archives Branch, Federal Records Center, Denver, Colorado.

Records of the U.S. District Court, Crook County, Wyoming. Case No. 33, *Territory of Wyoming vs. Harry Longabaugh.* Crook County Courthouse, Sundance, Wyoming.

Records of the U.S. District Court, Fremont County, Wyoming. Case Nos. 144, 166, *State of Wyoming vs. George Cassidy and Albert Hainer.* Fremont County Courthouse, Lander, Wyoming.

Records of the U.S. District Court, Fremont County, Wyoming. Case No. 167, *State of Wyoming vs. Thomas Osborne, aka. Thomas Osborne Shepheard.* Fremont County Courthouse, Lander, Wyoming.

Related Archives

American Legation, Bolivia. Correspondence, 1904–1906. Microfilm T51, Roll 22. Archives Branch, Federal Records Center, Denver, Colorado.

United States Census Records: 1870, 1880, 1900. Microfilm. Archives Branch, Federal Records Center, Denver, Colorado.

Records. Idaho State Correctional Institution. Boise, Idaho.

Marriage License: William T. Phillips to Gertrude M. Livesay. County Clerk's Records, Lenawee County Courthouse, Adrian, Michigan.

Records. Montana State Penitentiary. Deer Lodge, Montana.

Certificate of Death: William Phillips, Washington State Department of Social and Health Services. Olympia, Washington.

Wyoming Territory. Governor Moonlight record of pardons: Harry Longabaugh. February 4, 1889. Wyoming State Archives, Cheyenne, Wyoming.

Bertillion Book. Wyoming State Penitentiary. Rawlins, Wyoming.

Certificate of Death: Henry Wilbur Meeks. November 22, 1912. Wyoming Vital Records Services. Cheyenne, Wyoming.

Sheriff's Records. Carbon County. Rawlins, Wyoming.

Sheriff's Records. Crook County. Sundance, Wyoming.
Sheriff's Records. Fremont County. Lander, Wyoming.
Sheriff's Records. Johnson County. Buffalo, Wyoming.
Sheriff's Records. Natrona County. Casper, Wyoming.
Sheriff's Records. Sheridan County. Sheridan, Wyoming.
Police Department Records. Sheridan, Wyoming.
Parker family genealogy records. The Church of Jesus Christ of Latter-day
    Saints. Salt Lake City, Utah.
Membership Application: William T. Phillips. Spokane Lodge 228, Elks
    Lodge. April 8, 1925. Spokane, Washington.

Pinkerton Archives

Ayres, Charles. Informant report. Dixon, Wyoming, October 1900.
Dimaio, Frank P. Memorandum. New York, undated (June 1903).
————. Memorandum. Philadelphia, September 17, 1941.
Informant #85. Report. San Francisco, April 5, 1909.
JTC. Memorandum. Philadelphia, April 3, 1902.
Pinkerton, Robert. Memorandum. New York, July 29, 1902.
————. To Dr. Francis J. Beasley, Buenos Aires Chief of Police. New
    York, July 1, 1903.
————. Confidential memorandum. New York, January 15, 1907.
Pinkerton, William. To Robert Pinkerton. Chicago, July 9, 1904.
————. "Train Robberies, Train Robbers, and Holdups," speech before
    convention of International Association of Chiefs of Police. Jamestown,
    Virginia, 1907.
Pinkerton memorandum, New York, undated.
Roberts, Milton. Informant report. Chubut, Argentina, January 29, 1910.

Related Correspondence and Records

Anderson, Nema, to James Dullenty, March 26, 1974.
Button, I. V., to Pearl Baker, December 28, 1970.
Cassidy, Butch, to Mrs. Davis, August 10, 1902. Utah State Historical
    Society.
————, to "The Boys at Concordia," November 12, 1907. Percy Seibert
    Scrapbook, in possession of Mrs. Robert W. Cline, Williamsport, Mary-
    land.

————, to C. R. Glass, February 16, 1908. Percy Seibert Scrapbook, in possession of Mrs. Robert W. Cline, Williamsport, Maryland.

Christensen, Mart T. Memorandum. Wyoming State Archives.

————, to Charles Kelly, December 1, 1936. Utah State Historical Society.

————, to Charles Kelly, June 19, 1937. Utah State Historical Society.

Cranston, Mrs. George F., interview with James Dullenty, Daisy, Washington, July 11, 1973.

Fitzharris, Ben, interview with James Dullenty, North Hollywood, California, July 6, 1973.

Harris, Ellen, to Will and Minnie Boyd, October 8, 1940. Roy Jones Collection.

James, Millicent, interview with James Dullenty, Kaycee, Wyoming, April 1974.

Lundstrom, William, to Mrs. O. Rhodes, August 28, 1937. Letter in possession of Mrs. Ione Manning, Casper, Wyoming.

McCurry, Elsie, to James Dullenty, June 11, 1974.

Marcinck, Evelyne Currie, to James Dullenty, October 28, 1974.

Parker, Ellnor, interviews with James Dullenty, June 30, July 12, 1975.

————, to James Dullenty, July 20, August 11, 1975.

Phillips, Gertrude M., to Charles Kelly, October 4, 1938. University of Utah Marriott Library.

Piper, Ada, to Blythe H. Teeple, February 6, 1963. Kerry Ross Boren Collection.

Rhodes, Mary Boyd, to W. Fields, August 20, 1937. Letter in possession of Mrs. Blanche (Lundstrom) Glasgow, Medical Lake, Washington.

Russell, Gerald, interview with James Dullenty, Fayette, Ohio, May 29, 1974.

Seibert, Percy A., to "Dear Elizabeth," January 15, 1964. Percy Seibert Scrapbook in possession of Mrs. Robert W. Cline, Williamsport, Maryland.

Walker, Tacetta B., to Mart T. Christensen, August 8, 1936. Utah State Historical Society.

————, to Charles Kelly, August 1, 1936. Utah State Historical Society.

Interviews with Author

Baldwin, Ted, Lander, Wyoming, March 9, 1974.

Bengtson, Helen, Lander, Wyoming, March 12, 1973.

Betenson, Lula, Kanab, Utah, August 10, 1973.

Boedeker, Henry, Jr., Dubois, Wyoming, March 14, 1973.

Boyd, Phil, Lodge Grass, Montana, September 28, 1975.

Brown, Vince, Riverton, Wyoming, July 26, 1974.

Bullock, Nell, Riverton, Wyoming, August 25, 1974.

Burnaugh, Bud, Riverton, Wyoming, November 1, 1972.

Chamberlin, Esther, Arapahoe, Wyoming, August 7, 1973, July 25, 1974.

Charter, Boyd, Billings, Montana, December 1, 1973.

Daugherty, Ivan, Baggs, Wyoming, May 29, 1974.

Evans, Athol V., Spokane, Washington, August 17, 1974, September 10, 1976.

Glasgow, Blanche (Lundstrom), Spokane, Washington, August 16, 1974.

Gourley, Harry, Lost Cabin, Wyoming, November 8, 1972.

Hamilton, Bill, Lander, Wyoming, July 27, 1972.

Harris, Mary B'Hat, Riverton, Wyoming, July 26, 1974.

Hilman, Fred W., Big Horn, Wyoming, July 6, 1972.

Jackson, Harry, Billings, Montana, March 6, 1976.

Jebens, Carley, Baggs, Wyoming, May 29, 1974.

Jones, Roy, Fort Washakie, Wyoming, August 28, October 22, 1973.

Kegerris, Pete, Sheridan, Wyoming, August 24, 1974.

Kirk, Florence, Jeffrey City, Wyoming, June 11, 1974.

LaJeunesse, Herman, Fort Washakie, Wyoming, March 8, October 22, 1973.

Logan, Reg, Riverton, Wyoming, August 7, 1974.

Magor, Janette, Denver, Colorado, October 13, 1974.

Manning, Ione, Riverton, Wyoming, September 11, 1973.

McCullough, Essie, Kinnear, Wyoming, June 27, 1974.

McIntosh, Jim, Jeffrey City, Wyoming, June 9, 1974.

Meeks, Louis, Thermopolis, Wyoming, February 3, 1974.

Milburn, Ken, Hudson, Wyoming, January 1, 1974.

Miles, Harold, Colville, Washington, September 8, 1976.

Moriarty, Frankie, Dubois, Wyoming, June 15, 1974.

Nipper, "Dutch," Crowheart, Wyoming, January 11, 1973.

Otte, Hugh, Lander, Wyoming, July 6, 1973.

Parker, Max, Billings, Montana, September 12, 1975.

Peck, George, Dubois, Wyoming, June 8, 1974.

Pence, Charles, Sheridan, Wyoming, August 24, 1974.

Phillips, William R., Spokane, Washington, September 9, 1976.

Picard, Ray, Lost Cabin, Wyoming, November 21, 1972, October 20, 1973, March 31, 1974.

Reynolds, George, Riverton, Wyoming, May 7, 1974.

St. John, Tom, Lander, Wyoming, March 22, 1973.

Shippen, Mae, Dubois, Wyoming, January 11, 1973.

Smith, Ronald L., Spokane, Washington, September 10, 1976.

Stagner, Elmer, BarGee, Wyoming, August 12, 1972.

Taylor, Ethyl, Blue Creek Ranch, Wyoming, July 5, 1974.

Trosper, Jay, Lander, Wyoming, April 3, 1974.

Warnock, Leon, Riverton, Wyoming, August 9, 1974.

Welty, Frank, Dubois, Wyoming, August 9, 1974.

Woolery, Harriet, Kinnear, Wyoming, June 27, 1974.

Zimmerman, Jeannine, Denver, Colorado, June 15, 1975, September 24, 1976.

Letters to Author

Egan, G. F., May 1, 1974.

Fitzharris, Ben, undated (July 1973).

French, Graham K., Cultural Attache, American Legation, Bolivia, March 18, 1974.

Ullman, Ardythe Kennelly, April 5, 1976.

Zimmerman, Jeannine, November 19, 1973.

Index